CONTENTS

July 9, 2017. Israeli soldiers close military gate No. 623. The gate is used by the famers of Deir Al Ghusun and Attil, as it separates the towns' built-up areas from 500 acres of agricultural fields—despite the fact that both are located in the West Bank. Palestinian farmers have staged protests at the gate, demanding the Israeli army allow them to more easily access and tend their fields.

Ahmad Al-Bazz/ActiveStills

The Vital Contribution of International Law to Sustainable Palestinian/Israeli Peace

Richard Falk

The large, long-established body of international law governing relations among states and the protection of human rights is comprehensive enough to provide a reliable marker for how competing nationalisms could live normally together. In the enduring confrontation between the Palestinian Arab people and Israel, international law would support the redress of Palestinian grievances against Israel while providing a framework for shaping a future beneficial to both peoples, were there the political will to achieve a just and sustainable peace on both sides. An awareness both of history and of how international law has evolved over the last century is crucial for a clear perspective on the struggle.

The Relevance of History

2017 was the anniversary of three crucial milestones in this narrative: (1) the issuance of the Balfour Declaration by the British Foreign Secretary a hundred years ago pledging support to the World Zionist Movement in their campaign to establish a homeland for the Jewish people in Palestine; (2) the passage of UN General Assembly Resolution 181 seventy-one years ago proposing the partition of Palestine between the two peoples along with the internationalization of the city of Jerusalem as a political compromise between Palestinian Arabs and Jews; and (3) the Israeli military occupation of the West Bank, East Jerusalem, and the Gaza Strip of over fifty years ago after the 1967 War.

As Zionism has succeeded at each stage in gaining greater control over all of Palestine as a state for the Jewish people, Palestinian Arabs have continued the struggle to maintain their own presence and assert their own rights in the land.

Each of these milestones represents a major development in the underlying struggle and combines an Israeli disregard of international law that inflicts major injustices on the Palestinian people. Without due regard for this past, it will not be possible to understand the present encounters between Israelis and Palestinians or to shape a future beneficial for both peoples. Palestinians have suffered continually over the last century because of this non-compliance and failure of enforcement. While it is also the case that Palestinian resistance efforts have at times exceeded legal limits, especially by reliance on terrorism, these violations do not provide any justification for the basic pattern of Israeli non-compliance, expansionism, and failure to acknowledge or uphold fundamental internationally mandated Palestinian rights.

To gain perspective, history is crucial. Law and practice have changed significantly since the era one hundred years ago when colonial powers could impose international borders—when, for instance, the Balfour Declaration promised British support for establishment of a Jewish homeland in Palestine at a time when not only was Palestine overwhelmingly populated by Arabs, with a only a minuscule Jewish population, but when Britain did not yet even control the land. Today, the addition of such critical principles as the self-determination of peoples would have rendered such arbitrary colonial impositions politically unacceptable.

Following World War I, when the international community, led by the victors in war, Britain and France, divided the territorial possessions of the defeated Ottoman empire and took these over as colonies, US President Woodrow Wilson introduced the then-innovative idea of giving these regions and peoples self-determination. This led to a slippery compromise among the imperial powers, which established a "mandate" system authorizing the colonial powers to administer the territories more or less as they wished, but as ostensibly temporary trustees rather than explicitly as colonial powers. The rejection of self-determination implicit in this subjugation of foreign countries to mandatory tutelage was not then perceived to be a violation of international law, as it would be today.

In Palestine, this post-World War I realignment of

As Zionism has succeeded at each stage in gaining greater control over all of Palestine as a state for the Jewish people, Palestinian Arabs have continued the struggle to maintain their own presence and assert their own rights in the land.

colonial control coincided with the rise of nationalist impulses among both Palestinian Arabs and Jews—a phenomenon that ultimately gave rise to a century of conflict. Palestinians joined a rising tide of nationalist feeling throughout the Arab world and began to push for political independence for themselves, although they lacked credible political leadership. At the same time, and even before the threat from Nazi Germany, Zionism began vigorously lobbying for a Jewish place in Palestine, in fulfillment of Britain's pledge to support this and, as the years went on, as a safeguard for Jews against the Nazi threat. To the rising concern of Palestine's native Arab population, Jewish immigrants from Europe began flooding into Palestine in the 1920s and '30s.

An ultimately irreconcilable nationalist clash was inevitable. The notion of partition—of dividing the two peoples on the basis of ethnic identity—came to the fore in 1937 with the recommendation of a British royal commission, the Peel Commission, and became the policy carried out in 1948 when the international community, under the authority of the United Nations and again acting without consultation with the Palestinian Arab population, forced the division of Palestine into a Jewish and an Arab state. Diplomats have striven off and on since then to forge a peace agreement based on a two-state solution, and the Palestinian leadership finally accepted this notion in 1988.

I would personally offer this central explanation for the fact that a two-state resolution has never come to be: The main leaders of the Zionist movement before and after the establishment of the state of Israel in 1948 never subjectively accepted the two-state approach that Israeli political leaders endorsed publicly. In this respect, it is necessary to appreciate two facts. First, the right of a people to self-determination had become incorporated into international law, most authoritatively in common Article 1 of the two human rights covenants adopted by the UN in 1966. Second, that colonialist patterns of foreign rule and settlement had become unlawful in the decades following World War II, making Israel's

settlement project in the Middle East an anachronism. A central historical paradox is that Israel established itself as an independent state, admitted to the UN, in the very historical period during which European colonialism was collapsing throughout the world, and losing any claim to political legitimacy.[1]

In the decades after World War II and the Holocaust, international law was expanded to incorporate the right of a people to self-determination, and colonialist patterns of foreign rule and settlement became unlawful. Nonetheless, Israel has successfully manipulated these laws, or defied them, with the implicit consent of the laws' custodians. The UN partition resolution itself violated the principle of self-determination because the Palestinians were not consulted in advance, and at the time the Jewish population in Palestine numbered no more than thirty percent of the total. Nor was Israel's acquisition of additional territory during the war that followed partition legitimate under international law, which forbids the acquisition of territory by the use of force. By the conclusion of that conflict, Israel's sovereign territory had grown from the fifty-five percent granted by the partition resolution to seventy-eight percent, and fully two-thirds of the native Palestinian Arab population had fled their homes and land or been forcibly expelled and has never been allowed to return. The international community put up no politically meaningful objections to these major infringements of the law.

Lawless Occupation, Lawless "Peace Process"

Israel's capture during the 1967 war of the remaining twenty-two percent of Palestine—the West Bank, East Jerusalem, and Gaza—is equally illegitimate. After fifty years of occupation, Israel's various unlawful encroachments on these Palestinian territories, especially the establishment of an archipelago of Israeli settlements, must cast serious doubt on whether Israel has ever intended to comply with the basic thrust of the post-war Security Council Resolution 242, which called for withdrawal from captured territories.

With respect to Jerusalem, Israel defiantly declared its intentions immediately at the conclusion of the 1967 war by unlawfully enlarging the area of the city and then proclaiming it the "eternal capital of the Jewish people." Israel has continuously undermined the stability of Palestinian residence in Jerusalem while engaging in a series of cleansing and settlement policies designed to give the city a more Jewish demographic profile.

The Fourth Geneva Convention Relative to the Protection of Civilian Persons in Time of War, a widely ratified treaty governing situations of belligerent occupation, should govern Israel's actions in the occupied territories but stands out as a treaty flagrantly violated. The continuing establishment of numerous Israeli settlements in the West Bank and East Jerusalem (and until 2005 in Gaza) is a violation, for instance, of the Convention's Article 49(6). Article 33 forbids the

June 5, 1967. Israeli troops guard captured Egyptian troops and Palestinians in Rafah, Gaza Strip at the start of the Six-Day War.

Gallo/Getty

imposition of collective punishment; actions such as the comprehensive blockade of Gaza imposed in 2007, the periodic curfews imposed on Palestinian cities and neighborhoods, widespread house demolitions, construction of the Separation Wall inside the West Bank, all fall under this prohibition. Numerous other Israeli actions make Palestinian lives miserable; these include actions ranging from administrative detention of Palestinians without charge or proper legal action and the movement of Palestinian prisoners to jails inside Israel, to the imprisonment of hundreds of child detainees, prohibition on family visits to prisoners, restriction of Palestinian movement through the establishment of hundreds of checkpoints across the territories, and various other arbitrary closures. Israeli settlers in the occupied territories enjoy the full protections of Israeli law, while Palestinians are essentially without rights and without legal protection.

It should be noted that there are some serious deficiencies in the architecture of international law as it applies to prolonged occupation. The Geneva Conventions, by giving the occupying power an administrative mandate, automatically deprive the occupied society of normal civil and human rights, as well as the rule of law, but this is supposed to be temporary. While perhaps a reasonable practice for up to five years, this is totally unreasonable for fifty years with no end in sight. There is a serious need for a new international treaty addressing situations of prolonged occupation in ways that protect a civilian society under military rule.

Although the Oslo Framework of Principles agreed to in 1993 was widely hailed at the time as a breakthrough that would begin a conflict-ending process, in retrospect the agreement must be viewed quite critically. The Oslo Framework never acknowledged a Palestinian right of self-determination; it divided the West Bank into areas of differing Palestinian and continued overarching Israeli control; and the diplomatic process relied totally on the United States to serve as intermediary in peace talks, despite its continuing special military and diplomatic relationship with Israel.

Significantly, any consideration of international law was deliberately excluded throughout the years of Oslo diplomacy. This enabled Israel to continue its policy of creeping annexation via settlement construction, creating facts on the ground that made any prospect of withdrawal increasingly unlikely. Without any protection from international law, Palestinians were prevented by US diplomats from objecting to Israel's actions or invoking the law, on the premise that this would "disrupt the peace process." This failure of the falsely labeled peace process to move one step closer to either peace or Israeli withdrawal was immensely helpful to Israel and hurtful to Palestine.

Many Palestinian resistance tactics have also violated anti-terrorist laws and are inconsistent with

Fundamental Palestinian Rights Are Not Negotiable

Palestinians are mired in a one- or two-state debate that leapfrogs the need for a process of decolonization and reparations.... At this stage of the Palestinian struggle for self-determination, when the ultimate political solution cannot be defined, the concept of apartheid provides a clear analytical framework for a struggle for decolonization and self-determination that can isolate and weaken the oppressive practices of the Israeli state and—at the same time—preserve and strengthen the fundamental Palestinian rights that are not negotiable: The right to freedom from occupation and colonization, the right to full equality of Palestinian citizens of Israel, and the right of the refugees to return to their homes and properties.

Excerpted from "Talking Palestine: What Frame of Analysis? Which Goals and Messages?" Nadia Hijab and Ingrid Jaradat Gassner, Al-Shabaka Palestinian Policy Network, April 12, 2017

international laws governing the use of force.[2] Although this Palestinian violence must be taken seriously, it should not distract from the reality of Israel's overriding denial of fundamental Palestinian rights or its imposition of discriminatory structures of domination far in excess of any reasonable security justifications.

The Present Relevance of International Law: From Occupation to Apartheid

After fifty years, and numerous encroachments on the territorial integrity of the Palestinian remnant remaining after the 1948 War, it is no longer descriptive of the basic reality to refer to the Palestinian people as living under "occupation." Focusing on "occupation" creates the misleading impression that Palestinian grievances under international law are limited to the situation since Israel's capture of territories in 1967, thereby ignoring the plight of several million displaced Palestinians still living in refugee camps after seventy years. Denying involuntary exiles a right to return to their native country is a grave violation of international refugee law, which confers a right of repatriation.

The term "occupation" overlooks several aspects of Israel's control over Palestinian territories. Fundamentally, Israel's policies constitute a "creeping annexation" in which areas under supposed temporary control, but fifty years on, are being incrementally incorporated into territorial Israel. Israel has also fragmented Palestinians in the West Bank into Areas A, B, and C, as well as separating residents of the West Bank, East Jerusalem, and Gaza from one another. Further, focus on the occupation also overlooks the situation of the approximately two million Palestinians living in Israel under a regime of discriminatory laws. The overall purpose of this fragmentation and systematic discrimination has been to enable the domination of the Palestinian people by the Jewish state of Israel.

The term "apartheid," designating a structure of control, extends to all of these distinct domains in which Palestinians are being actively subjugated in violation

Although...Palestinian violence must be taken seriously, it should not distract from the reality of Israel's overriding denial of fundamental Palestinian rights or its imposition of discriminatory structures of domination far in excess of any reasonable security justifications.

Israeli soldiers block Palestinian activists during an action against the separation policy between Palestinians living in the West Bank and Palestinians living in Jerusalem, Hizma checkpoint, March 9, 2012. Under military order 101, all protests organized by Palestinians in the West Bank are deemed illegal by the Israeli authorities and are routinely dispersed violently, leading to countless fatalities, injuries, and arbitrary arrests.

ActiveStills/Oren Ziv

...the weight of international law now clearly mandates that negotiation of a sustainable peace depends on the prior disavowal and abandonment of the apartheid regime that Israel relies upon to subjugate the Palestinian people.

of international law. This pattern of fragmenting and exercising domination over the totality of the Palestinian people is a violation of the 1973 International Convention on the Prevention and Punishment of the Crime of Apartheid. Although the concept of apartheid and the word are borrowed from the South African experience, the clear intention of the international community has been to broaden the law to mark apartheid anywhere as an international crime and to associate its occurrence with "inhuman acts" committed for the purpose of maintaining one race's domination over another. For purposes of international criminal law, the distinct ethnic identities of Jews and Palestinians are enough to satisfy the international law understanding of "race."

Conclusion

The historical milestones marked in 2017 call attention to a critical aspect of international law's relevance for Palestine/Israel: what was acceptable under international law one hundred, seventy, and fifty years ago is no longer acceptable in 2017, and the fact that the Palestinians' right under international law to self-determination has never been respected is of surpassing importance. Palestinian grievances falling under the international legal regime must be taken into account in any diplomatic solution of the conflict. The Palestinian right to self-determination must, of course, be realized in a context sensitive to the corresponding right of the Jewish people resident in historic Palestine, and giving proper effect to this double right of self-determination is a central challenge facing any authentic diplomacy. Unlike the Balfour Declaration or the UN partition

resolution, no peace treaty in this post-colonial era will be acceptable under international law if it is imposed by violent force or under the authority of an outside party.

A solution that brings peace in accord with international law and global justice must also center on ending apartheid—that is, on dismantling the structures of domination and discrimination that have victimized the Palestinian people as a whole in the various fragmented domains where Palestinians have been confined. Implementing such a process would require a diminished Zionist policy agenda, including recognition that any legitimate state or states that emerge in Palestine formally must be neither religious nor ethnic. It would not be inconsistent with international law to establish a Jewish homeland within such a post-apartheid secular state, but this would have to be based on religious and ethnic equality with the rest of society, as well as on adherence to a rule of law that upheld human rights.

It is critical to keep in mind that the goal merely of "ending the occupation" is an outmoded way of moving toward peace, and that the weight of international law now clearly mandates that negotiation of a sustainable peace depends on the prior disavowal and abandonment of the apartheid regime that Israel relies upon to subjugate the Palestinian people.

Richard Falk is the Albert G. Milbank Professor of International Law Emeritus, Princeton University, and Former Special Rapporteur for Occupied Palestinian Territories, UN Human Rights Council.

Intersectionality and the Shared Struggle for Human Rights

The links among resistance movements opposing empire have brought the currents of racial, economic, gender, immigration, education, mass incarceration, and climate and environmental global justice together in a way never before witnessed.

The quest for justice in Palestine is rooted in values found not only in religious texts of all Abrahamic faiths, but in the secular founding documents of the United States and other democratic nations, and in the founding principles of the United Nations. Justice is indivisible. Peace is indivisible. Justice in one place is not enough without justice everywhere; peace in one place is insufficient without peace everywhere.

Consider the metaphor of a single global fabric. The various rights enumerated in the Universal Declaration of Human Rights are interwoven into that interdependent fabric. These rights are universal. They apply to everyone in every society. Each right is one strand of that fabric. When one strand is broken or pulled out of place, the entire garment is weakened. Scholars now use the term *intersectionality* for this interwoven web of rights and the common struggle to realize these rights all over the world.

In that spirit, and reflecting on the unprecedented political moment presented by a new administration in the US, a global situation of virtually constant warfare, and a global political climate in which resistance to oppression of all sorts is notably increasing, the leaders from the Israel Palestine Mission Network (IPMN) who produced the study guides *Steadfast Hope* (2009, 2011) and *Zionism Unsettled* (2014) have broadened the scope of this current study and the composition of the study guide. Faith-based advocacy is a centerpiece of IPMN. Faith-based communities and networks are at the epicenter of our advocacy work for justice in Palestine. We invite you to walk with us as we use a wide angle lens to put Palestine in a global context and expand the reach of our work to include secular and non-Christian communities.

Struggles for justice today have become collaborative. Whereas *Steadfast Hope* addressed facts on the ground from a largely Christian perspective and *Zionism Unsettled* reframed the discussion of facts by explaining the political ideology of Zionism, *Why Palestine Matters: The Struggle To End Colonialism* offers a global perspective on the issue of justice for Palestine, expanding the prospective study groups to include wider secular and faith-based audiences. Colonialism and empire are phenomena that trace their origins

> Injustice anywhere is a threat to justice everywhere. We are caught in an inescapable network of mutuality, tied in a single garment of destiny. Whatever affects one directly, affects all indirectly....
>
> Martin Luther King Jr.

to centuries past but that continue to have a global impact in a new guise today—through, for instance, neocolonial and neoliberal economic policies, through settler colonialism as practiced by Israel in Palestine, and through US military dominance.

The cross-fertilization and intersectionality of activism among new movements such as Black Lives Matter and the water protectors at the Standing Rock Sioux Reservation, as well as the older quest for justice through Liberation Theology, have linked the Palestinian quest in a global struggle against the overarching domination of colonial and imperial interests. The links among resistance movements opposing empire have brought the currents of racial, economic, gender, immigration, education, mass incarceration, and climate and environmental global justice together in a way never before witnessed.

The challenge to see Palestine in a global context is the impetus for this current study guide. We are educators, theologians, and Palestine solidarity activists, and we recognize that an intersectional approach to justice in Palestine demands both a laser focus on Palestine and a zooming out beyond Palestine.

Undergirding this project is a basic assumption that people matter. Black lives matter. Palestinian lives matter. Israeli lives matter. All lives matter. The infrastructure of injustice is not circumscribed by ethnicity, gender, race, class, nationality, or place. Efforts to dismantle injustice must connect the dots. We are in this together; our work must be for the betterment of us all. If we fail to take all of us everywhere into account, we have failed overall.

The project of human emancipation is not limited to Palestine, but it also cannot proceed without Palestine. This study guide is intended for and inspired by all who seek and work toward justice.

CHAPTER 1

Palestine Through the Lens of Colonialism and Intersectionality

Rethinking Narratives
Martina Reese

Before the British Mandate was established in Palestine or the Holocaust devastated European Jewry, waves of Jews migrated from Europe to Palestine to make a permanent homeland where their biblical forebears lived 2,000 years earlier. In the early twentieth century, further waves of Eastern European Jews arrived in Palestine seeking refuge from antisemitism.*

Over the decades, most western observers have perceived the Israeli state-building project as an appropriate, even necessary, manifestation of Jews' desire for self-determination in a hostile world. This pro-Zionist understanding of the entwined history of

> If the roots of a conflict show you that it's not really a conflict but rather a case of colonial aggression, then you have to think differently about its historical extension into the present…. [T]he current state of Israel is an extension of that original massive 1948 ethnic cleansing, with its subsequent 1967 ethnic cleansings, and on to present-day ethnic cleansings which occur even in what is called "Israel proper," targeting Israeli citizens who are non-Jewish.
>
> Jonathan Ofir, Israeli writer, 2017

* Throughout *Why Palestine Matters: The Struggle To End Colonialism*, the IPMN uses the spelling "antisemitism." Jewish Voice for Peace explains that the use of the hyphen and upper case, as in "anti-Semitism," legitimizes the pseudo-scientific category of Semitism, which sorts humans into different races, justifies racial hierarchies, and argues for discrimination, supremacist policies, and worse. The IPMN affirms this reasoning and has used it to guide our own decision-making regarding the spelling of antisemitism in this study guide. See "A Note about the Spelling of 'Antisemitism'" in *On Antisemitism: Solidarity and the Struggle for Justice*, page xv, Haymarket Books, 2017.

Palestinians and Israelis, known as the "Israeli narrative," has dominated international discourse. A complex set of historical conditions has made it so: Christian identification with biblical Israel, the presence of Jewish and non-Jewish advocates for Israel within western power elites, underrepresentation of persons of Arab ancestry within mainstream western institutions, racist perceptions of Arabs, and Holocaust guilt.

The Israeli narrative, while deeply rooted in American culture, obscures the largely untold other side of the story, known as the "Palestinian narrative." By 1949, 750,000 Palestinians whose ancestors had inhabited the region for centuries were dispossessed of their land and property. Palestinians experienced the proliferation of the predominantly European Jewish Zionists as settler colonialism—much as had colonized peoples elsewhere throughout the Western and "non-white" world. While colonial structures were toppling in the postwar decades, the same period saw an expansion of Zionist encroachment, ethnic cleansing, and domination of the indigenous Arab peoples in Palestine. The departure of the British Mandate governors from Palestine in 1948 was not followed by the promised Palestinian self-determination, but by another form of European colonialism: Zionism.

Colonial domination of non-whites by European powers proved unsustainable after the new post-WWII world order: over the course of two decades, most of the colonial enterprises in Africa and Asia collapsed (Indonesia in 1945, India in 1947, African colonies

Nicolas Tikhomiroff/Magnum Photos

The impulse of indigenous peoples to resist and expel their colonizers is generally accepted as a justified and necessary response to domination and oppression; it is a right enshrined in international law. Nonetheless, the Palestinian struggle for self-determination has, in the minds of many, been detached from the wider global struggle of indigenous peoples against colonialism.

The time is past due for Americans and global citizens to undertake an open exploration of Palestinians' historical and contemporary situation seen through a wide-angle lens. Westerners who support the Zionist project in Palestine as a remedy for antisemitism do so at little cost to themselves. Indeed, the culturally Christian West must continue to critique its role in the heinous history of antisemitism. At the same time, it is essential to reckon that, with the creation of an ethnocentric Jewish state in their millennial homeland, Palestinians are paying the moral and physical price for abhorrent acts of antisemitism they did not commit. It is time to hear the narrative of the colonized with open hearts and minds.

1960. French troops of "Les Gardes Mobiles" use military force to suppress a demonstration in Algiers. The Algerian War for Independence lasted from 1954-62 and ended with France's withdrawal from the colony it had declared in 1838 to be an "integral part of France."

throughout the 1960s). Because white colonizers throughout Asia and Africa were a small—if privileged and powerful—minority in their respective colonies, it is perhaps inevitable that these colonial projects were ultimately abandoned as unsustainable, unlike the cases of the United States, Canada, and Australia, where the unstoppable influx of white settler-colonists and the decimation of the indigenous populations resulted in irreversible victory for the colonizers.

From a Palestinian Perspective
G.J. Tarazi

The history of colonialism has shared intersections in places that will surprise, anger, and, it is hoped, motivate some readers to action. In this article, G.J. Tarazi describes some justice struggles from a Palestinian perspective.

Colonialism uses methods that are intentional, purposeful, destructive, and long lasting. The United States has its own colonial history and fits the definition of an empire. Israel's now century-old settler colonial experiment also fits into this paradigm in what is for many a Holy Land. The methods by which the United States and Israel have gained power and retain dominance have striking similarities: the manner in which they interact with the indigenous populations; the attitude of "exceptionalism"; the dehumanizing maltreatment of those who are not like them; and the exploitation of natural resources. There is hope that critically evaluating elements of colonialism in both these countries will inform and inspire a much-needed healing process.

Tools of Domination
In an uneven power structure, racism feeds the exceptionalism of the powerful and the dehumanization of the powerless. "Race" is a social construct used for identifying and segregating people based on skin color and/or physical features; geography and/or

nationality; language and/or culture; and sometimes religion. Using these designations often leads to feelings of superiority, which in turn fosters dehumanizing and even demonizing of others to reinforce feelings of exceptionalism.

There are clear parallels between the experiences of Palestinians living under Israeli settler-colonialism and Native Americans living in the settler-colonial United States. Early European settlers who colonized the land that became the United States referred to the indigenous people they encountered as "Indians." Indians did not look like the colonizers, speak the same language, or have the same social practices. They did not worship the same god. Stealing their ancestral lands, the settler-colonizers called the indigenous people "savages," took it upon themselves to "civilize" them by imposing the colonial language on them, converting them to Christianity, and forcing them into new economic and educational systems. They considered these efforts a moral obligation—their "White Man's Burden," as described by Rudyard Kipling for British colonialism.

When these efforts failed, the colonizers used their

In an uneven power structure, racism feeds the exceptionalism of the powerful and the dehumanization of the powerless.

Water Protectors camp out at Oceti Sakowin Camp on the edge of the Standing Rock Sioux Reservation, outside Cannon Ball, North Dakota, in December 2016. Palestinians and Palestine solidarity activists were there to support the rights of Native Americans for their ancestral lands.

For decades, Israel's official policy has been one of keeping the local indigenous population separate from the settler colonizers....In addition, Israeli/Zionist policy has been to take the land of Palestine with as few Palestinians as possible.

army to force the indigenous people into reservations, started wars against them, and continued to steal their lands. White Man's Burden became the more specific "Manifest Destiny," a belief that God had given them a mission to 'civilize' this massive new land "from sea to shining sea."

Then and Now
This past treatment of Native Americans is believed to be grounded in racism. Unfortunately, it continues to be visible and do damage in the United States today. In 2016, powerful oil companies and their financial backers planned the construction of pipelines carrying crude oil through Standing Rock, a Native American reservation in North Dakota. The Sioux Nation resisted what they believed to be an illegal and immoral enterprise. When the courts sided with the powerful oil companies, the Sioux and their supporters used nonviolent tactics—on their own land—to stop the construction. They called themselves "Water Protectors," describing their attempt to keep their water supply clean and their land sacred. Joined by large numbers of American and international activists, the Water Protectors built encampments to block the construction crews. The oil companies, supported by state and local police forces, initially could not impact this nonviolent resistance. Not completing the pipeline on schedule cost the oil companies millions of dollars a day. However, the oil companies successfully lobbied the federal government to add the Water Protectors to the official "terrorist organizations" list, which enabled federal forces to break up the peaceful protestors. Aided by the severe North Dakota winter, these combined company, local, and federal forces used military equipment and dogs to violently destroy the encampment. The pipeline was eventually built.

Here and There
The tools of domination are strikingly similar in Israel.

An exceptionalist theology has led to a settler people dominating an indigenous people. European Ashkenazi Zionist Jews began to settle the land in the 19th Century. Their belief, based on the Hebrew Bible, that they were chosen by God to be "a light unto the nations," which is associated with Jews being known as the "chosen people." Ashkenazi Jews, the ruling elite in Israel today, are not Middle Eastern but are European settlers; they control all aspects of life in Israel as well as the territories taken in the 1967 War (the West Bank, Gaza Strip, East Jerusalem, and the Golan Heights). In the post WWII era, as independence came one-by-one to all colonies of Western powers, Israel remained a Western settler-colonial state. Decades later, this colonial power is backed by unconditional military, economic, and political support by the United States. The seemingly unbreakable bond between Israel and the United States is said to be based on their "shared values," which Palestinians see as imposed archaic settler values.

Occupation to Apartheid
What began as a military occupation in 1967 was then and is now a policy of separation also known as apartheid, an Afrikaans word meaning "separate." For decades, Israel's official policy has been one of keeping the local indigenous population separate from the settler colonizers. This is reminiscent of settler colonialism in North America, Africa, and South Africa, where European settlers forced the indigenous populations into separate areas. The system of government which rules different peoples with different laws is known as an apartheid government; it is a crime under international law. Naming the issue of separation as apartheid— rather than occupation—corrects the whitewashing and normalization of what is happening on the ground today. This point is reinforced by a comprehensive March 2017 United Nations report which labeled Israel an "apartheid state" for the first time. However, the report was pulled from the UN system as a result of intense pressure from Israel and the United States.1

Apartheid is justified by ethnocentric and supremacist ideologies. In the Israel/Palestine situation, it is compounded by the Israeli government's calculated, purposeful, and meticulous dehumanization of Palestinians. Mirroring the labels such as "savages" for Native Americans, Zionist politicians have publicly called Palestinians "snakes"—and worse. There is documentation and video showing the Jewish Israeli settlers treating Palestinians as less than human.2 Veterans of the Israeli Defense Forces have come forward to share their experiences of how abuse of Palestinians is intentional and systemic. These IDF veterans share their stories publicly through an organization called Breaking the Silence.

In addition, Israeli/Zionist policy has been to take the land of Palestine with as few Palestinians as possible. This has been documented by Israeli historian Ilan Pappe, in his book, The Ethnic Cleansing of Palestine.

This practice of ridding Palestine of its indigenous population through transfer, deportation, and massacres began prior to the creation of the State of Israel based on the ideology of the first Zionist settlers.

Reminiscent of Jim Crow Laws in the United States, Israeli laws today specifically designed for Palestinians living in Israel discriminate and disadvantage Palestinians at every turn.[3] In the apartheid areas of the West Bank and Gaza Strip, Palestinians live under strict and harsh Israeli military laws that control all aspects of their daily lives—including access to water and electricity, restricted movement within their own areas, even where cell phone service works.

More Parallels

As with Native American and African populations, Palestinians' ancestral land continues to be taken by force. And completing the segregation on the land, settlements which are illegal Jewish-only colonies are built with highway systems connecting them to each other. These highways can only be accessed by travelers in cars with Israeli license plates. These Jewish-only settlements in the West Bank are built on 42 percent of the Palestinian territory, and Israel controls a total of 60 percent of the West Bank. Palestinians are confined to live in ever-shrinking, isolated, non-contiguous areas, reminiscent of South Africa's Bantustans during their apartheid era.

In another parallel with the Native American experience, the narrative of the colonized is erased. Following Zionist policies, Israel's education system has erased Palestinians and Palestine from their textbooks. They use the word "Arab" instead. They refuse to use the name the Palestinians prefer for themselves. This is a blatant tool of domination. Furthermore, the border line separating the West Bank and Golan Heights from Israel is no longer in Israeli school textbook maps; those lands acquired through the 1967 War are now fully incorporated into the map of Israel. As history is often told by the victors, under Israeli law, it is illegal to commemorate or speak about the "*Nakba*," a word which means catastrophe in Arabic, and refers to the experience of dispossession, transfer, and massacre of Palestinians that began with the creation of Israel. Israeli historians, using declassified documents, have discovered that during the creation of Israel, various terrorist militias destroyed more than 601 Palestinian villages and drove more than 750,000 Palestinians from their homes. These forces were Zionist, and Zionism was their driving force. In what has been referred to as "Judaizing the land," Palestinian names of villages, towns, and roads have been erased from official Israeli maps and documents, compounding the assault on identity, history, and narrative. Carrying this assault into the future, Israel refuses to grant Palestinians their Right to Return to their homes and homeland, a right enshrined in international law and one that has not been denied to other refugee groups.

More parallels can be seen in the history of slavery in the United States. This history is thoughtfully presented in the National Museum of African American History and Culture in Washington, DC. Walking through the subterranean floors of the museum is depressing, with stark displays of the realities of slavery. Those floors are dark and dingy, with messages at each display depicting the long history of racism and its deplorable byproduct, slavery.

During the time of slavery, many political, economic, and religious colonial leaders thought of themselves as superior beings and masters of their world and everything within their world. They defined African Americans as less than human. Politicians enacted laws, which defined the Negro as three-fifths human. To the economic leaders of the time, African Americans were just property to be used to advance the welfare of their owners. Slaves were critical cogs in the cotton and sugar-based economy, and their owners used a variety of justifications to maintain this system. With self-serving interpretations of scriptures, the religious leaders of the time did what was required to justify misguided beliefs on slavery and inhuman actions. As with the establishment of the modern state of Israel, those who oppressed others used the Bible as a weapon and forced their control over people whom they considered inferior. This type of domination is often the source of racism that takes root in a society.

Mass Incarceration

After a very bloody and costly civil war, legal slavery in the United States was brought to an end; once-blatant aspects of racism became more subtle but no less controlling and vicious. The 13th Amendment to

As history is often told by the victors, under Israeli law, it is illegal to commemorate or speak about the "*Nakba*," a word which means catastrophe in Arabic, and refers to the experience of dispossession, transfer, and massacre of Palestinians that began with the creation of Israel.

Palestinian boys wave national flags near the Erez border crossing between Gaza and Israel. Innocent children are captive to collective punishment in Gaza since 2006 when Israel put a population of now close to 2 million under military siege and blockade.

Hatem Moussa/AP

The most serious discriminatory laws were enacted very quickly after the creation of the State. These laws relate to land ownership/control and Israeli citizenship.

the Constitution in January 1865 outlawed slavery. Unfortunately, the hateful products of racism morphed from slavery to yet another legal system under the guise of "law and order" or "war on crime" or "war on drugs." The 13th Amendment abolished slavery and involuntary servitude, *except as punishment for a crime*. This provision created the insidious prison industrial complex.

Shortly after the 13th Amendment was passed, there was a swift en masse arrest of African Americans, mostly for minor violations. This led to a system called "convict leasing" whereby incarcerated African Americans were forced to do work previously done by slaves. This included farming, road-building, industrial work, and other punishment for their "crimes." In addition, Jim Crow Laws were enacted that made African Americans second-class citizens. A century after the end of slavery, with the passage of the Civil Rights Act and Voting Rights Act, the US ended the era of *de jure* racism by ending the use of racist laws. However, scholar John L. Jackson, Jr. concludes that this began the era of "de cardio racism," the racism "of the heart," a more insidious racism that cannot be changed through public policy and laws.[4]

In Israel and the Palestinian areas it controls both *de jure* and *de cardio* racism are visible. There are dozens of discriminatory laws that treat Palestinians differently from Jews. Palestinians who remained in Israel after 1949 were subject to martial law governing their travel, curfews, administrative detentions, and expulsions. In 1966, however, overtly discriminatory laws replaced martial law. These laws clearly defined the primacy of ethnically Jewish Israelis, giving statutory recognition to Jewish cultural and educational institutions at the

expense of minorities, including indigenous peoples.

Disregarding millennia of connection of Palestinians to this land, the Knesset (parliament) sessions open with a reading of portions of Israel's Declaration of Independence, emphasizing the exclusive connection of the State of Israel to the Jewish people. Any political party that advocates equal rights for all citizens of Israel regardless of ethnicity is denied participation in the Knesset. New laws were enacted that unequally administered and funded established separate educational systems for Jews versus non-Jews, completing the separation/segregation of peoples.

As Max Blumenthal has shown in his book, *Goliath: Life and Loathing in Greater Israel*, de-cardio racism (racism "in the heart" not reachable by law) is rampant in Israel. The racial domination that took centuries to develop in the United States has been concentrated and accelerated in Israel and Palestine. This reality makes a mockery of Israel's claim to be "the only democracy in the Middle East," a state where one's religion determines the level of rights one can exercise.

Advocates for a "Jewish and democratic" state admit that even if the occupation of Palestinian territories and people ended and a separate independent Palestinian state emerged alongside Israel, a "Jewish and democratic" state would still privilege Jewish (currently 75% of the population) over non-Jewish citizens of the state of Israel. This discrimination would also be seen in Israel's symbols (national flag and anthem), in its national holidays, race-based laws, and, above all, in its immigration policy.

In 2012, Adalah, the Legal Center for Arab Minority Rights in Israel, published a report entitled "The Discriminatory Laws Data Base," which collected and analyzed more than 50 laws enacted since 1948 that discriminate against Palestinian citizens of Israel. The most serious discriminatory laws were enacted very quickly after the creation of the State. These laws relate to land ownership/control and Israeli citizenship. Israel took over and controlled about 93% of all land within the 1949 armistice line known as the "Green Line." This law gave preferential treatment to Jews and denied Palestinians the ability to develop and build on their own land, some of which were deeded during the Ottoman Empire or during the British Mandate.

The 1950 Absentee Landlord Property Law defines as "absentee" Palestinians who were expelled, fled, or left Palestine, but their land and property was claimed by the very people who expelled them. Today, Israel continues to use this law to justify its colonization and "Judaization" of East Jerusalem, and the taking of land belonging to Palestinian refugees living in Israel and the Diaspora.

There are striking parallels in the United States in using laws to oppress "other" peoples. In our living memory, political parties have used racist dog-whistle statements during the 1970s and 1980s to

July 3, 2016. **Protesting police terror, Ethiopian-Israelis in Tel Aviv block traffic on Kaplan Street.**

Benny Woodoo

maintain racial segregation, and more recently in the 2016 election by Trump supporters against Hispanic and Muslim immigration. Incarceration figures and demographics illustrate that African American communities were targeted by law and order policies in order to control them. African American men living in the urban ghettos were called "super predators" and were seen being arrested every night on the evening news. The reported "lawlessness" of African Americans was labeled "wilding," which reinforced and advanced their criminalization myth.

Further evidence of the targeting of African Americans in the US is apparent in laws dealing with cocaine. Powder cocaine, the expensive drug of white, suburban dwellers, and crack cocaine, the less expensive drug of African Americans, have very different legal consequences. Crack cocaine was criminalized, and African Americans who were arrested were subjected to mandatory sentencing. Intentionally, 97% of African Americans arrested for possession of crack cocaine never made it to trial. Plea bargains may have reduced their jail time, but with the racially targeted "three strikes and you're out" policy, African Americans who were arrested the third time did not have any chance for release. In addition, President Bill Clinton's 1994 Omnibus Crime Bill militarized policing and severely aggravated the conditions of African Americans.

As mass incarceration became privatized, it quickly became the financial lifeline for the prison industrial complex. In addition to the direct logistical running of for-profit prisons, an entire support structure developed around it. This included providing for-pay landline phones, food services, health care, uniforms and laundry services, GPS with ankle/wrist home-confinement bands, etc. These businesses supported and are supported by private, for-profit prisons. Michelle Alexander's *The New Jim Crow* exposes how the so-called "war on drugs," begun in the Reagan era, was actually a new way of keeping African Americans incarcerated for minor drug offenses which in turn kept them from voting on election day and from the equality promised after the dismantling of Jim Crow laws.

The treatment of African Americans in the United States and Palestinians by Israel is shockingly similar. Since the June 1967 war, Israel has imprisoned nearly a million Palestinians, including nonviolent human rights activists. According to the prisoners' rights group Addameer, as of May 2017 there were 6,200 Palestinian political prisoners in Israeli jails.[5] The Israeli justice system is two-tiered, administered differently for Palestinians and Israelis. Jews have "more rights" and are subject to Israeli civil law, while Palestinians - Muslims or Christians - are subject to military law. Human rights organizations have condemned this system as falling far short of the minimum standards required for a fair trial.[6] The military court system, which Palestinians are

January 2018. Ahed Tamimi, a 16-year-old Palestinian protester from the West Bank village of Nabi Salih, is booked in Ofer Military Court. Since Ahed's incarceration began, Ahed marked her 17th birthday in prison. Despite an international outcry for her release, she remains jailed as she awaits trial.

forced into, has an unbelievable conviction rate of more than 99%.[7]

Using the practice known as "administrative detention," Israel also imprisons Palestinians *without charge* or trial for up to six months; this can be extended indefinitely. Israel has used administrative detention against Palestinians more than 50,000 times since 1967.[8] This process has been condemned by human rights organizations such as Amnesty International and Human Rights Watch.[9]

Mass incarceration of the African American community in the US and of Palestinians by Israel each bear remnants of colonialism and maintain systems of power and domination. Both systems impose a harsh reality of extreme incarceration and subjugation as a means to an end, with no apparent way out.

Abuse of Children

A matter of particular concern, both in Palestine today and under the system of segregation in the US pre-Civil Rights legislation, is the treatment of children. All racism is abhorrent, but the abuse of children is most egregious, especially when children are abused simply because of who they are.

Emmett Louis Till, an African American child, was murdered during August of 1955, one month after his fourteenth birthday. His story is but one stark example of how African American children have been the victims of racism throughout American history. Emmett was born outside Chicago. While visiting family in Mississippi, he was kidnapped, beaten, shot in the head, and thrown into the Tallahatchie River. His deformed body was found three days later. His "crime" was making eye contact with a white woman who was offended by this behavior. She was the cashier at a store from where he was making a purchase. A jury of all white

Mass incarceration of the African American community in the US and of Palestinians by Israel each bear remnants of colonialism and maintain systems of power and domination.

[M]ore than 92.6 percent of complaints Palestinians lodge with the Israeli police go without charges being filed, so in reality, attacks by Jewish settlers are far more prevalent than recorded.

men acquitted the two white men who later confessed to killing Emmett. The brutality of his murder and the fact that his killers were acquitted underscore the long history of violent persecution of African Americans in the United States. Posthumously, Till became an icon of the Civil Rights Movement. His original casket is on display at the National Museum of African American History and Culture.[10]

There are similar examples of racism and the abuse of children in Israel today.

One example of Israeli brutality toward children is the murder of an eighteen-month-old Palestinian infant, whose name was Ali Saad Dawabsheh. He was burned to death when his family's home in the West Bank village of Duma, near Nablus, was attacked before sunrise and set on fire by illegal settlers. The toddler's parents were able to grab their older son and escape the deadly blaze. They were taken to hospital with burns over seventy percent of their bodies. Both parents died shortly after this attack but their older son survived. According to witnesses, two masked men from the nearby illegal settlement

of Migdalim smashed the windows and threw two firebombs into the house. They sprayed painted graffiti on the outside walls of the house reading "revenge" and "long live the Messiah" in Hebrew. Incredibly, Jewish settlers celebrated this murder of a toddler and his parents. A group of Israeli settlers recorded themselves rejoicing at a wedding party over the killing of this Palestinian baby, stabbing his photograph, with footage airing on Israeli news stations. Palestinians call these settlers terrorists.

According to the UN, at least 120 attacks by Israeli settlers have been documented in apartheid West Bank since 2015. A recent report by Yesh Din, an Israeli human rights organization, showed that more than 92.6 percent of complaints Palestinians lodge with the Israeli police go without charges being filed, so in reality, attacks by Jewish settlers are far more prevalent than recorded.

Palestinian children and youth living in segregated/apartheid West Bank and Gaza are experiencing brutal treatment by police and occupation soldiers daily. (The Israeli military are referred to as Occupation Forces because they are there to defend the settlers, not the Palestinians from the settlers). Palestinian children are subjected to very strict and repressive laws. One such law is the stone-throwing law. A Palestinian child in Israel or East Jerusalem can be sentenced to a minimum of three years for throwing a stone at tanks, armored jeeps, armored police, and soldiers. This law only applies to Palestinians and is not applied to Jewish settler youth who throw stones at Palestinian children going to school in the West Bank. In the big picture, this law is mind-boggling since, in Israel, there are no minimum sentences for such crimes as bribery, manslaughter, or rape.[11]

In addition, detained Palestinian children and youth from the West Bank aged 16 and up are subject to adult military law. Children as young as 12 years old have been taken in pre-dawn raids on their homes, traumatizing the entire family. Children are jailed without parental or legal representation and spend weeks or months without going to trial or even being charged with a crime.[12] Many children who go through this inhumane process, which is defined as illegal under international law, also report mental and physical torture. Many children describe the same torture techniques used by the Israeli police and soldiers[13] —including beatings, being tied to a wooden chair for long periods of time, and being deprived of food, sleep, and light.

In 2016 alone, 32 Palestinian minors from the West Bank and East Jerusalem have been killed at the hands of Israeli occupying forces.[14] It is also estimated that 500 to 700 Palestinian children and youth are detained each year in military jails.[15] A majority of them are prosecuted for throwing stones. This Israeli abuse of Palestinian children is unreported in American media. As a result, it is difficult to educate Americans of the incredible abuse that is ongoing, let alone to influence our legislators to help stop the abuse.

Militarizing Police Forces

In the presence of exceptionalism and dehumanization, racism flourishes. The Black Lives Matter movement in the United States came about as a result of on-going murders of black youth by police. The transformation of police forces into military-like forces has been seen as another tactic to dominate people. Israelis are actively cross-pollinating their policing and military tactics with other settler colonial cultures. The militarization of police forces in the United States is part of this process. Israel develops weapons for use against Palestinians. These weapons and surveillance techniques are sold to American police forces. In addition, for large sums of taxpayer money, US police forces travel to Israel to learn how to use these weapons and strategies. This militarization of policing, which results directly from this training, is considered to be the new face of racism. Police brutality on young black men in the US happens in plain sight, as has been witnessed in violent incidents in Ferguson,[16] Baltimore,[17] St. Louis,[18] and New York City.[19] All those police forces have been trained in Israel.

Domination and Water

Parallels can be found between how power structures in the United States and Israel use access to clean water to control and dominate the powerless.

News of the lead-poisoned water crisis in Flint, Michigan, has reached a wide audience around the world. The basic facts are known: Governor Rick Snyder nullified the free elections in Flint and deposed the Mayor, based on a state provision that applies when a city is facing financial challenges. He then appointed a businessman to run the city. Snyder and the unelected officials decided to unhook the people of Flint from their

Brendan Smialowski/AFP/Getty

fresh water source, Lake Huron, and hooked them to the Flint River. When the governor's office discovered how toxic the water was, they ignored the damage being inflicted on Flint's residents, most notably the lead affecting the children, which causes irreversible and permanent brain damage.

Michael Moore, author, documentary filmmaker, political and social activist, who is also a resident of Flint, provided some additional facts about this abuse of power in his blog. Here is a summary of some of the often-unheard facts he shared

While the predominantly African American citizens of Flint were given toxic water to drink, General Motors was given a special hookup to clean water. A few months after Governor Snyder removed Flint from the clean water source to save money, he spent $440,000 to hook

Baltimore County Sheriffs officers gather after Baltimore Officer Caesar Goodson Jr. was acquitted of all charges in his murder trial for the death of Freddie Gray at the Mitchell Court House June 23, 2016, in Baltimore, Maryland. The Baltimore police force, cited by the US Department of Justice for "widespread constitutional violations, discriminatory enforcement, and culture of retaliation," has received training on crowd control, use of force, and surveillance from Israel's national police, military, and intelligence services.

Library of Congress

On March 7, 1965, state troopers and a sheriff's posse in Selma, Alabama, attacked 525 civil rights demonstrators taking part in a march between Selma and Montgomery, the state capital. The march was organized to promote black voter registration and to protest the killing of a young black man, Jimmie Lee Jackson, by a state trooper during a February 18 voter registration march in a nearby city.

Upholding the Right to Resist

Thus when Palestinians resist the theft of the their land and the killing of their people by Israeli colonists, their response is defined as illegitimate violence that sparks support for Israel's "right to defend itself." When Africans waged national liberation struggles to free themselves from European colonial domination in places like Kenya, Angola, Mozambique, Zimbabwe, and South Africa, the West condemned their efforts as illegitimate. Furthermore, because those struggles were determined to be illegitimate, colonial powers felt justified to viciously attack those efforts with the support of the US government. And when African Americans organized against police violence and for self-determination and our own definitions of liberation in the '60s, our efforts were deemed illegitimate. We were brutally suppressed with the full range of state terror tactics including beatings, deaths, infiltration, surveillance, and the jailing of activists for decades.

Ajamu Baraka, national organizer of the Black Alliance for Peace, *Ferguson and the Right of Resistance*, *Counterpunch*, November 26, 2014.

Israel controls all access to water and how much water can be distributed. Israeli authorities determine annual quotas on the amount of water available to Palestinians.

A child transports water by jug during a water shortage crisis in Qarawat Bani Hassan village, May 23, 2015. Discriminatory water delivery quotas implemented by Mekorot, Israel's state-owned water distribution company, deprives West Bank Palestininans access to their own water resources while providing Israeli settlers with a plentiful supply. Boycott, divestment, and sanctions supporters have targeted Mekorot on the basis of its enforcement of "water apartheid."

up GM back to the Lake Huron water, while keeping the rest of Flint on the Flint River water. The GM factory was the only address in Flint hooked to the clean water of Lake Huron.

For $100 a day, this crisis could have been prevented. Federal law requires that water systems that use lead pipes must contain an additive that seals the lead into the pipe and prevents it from leaching into the water. It would have taken $100 a day for just three months to add this anti-corrosive treatment to the water coming out of the Flint River. The Governor and his staff rejected this option. As a result, the State had to pay more than $1.5 billion to remedy the situation of their own making.

There's more than lead in Flint's water. In addition to exposing every citizen of Flint to lead-poisoning on a daily basis, there are signs of other diseases. For example, Legionnaires Disease has increased *tenfold* since the misguided switch to the Flint River water. Doctors are discovering other toxins in the blood of Flint's citizens, causing concern that there are other health catastrophes, which may soon affect these innocent victims.

While they were being poisoned, Flint citizens were being bombed. During the years of water contamination, residents in Flint have had to also contend with a decision made by the Pentagon to use Flint for unannounced military exercises, complete with live ammunition and explosives. The army conducted urban warfare tactics on Flint, targeting abandoned homes on which they could drop bombs. Flint citizens reported that the exercises sounded as if the city was under attack from an invading army or from terrorists. People were shocked this could be going on in their neighborhoods. Flint, Michigan, a predominately African American city, is but one example of how access to clean water is used

to maintain domination of an underclass.

The use of water as a tool of Israeli domination is similar. Since the occupation of the West Bank in 1967, Israel grabbed control of Palestinian water resources through discriminatory water-sharing agreements that prevented Palestinians from maintaining or developing their own water infrastructure. As a result, thousands of Palestinians do not have access to clean water and have become dependent on a hostile power for a life-critical resource.

Israel has promulgated the myth that Israel-Palestine is a water-scarce region. The reality is that Ramallah has more annual rainfall than London. Israel has denied Palestinians control over their own water resources and successfully controlled all water aquifers in the region, both in Israel and the Palestinian territory. Israel prevents Palestinians from accessing the Jordan River or the Mountain Aquifer. The 1995 Oslo II interim agreement, which defines the water-sharing relationship between Palestine and Israel, gives Israel total control. In addition, Israel was granted access to over 71 percent of aquifer water, while Palestinians were granted only 17 percent. While the agreement was supposed to last only five years, it is still in effect today.

Israel controls all access to water and how much water can be distributed. Israeli authorities determine annual quotas on the amount of water available to Palestinians. While the UN's World Health Organization recommends a daily allotment of 100 liters/day/person, Palestinians are limited to 70 liters/day/person. However, Israelis are given access to 300 liters/day/person. Israelis also control and/or obstruct Palestinians from repairing or developing their infrastructure. For example, Palestinians are not permitted to build or repair cisterns to collect surface rainfall flow.

Most critical is the Israeli use of water to dominate

Ahmad Al-Bazz / ActiveStills

Flint and Gaza: Water Crises of Colonialism

...In spring of 2015, a year into one of the great public-health debacles in American history, the Flint [Michigan] City Council staged a symbolic protest vote in favor of abandoning Flint River water and spending $12 million a year to reconnect with the Detroit Water and Sewage Department....Only when physicians and scientists like Dr. Mona Hanna-Attisha went public was the governor finally forced to acknowledge the crisis and begin taking steps to address it....

Just as Flint residents were disenfranchised by the Emergency Manager Law and had their access to a basic staple like clean water denied by decisions made by bureaucrats they did not elect, so the Palestinians of Gaza lack the basic rights of citizenship. Israel invaded Gaza and ruled it directly from 1967 to 2005. It still prevents Palestinians from farming one-third of its land, denies it a seaport and an airport, and closely controls building and other materials going into the surrounded territory. Palestinians do not control their land, their water, or the air over their heads.

Since 2007, the people of Gaza have been under siege by the Israeli government, which is recognized as the occupation power. The Geneva Convention on the treatment of occupied populations of 1949 were enacted to forestall further crimes of the sort the Axis powers committed in the places they occupied during World War II. The convention makes occupying powers responsible for the health and well-being of the peoples they dominate. The Israeli government's fiction that it withdrew from Gaza in 2005, and may now treat the small strip and its trapped population as a belligerent independent state, has been repeatedly rejected by the international community. Israel is responsible for the Palestinians of Gaza.

Residents of Flint, Michigan, and supporters participate in a national mile-long march in February 2016 to demand for clean water in the majority-black city. Lead seepage into the drinking water has caused a massive public health crisis and prompted then-President Obama to declare a federal state of emergency.

"Flint and Gaza: Water Crises of Colonialism," Juan Cole, *The Nation*, February 3, 2016. Juan Cole is a professor of history and director of the Center for Middle Eastern and North African Studies at the University of Michigan.

Palestinians living in Gaza. Under Israel's military siege since 2007, Gazans have endured three Israeli military incursions and assaults in which power plants and water treatment plants were destroyed or badly damaged. The military blockade and siege of Gaza prevents repair materials and building supplies from entering the devastated Gaza Strip, creating a human crisis of catastrophic proportions. A report published by Oxfam International stated that Palestinians in Gaza were once able to drink clean water from the tap. Now less than 4% of tap water is drinkable and the surrounding sea is polluted by sewage. The report laments that the international community is failing to do enough to protect the health and dignity of almost 2 million people who are imprisoned under an airtight siege since 2007.[20]

Further, the report added that Gaza's water and sanitation crisis is escalating dangerously with clean water increasingly scarce, and almost a third of households are not connected to a sanitation system. Gaza's only functioning power plant creates even more urgency, with the water utility warning that it does not have the fuel to run water and sanitation facilities when the power is off. Water pollution is among the factors causing a dramatic increase in kidney problems in the Gaza Strip, with a 13-14% increase every year in the number of patients admitted with kidney problems to Gaza City's Shifa Hospital.

Access to clean water has been effectively used by Israel as a colonial tool to control a defeated people under its control and to further its domination over them.

Conclusion

Colonialism produced systems of domination of the colonizer over the colonized. This has been witnessed and documented in Israel and the United States, where there are strikingly similar rationales, foundations, and practices. In both countries, power was established and retained over indigenous populations based on exceptionalist ideologies that dehumanized "other" peoples under their control. In both countries, there has been exploitation of natural resources, to the point of deprivation and human rights abuses. In both countries, children have suffered disproportionately, with cruel and unusual punishment. In both countries, the law has been skewed to benefit the dominant power, leaving the oppressed and often powerless without any remedy for the deplorable conditions these countries have created and are creating.

Those who desire peace with justice are called upon to name, examine, and repair these failures and begin a much-needed healing process. Beginning with acknowledging the stories of the people who are under domination, the healing and reconciliation can begin.

...the international community is failing to do enough to protect the health and dignity of almost 2 million people [in Gaza] who are imprisoned under an airtight siege since 2007.

CHAPTER 2
An Intersectional Approach to Justice

A New Moment, A New Lens
Susan Landau and Rachael Kamel

The particularities of any struggle for justice do not exist in a vacuum. Threads of connection exist across issues and geography. These tangled knots of oppression, once made visible, together weave a new fabric of liberation.

Today's activist discussions, as well as current social theory, have identified "intersectionality" as the most fruitful way of understanding these threads of connection. This introductory chapter puts that discussion in context, offering a brief history of the concept, complemented by contemporary examples of how the vision of intersectionality has worked to build new connections among social movements in different locations.

The impulse to offer intersectional understandings of the drive toward social justice dates back to the late 1970s when Black women offered a powerful critique of the feminist movement of the day, charging that it was constrained by the perspectives of economically privileged white women. The Black liberation movement of that time, they also argued, was limited by its reliance on the experience and perspectives of Black men.

This activist critique was distilled in the statement of the Combahee River Collective.[1] Published in 1977, this critique continued as part of a Black feminist discussion over the years. In 1989, legal scholar Kimberlé Crenshaw coined the word "intersectionality" as a way of articulating this critical perspective.[2]

The concept of intersectionality has been widely accepted as a key approach, across activist communities as well as in discussions among academic researchers of different disciplines. Crenshaw's landmark essay "placed into sharp relief how discourses of resistance —e.g., feminism and antiracism—could themselves function as sites that produced and legitimized marginalization,"[3] whenever such discussions discounted the intersectional nature of social problems.

From its very beginnings, the call for an intersectional understanding of politics has been grounded in the call for coalition efforts. The very idea of intersectionality calls on us to see that even the terms we used to describe our experiences cannot be separated without doing violence to the realities they evoke. Simply put, it is impossible to speak of the experience of women without specifying whether one is referring to the situation of Black women, of white women, or of women of color in general. By the same token, there is no generic "Black" experience, but only the experience of Black women, Black men, and so on.

Part of what this means is that coalition politics is not additive. Human experience, for example, cannot be parsed as female + Black + impoverished; instead, each of these dimensions of experience co-create one another (or, in the language of social theory, they are "mutually constitutive").

> Employing an intersectional lens invites us to focus on creating effective alliances based on an understanding of our historical legacies of racism, patriarchy, and colonial expropriation.

> Intersectionality promotes an understanding of human beings as shaped by the interaction of different social locations (e.g., 'race'/ethnicity, Indige-neity, gender, class, sexuality, geography, age, disability/ability, migration status, religion). These interactions occur within a context of connected systems and structures of power (e.g., laws, policies, state governments and other political and economic unions, religious institutions, media). Through such processes, interdependent forms of privilege and oppression shaped by colonialism, imperialism, racism, homophobia, ableism and patriarchy are created.
>
> Olena Hankivsky, PhD, The Institute for Intersectionality Research and Policy, SFU, April 2014

From its very beginnings, the call for an intersectional understanding of politics has been grounded in the call for coalition efforts.

From the 1990s onward, both theoretical and practical applications of intersectionality have proliferated, across social movements, across academic disciplines, and across national and international boundaries. A useful discussion of how this concept has traveled across multiple boundaries is presented in "Intersectionality: Mapping the Movements of a Theory," a 2013 special issue of the *Du Bois Review*.[4] As the editorial introduction comments,

> [both] scholars and activists have broadened intersectionality to engage a range of issues, social identities, power dynamics, legal and political systems, and discursive structures in the United States and beyond....These movements of intersectionality have left behind a lively and provocative travelogue characterized by adaptation, redirection, and contestation.[5]

Some skeptics have questioned whether "Black women are too different to stand in for a generalizable theory about power and marginalization."[6] As the editors of this special issue have noted, however, "the travels of intersectionality belie that concern."[7]

As the editors go on to say, "paying attention to the movement of intersectionality helps to make clear that the theory is never done, nor exhausted by its prior articulations or movements; it is always already an analysis-in-progress."[8]

This book encourages a discussion of intersectionality because we believe this is a profoundly intersectional moment in the world of social movements. In the United States and beyond, the politics of austerity, as well as the depredations neoliberal economic policies, have forced social activists to rethink the single-issue model of political struggle. Attention to the perils of militarization, particularly in the quest for a sustainable and equitable peace in Israel-Palestine, has prompted us to explore the unprecedented levels of connection that are being forged across movements, borders, and other types of divisions.

Audre Lorde, black feminist poet and civil rights activist, observed,

> Intersectionality has evolved from a theory of how oppression works to a notion of how people can fight it....There is no such thing as a single-issue struggle because we do not live single-issue lives.

Employing an intersectional lens invites us to focus on creating effective alliances based on an understanding of our historical legacies of racism, patriarchy, and colonial expropriation.

The drive toward war, domestic repression, and the militarization of society can only be stopped by the people. But that will not occur until there is a shift in the culture and consciousness of the public. A shift in which the inherent value of all lives is recognized and a new kind of politics is practiced in which the people are able to recognize that their interests are not the same as the interests of the capitalist oligarchy and that they have a responsibility to victims of US imperialism around the world.

Ajamu Baraka, national organizer of the Black Alliance for Peace, May 10, 2017

The tendency has been to consider Palestine a separate—and unfortunately too often marginal—issue. This is precisely the moment to encourage everyone who believes in equality and justice to join the call for a free Palestine.

Angela Y. Davis. *Freedom Is a Constant Struggle*, 2016

This quote by Martin Luther King, Jr. appears in support of the Standing Rock Sioux in a protest against the Dakota Access Pipeline, August 31st, 2016.

Justin Deegan

...if we put identity politics ahead of the requirement to be intersectional and to connect to other struggles, we harm ourselves, our cause, as well as other causes.

Excerpt from a public talk by Omar Barghouti, delivered May 2, 2017, as told by Philip Weiss on *Mondoweiss*

Inspired J. Howard Miller's iconic "We Can Do It!" wartime poster of "Rosie the Riveter," this image was rediscovered in the '80's and used as a symbol of the feminist movement. This version has become a powerful image of feminism today as influenced by intersectionality and inclusion.

Like Jim Crow (and slavery), mass incarceratio operates as a tightly networked system of law policies, customs, and institutions that operate collectively to ensure the subordinate status o a group defined largely by race.

Michelle Alexander, *The New Jim Crow: Mass Incarceration in the Age of Colorblindness*, 2010

INTERSECTIONALITY THREADS OF CONNECTION

Islamophobia is one branch on the tree of racism. Islamophobia, homophobia, anti-Black racism, and antisemitism are all connected, and we cannot dismantle one without the other. Our liberation is intertwined, our stories are intertwined, our identities are intertwined.

"Our Liberation Is Intertwined," An Interview with Linda Sarsour, *On Antisemitism: Solidarity and the Struggle for Justice*, p.93, 2017

Tess Scheflan/ActiveStills

Fadi Arouri/Xinhua

If you have come to help me, you are wasting your time. If you have come because your liberation is bound up with mine, then let us work together.

Lilla Watson, Aboriginal activists group, Queensland, Australia

Palestinians wait to cross Qalandia checkpoint on their way to attend Ramadan Friday prayers in Jerusalem on August 3, 2012.

But now something new is happening. There may be new energy and clearly anger, fear, and hopefully sustained resistance to our failed political system on multiple levels. While we are not united as yet, people more readily see the connection of these noble causes and how the causes intersect with the Palestine question.

Letter by Don Wagner, Presbyterian theologian and Palestine advocate, to fellow Palestine justice seekers, January 2017

The hard truth is: Environmentalists can't win the emission-reduction fight on our own.... To win that kind of change, it will take powerful alliances with every arm of the progressive coalition.

Naomi Klein, influential voice on climate change and author of "This Changes Everything," "We are Hitting the Wall of Maximum Grabbing," *The Nation*. December 14, 2016

The London Protest Exposes Israeli Government "Brand Israel" propaganda in #TLVinLDN Festival, an example of a cultural boycott, September 2017.

Above: Protesters gathered in Copley Square in Boston, MA, January 29, 2017, to demonstrate against President Trump's immigration order.

Native Americans Take a Stand for Gaza. Tony Gonzales of the American Indian Movement (AIM): "with a common legacy of *bantustans* (homelands)—Indian reservations and encircled Palestinian territories —Native Americans understand well the situation of Palestinians."

Image via Sharat G. Lin

You who come from beyond the sea, bent on war,
don't cut down the tree of our names,
don't gallop your flaming horses across
the open plains.
You have your god and we have ours,
you have your religion and we have ours.
Don't buy your God
in books that back up your claim of
your land over our land...

The stanzas above are excerpted from Mahmoud Darwish's poem, "Speech of the Red Indian." Read the complete poem as translated by Sargon Boulos at https://www. poemhunter.com/poem/speech-of-the-red-indian/

Cornell Daily Sun/Michael Wenye Li

Professor Has No Regrets After Controversial Chant

...at a knee-in, Rickford led the chant "Free Palestine" just before the crowd kneeled.... "All the great structures of US violence—mass incarceration, militarism, police terror, racism, etc.—converge in the occupation of Palestine....I always invoke Palestine when I speak publicly. It is part of my attempt to demonstrate solidarity, as the Palestinian people have long done in relation to the black freedom struggle."

John Yoon, *Cornell Daily Sun*, October 5, 2017
http://bit.ly/Rickfordnoregrets

Activist and scholar of black American history, [Russell] Rickford joined Black Lives Matter in Ithaca in 2015 and became a founding member of Cornell Coalition for Inclusive Democracy.

To stand one's ground acknowledges the right to defend one's beliefs or rights through acts of resistance and protest. Here, a protester at Standing Rock holds a sign which demonstrates the importance of their ancestral lands to the indigenous Dakota.

H. Samy Alim
@HSamyAlim

Follow

The interconnected events of the summer of 2014 have brought a collective moment of clarity. #Ferguson #Gaza #USBorder #MakeTheConnections

3:34 PM - 14 Aug 2014

Posts showing solidarity have continued to erupt over social media as others become aware of the situation in the US, and as groups around the world find commonality in their struggles.

INTERCONNECTED STRUGGLES INTERSECTIONAL POLITIC

Standing Rock and Palestine: The Struggle for Justice is One

Because it raises such fundamental issues of justice and history, Standing Rock has become the epicenter for a protest movement that has drawn thousands of Native Americans from across the US and won the support of indigenous peoples around the globe. The protesters who refer to themselves as "Water Protectors" have engaged in massive and peaceful acts of civil disobedience only to be met with a heavily militarized police force using rubber bullets, tear gas, and power hoses spraying demonstrators with water in below freezing weather. And so as an American, and especially as an Arab American, I am proud to stand with the Standing Rock Sioux because the struggle for justice is one and is playing out daily in North Dakota and across the occupied Palestinian lands.

James J. Zogby, November 28, 2016, *Washington Watch*

September 7, 2017. At Standing Rock, protesting the Dakota Access Pipeline, water protectors described uncanny connections between the obstacles and oppressions facing the in Standing Rock and Palestinians under occupation and apartheid. Palestinian activists authored and circulated a statement of solidarity with the Great Sioux, "We condemn forms of state violence against our Nation siblings and denote that the undermining of their sovereignty an livelihood is a part of the continuin dialectic of settler-colonialism transnationally."

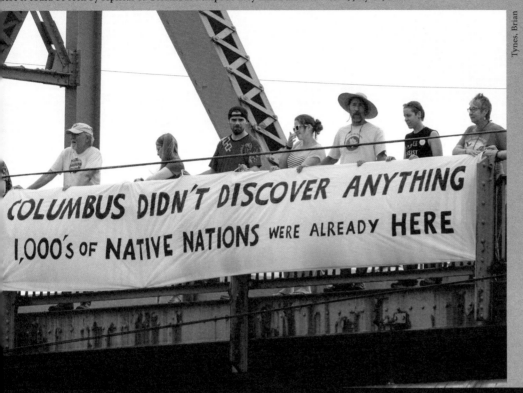

Christopher Columbus's controversial place in history was highlighted in Brewerton, a town in upstate New York, when the group "Neighbors of the Onandaga Nation" displayed this banner from a bridge where it could be seen by replicas of Columbus's ships as they sailed into New York, July 21, 2017.

Tynes, Brian

In Standing Rock I Saw Something of Tahrir

It was unmistakably there: the clear sense of purpose; the transformative feeling of community; the fearlessness in the face of police brutality,...the indescribable joy in being a part of something...the sheer sense of possibility; the feeling that one would never be the same again.

...Something real and effective had been created through months of grassroots organizing, movement building, and leadership from indigenous people. They had used their bodies as a form of resistance....They had made a stand in defense of the environment and Native American sovereignty against corporate and government power that reverberated across the country....

Sharif Abdel Kouddous, "What Standing Rock Can Tell Tahrir," January 2, 2017

GROUNDED IN EFFECTIVE ALLIANCES

Right to Education, from Pine Ridge to Palestine

In April 2016...Palestinian students came to speak at US university campuses about their experiences studying under Israeli occupation and the impact of colonialism on their education. [The Right to Education Tour] aimed to create links between student movements in the US and Palestine... and social movements (*e.g.*, indigenous, migrant, and black struggles)....Palestinian students and organizers reached the understanding that Black-Palestinian solidarity is a praxis to be adopted in a joint liberation struggle against interconnected forms of racial supremacy, state violence, and Empire....As indigenous people living under settler-colonial states, Palestinians, American Indians, and Hawaiians experience and struggle against illegal occupation, dispossession, and erasure.

Osama Mor, Amira Sakalla and Kristian Davis Bailey, http://mondoweiss.net/2016/03/right-to-education-from-pine-ridge-to-palestine/

From Mexico to Palestine, All Walls Will Fall

...Just as the "Gaza to Ferguson" connection that surfaced during the riots against police murders of African Americans in various US cities, the chant linking the Mexico Wall to the Israeli Annexation and Apartheid wall is a sign that points in the right direction, one of global struggle, global solidarity, global alliances.

Nada Elia, *Mondoweiss*, January 31, 2017 http://bit.ly/No2Ban

November 2016. Morton County, North Dakota, police assault Standing Rock Water Protectors with tear gas and pepper spray. The Standing Rock Sioux and allies from around the world amassed to fight to protect their water rights and treaty land from the Dakota Access Pipeline.

Since white Ferguson police officer Darren Wilson shot and killed unarmed Black teenager Michael Brown last August, sparking an uprising for racial justice that swept the nation, there has been growing awareness about Israel's role in training US law enforcement agencies in the methods of domination and control that have sustained Israel's decades-long occupation and disenfranchisement of Palestinians, enabled by billions of dollars in military aid from the United States. The growing realization that their oppressors—the United States and Israel—are working together has ignited an outpouring of mutual solidarity between a younger generation of Black Americans and Palestinians…

Rania Khalek, independent journalist and political commentator, January 2016

> **Rajai Abukhalil**
> @Rajaiabukhalil   [Follow]
>
> Dear #Ferguson. The Tear Gas used against you was probably tested on us first by Israel. No worries, Stay Strong. Love, #Palestine
>
> 11:24 PM - 13 Aug 2014

> **Rajai Abukhalil**
> @Rajaiabukhalil   [Follow]
>
> Don't Keep much distance from the Police, if you're close to them they can't tear Gas. To #Ferguson from #Palestine
>
> 12:02 AM - 14 Aug 2014

"As the protests in Ferguson have escalated over the past week, the international community has increasingly turned its attention to the demonstrations stemming from the fatal shooting of an unarmed 18-year-old black man. Surprisingly, the images and videos of the police crackdown on protesters have resulted in shows of sympathy and support coming all the way from Palestinians in Gaza," wrote David M. Brooks in the *New York Times*, August 14, 2014.

MILITARIZATION, REPRESSIVE POLICING UNPRECEDENTE

On December 2, 2016, Playgrounds for Palestine (PfP) dedicated a playground to two boys, one African American and one Palestinian, who were killed, ultimately, by institutional racism. Tamir Rice was killed by police in Cleveland, Ohio, as he played in a park. Abdurrahman Obeidallah was killed by an Israeli sniper as he walked home from school. Both boys were 12 years old. Neither the American police officers nor the Israeli soldiers who killed Rice and Obeidallah were indicted for killing the boys. A monument in their memory was erected at the Lajee Center, where PfP built a new playground. The Reverend Graylan Hagler, together with a group of Black pastors, participated in the ceremony. They were in Palestine as a delegation of church leaders there to bear witness.

Playgroundsforpalestine.org

playgroundsforpalestine.org

Monument in memory of Tamir Rice and Abdurrahman Obeidallah, erected by Playgrounds for Palestine inside the Aida Refugee Camp in Bethlehem. [See story at left.]

> مريم البرغوثي
> @MariamBarghouti   [Following]
>
> Always make sure to run against the wind /to keep calm when you're teargassed, the pain will pass, don't rub your eyes! #Ferguson Solidarity
>
> 11:07 PM - 13 Aug 2014

While Gaza residents sent tweets to the protesters in Ferguson with advice on how to handle tear gas, the Ferguson crowd chanted "Free Gaza."

This quote by W.E.B. DuBois, American sociologist, historian, civil rights activist, Pan-Africanist, and author, makes frequent appearances on social media platforms and protest placards.

In the global, post-9/11, permanent war economy, Israel has parlayed its permanent subjugation of the Palestinian people into a huge competitive advantage—deeply attractive to powerful elites within the "core" and far off in the periphery....More to the point, permanent occupation has necessitated the development of technologies and protocols for surveillance, policing, and population control that Israel can market around the world, generating healthy profits.

Jeff Halper, *War Against the People*, 2016

An Israeli soldier points his weapon at journalists and medics during confrontations between Palestinian protesters and occupation forces near al-Bireh and the Beit El checkpoint, December 22, 2017.

Oren Ziv/ActiveStills

ONNECTIONS ACROSS MOVEMENTS AND BORDERS

desrowvisuals

uly 12, 2014. upporters of alestinian rights lly in Denver protest Israeli tacks in Gaza.

he place where human rights forms the common ground for joint action mong Palestinians, Americans, and Israelis is in the area of police practices. 49 of 50 states...Israeli security consultants are training our city and state olice....The slogan "from Ferguson (or North Dakota) to Palestine, Apartheid a crime" rests on more than an idle juxtaposition of American and Palestinian vil rights. It rests instead on the recognition that the same forces, sometimes ven the very same companies, are acting to suppress human rights in alestine, in the United States, and against dissidents and refuseniks in Israel.

ve Spangler, "The Perfect Storm: Civil Rights in the Era of Trump, Netanyahu, and Abbas," *ondoweiss*, January 19, 2016

Palestinian protestors, experienced with the use of tear gas and rubber bullets by Israeli military personnel and police, have used social media to express solidarity with the protests against police brutality in Ferguson, Missouri.

Rana Nazzal رنا
@zaytouni_rana   ⊕ Follow

Hamde Abu tells #Ferguson that #Palestine knows what it means to be shot for your ethnicity

3:15 PM - 14 Aug 2014

مريم البرغوثي ⬡
@MariamBarghouti   Following

Made in USA teargas canister was shot at us a few days ago in #Palestine by Israel, now they are used in #Ferguson.

11:31 PM - 13 Aug 2014

4,892 Retweets 1,664 Likes

♡ 140   ⟲ 4.9K   ♡ 1.7K

Movement for Black Lives Endorses BDS

In the fight for dignity, justice, and freedom, the Movement for Black Lives is committed to the global shared struggle of oppressed people, namely the people of occupied Palestine and other indigenous communities who for decades have resisted the occupation of their land, the ethnic cleansing of their people, and the erasure of their history and experiences….We commit to global struggle, solidarity, and support of the Boycott, Divest, and Sanction (BDS) movement to fight for freedom, justice, and equality for Palestinian people and to end international support of the occupation.

#FreedomNow#BlackPalestinianSolidarity

From Palestinians we learn the importance of struggling for self-determination—This is a right that Palestinians refuse to let go of through their *sumud*, or steadfastness—and it is a right that Black people must claim as well….The call for boycott, divestment, and sanctions also models what it might look like for Black people in the US, across our varying political ideologies, to present basic criteria…and to present basic actions people around the world can take to help us actualize our self-determination….Full justice for Palestinians makes the case stronger for our own organizing in the US; full justice for Black Americans or South Africans makes the case stronger for Palestinians. I see each of these struggles as my own, because a victory for one group is a victory for us all.

Kristian Davis Bailey, "Our Palestine statement draws on history of Black internationalism," *Electronic Intifada*, September 2015

Anne Paq/ActiveStills

Left: November 25, 2017. People of African descent and supporters protest against against the slavery and human rights that refugees face in Libya, in front of the Libyan embassy in Berlin, the event took place as other demonstrations were organized internationally.

CROSS-MOVEMENT CONNECTIONS BUILDING A GLOBA

Statement of Solidarity with the Standing Rock Dakota Indians

We…hereby declare our unqualified and heartfelt solidarity with the Standing Rock Sioux Tribe in their epic struggle to protect what remains of their ancestral lands, waters, and sacred sites.

As an indigenous people, we recognize that Native American and First Nation peoples have endured centuries of violent settler colonialism that has dismantled and robbed them of home, heritage, dignity, security, narrative, land, language, identity, family, trees, cemeteries, animals, livelihoods, and life.

We recognize the multitude of ways that Native American and First Nation struggles to protect indigenous territories have ultimately been struggles on behalf of all of humanity to save the Earth we share from toxic globalization of neoliberal and capitalist ethos that threaten our collective survival…

http://bit.ly/PalestinetoStandingRock

Arundhati Roy, Indian human rights and environmental activist and author of *The God of Small Things* has inspired activists around the world with her statement, "Another world is possible. On a quiet day I can hear her breathing."

Sumud: Freedom Camp

We are a diverse community whose sacred values compel us to join in shared nonviolent resistance to discrimination, inequality, and occupation and build a future in which the civil and human rights of all people are recognized unequivocally. We envision a world in which the overwhelming violence, psychological trauma, and spiritual burden of endless occupation is abolished, and a beloved community can emerge beyond the walls, borders, and checkpoints of today. We envision a world in which all systems of violence, domination, and oppression have been dismantled, and the inherent value of all people is respected. We believe that the struggle for Palestinian civil and human rights is part of a broader struggle for a world in which all people can thrive, and resources are not distributed on the basis of class, race, ethnicity, nationality, gender, and ability.

https://sumudcamp.org

Economic activism calls upon banks and corporations to be socially responsible by stepping away from contracts that contribute to climate, racial, and economic injustice.

Friends of Sabeel North America (FOSNA) Solidarity Statement

Electronic Intifada/Rania Khalek

2014. Members of the Palestine contingent in St. Louis protest race-based police brutality. Over 9,000 American officials have trained with Israeli police and military units. Police responses to civilian protest often fail to distinguish between the police's duty to protect civilians and military responses to war.

Across the Globe: Solidarity with Palestinian Mass Hunger Strike

Palestine, in its struggle against the Israeli occupation, has long mobilized transnational solidarity among peoples who have shared experiences of living under colonial imperialism, government oppression, racial domination, and economic exploitation.... Oppression, repression, and brutality of state terror persist despite the existence of internationally recognized rights, as oppressed peoples continue to be denied basic human rights, including the right to self-determination....We salute all of the political prisoners around the world leading the movement for justice, freedom, and self-determination. Together, our global solidarity is crucial to collectively face repression and defeat racism, imperialism, and exploitation.

http://samidoun.net/2016/08/across-the-globe-transnational-solidarity-with-palestinian-mass-hunger-strike/

OVEMENT FOR JUSTICE

From the Platform for Black Lives

In the years since September 11 and the US-driven "global war on terror," US military spending has increased by 50 percent. This war has led to the killing of 4 million civilians in the Middle East. US arms and military corporations have made billions of dollars in profit from waging disaster and destabilization in the Middle East, while increasing western control over the land and resources of the region. In South America and the Caribbean the war on terror has combined with a long-running war on drugs intensifying forced migrations, land grabs, and political disenfranchisement....The US justifies and advances the global war on terror via its alliance with Israel and is complicit in the genocide taking place against the Palestinian people. The US requires Israel to use 75 percent of all the military aid it receives to buy US-made arms. Consequently, every year billions of dollars are funneled from US taxpayers to hundreds of arms corporations, who then wage lobbying campaigns pushing for even more foreign military aid. The results of this policy are twofold: it not only diverts much needed funding from domestic education and social programs, but it makes US citizens complicit in the abuses committed by the Israeli government. Israel is an apartheid state with over 50 laws on the books that sanction discrimination against the Palestinian people. Palestinian homes and land are routinely bulldozed to make way for illegal Israeli settlements. Israeli soldiers also regularly arrest and detain Palestinians as young as four years old without due process. Everyday, Palestinians are forced to walk through military checkpoints along the US-funded apartheid wall.

Joe Piette

Jerusalem is a spiritual wellspring, not a colonial prize

December 8, 2017. Hundreds protest in Philadelphia against President Trump's order to move the US embassy from Tel Aviv to Jerusalem.

December 6, 2016. National Students for a Democratic Society activists stand in solidarity with the Standing Rock Sioux Tribe in opposition to the Dakota Access Pipeline.

CHAPTER 3

Where We Are Now: Facts on the Ground

3.1

East Jerusalem, Neither Here Nor There

Jonathan Kuttab

Immediately after the Six Day War of 1967, Israel found itself in control of all of Palestine. It moved quickly to exert full sovereignty over East Jerusalem, and treated it differently from the rest of the West Bank, as well as Gaza. Its official position was that it had no territorial claims over the occupied territories and that the 1967 war was a preemptive, defensive war undertaken because they feared an imminent attack from the Arab countries bent on destroying Israel. Yet, no attempts were made to hide the glee at capturing the Old City and asserting religious and historic ties to it.

In the euphoria after the war Israel moved immediately to raze to the ground the entire Moghrabi Quarter in front of the Western Wall and turn it into a spacious plaza. The action was done in such a hurry that one old lady was in fact buried alive under the rubble as she failed to evacuate her home in time.[1] Israel then proceeded to incorporate East Jerusalem into the Jerusalem Municipality it had controlled since 1948 and expanded the borders of that Municipality to include a large portion of the land area of the West Bank. From that point on, it was to be known as East Jerusalem, to be treated differently from the rest of the West Bank and the other occupied territory in Gaza.

At the time, Israel loudly proclaimed that it was not "annexing" the Old City of Jerusalem, but it did announce that it was "applying Israeli law and jurisdiction" to the territory. Part of the reasoning for doing this was fear of the international outcry that would follow outright annexation, particularly given Jerusalem's importance to Muslims and Christians throughout the world. Abba Eban, Israel's eloquent representative at the United Nations, emphatically denied annexation and insisted that nothing will be done to affect the status quo but that freedom of religion and access to the holy places will be meticulously observed, contrasting this to the earlier Jordanian jurisdiction that prevented Israeli Jews from worshiping at the Western Wall.

While the legal issue of the status of East Jerusalem was left deliberately unclear, the line expanding the borders of the Jerusalem Municipality was being drawn very precisely and deliberately. The guiding principle behind the gerrymandering line of the expanded municipality was clearly the attempt to include as much land as possible, with as few Palestinians as possible.

In Israel's euphoria after the 1967 Six Day War, it moved immediately to raze to the ground the entire Moghrabi Quarter in front of the Western Wall and turn it into a spacious plaza.

The line therefore excluded Al Ezariyyeh, a close neighborhood from which the walls of the Old City and the Dome of the Rock are visible, as well as the Anata refugee camp, but extended as far north as the borders of the town of Al Bireh, in the far north, and the borders of Bethlehem in the south. The gerrymandering carefully excluded the densely Arab-populated areas of Arram, Dahyiet Al Barid, and the bulk of the Qalandia refugee camp. It was the Zionist plans of grabbing as much land with as few people as possible coming to life. To divide the conquered people, the population of East Jerusalem was given blue Israeli Identity cards, issued by the Ministry of Interior, while residents of the rest of the West Bank were given orange identity cards issued by the Military Government. Family members ended up under different jurisdictions with different rights.

The State of Israel then began their settlement project; they proceeded to build two rings of high-density multi-story buildings surrounding East Jerusalem. The inner ring included Ramat Ashkol, French Hill, the expanded Hebrew University, Attur, and Ramat Rahel. The outer ring included Atarot Industrial zone, Neve Yaccov, Maale Adumim, Gilo, and Har Homa. Maaleh Adumim continued to be technically in the West Bank (by Israeli definition), but administrative arrangements were made to insure that its inhabitants enjoyed all the privileges and services of Israeli citizenship. Unlike the other West Bank settlements, which were agricultural in nature and covered large areas of land, these urban settlements were highrise and high density. The intention behind these two rings was not only to cut off Arab Jerusalem from the rest of the West Bank, but also to create an influx of Jews into occupied Jerusalem so that there would be a Jewish majority even in East Jerusalem. These East Jerusalem settlements were treated a "neighborhoods," and even the leftist Labor Party and leftist Israelis often ignored them when speaking about settlements and treated them as part of Jerusalem and part of Israel. They "disappeared" the border.

The Arab population of East Jerusalem initially thought that their status provided them a number of advantages over other West Bankers: They did not need permits to work and travel in Israel, they used Israeli yellow license-plated cars, and enjoyed Israeli national insurance, social security, and health benefits, and were subjected to Israeli civil courts, not military courts. Soon, however, these advantages proved less appealing: high taxes were a burden; Israeli police and civil courts proved (in matters pertaining to political activities of Palestinians) no different from Israeli military courts; and any attempt to take advantage of Israeli laws was viewed as an affirmation and acceptance of Israeli annexation, which they did not support. Basically, from Israel's perspective, they were placed in a beautiful dilemma, either of foregoing the advantages or of affirming Israeli annexation and legitimacy in East Jerusalem.

In 1980, this situation was compounded when Israel announced the official annexation of Jerusalem and the enactment of a new Basic Law (Israel's equivalent of a constitutional law) declaring the unified Jerusalem to be its eternal capital. The international community rejected this move and responded by withdrawing their embassies from Jerusalem to Tel Aviv. They based this move on the international legal principle rejecting annexation of land that is taken as a result of armed activities. Even some Israeli scholars, including Yoram Dinstein, then Dean of the Tel Aviv School of Law, rejected the annexation as illegal. It is curious that he based his position on the fact that Israel did not grant East Jerusalemites automatic citizenship.

In fact, the precise legal status of East Jerusalemites remained in limbo until the Israeli high Court settled the matter in 1988 in the case of Mubarak Awad vs. Minister of Defense. In that case, which examined the deportation of Dr. Awad, an East Jerusalemite advocate of nonviolence, the court held that there was a lacuna in the law, in that it failed to define the status of those living in the areas that were annexed. The Court held that the status of such East Jerusalemites should be governed by the 1950 Law of Entry into Israel, and that they were free to live and work in Israel as permanent residents, but this was a tenuous status. They would lose that status if they, a) acquired another citizenship; b) acquired another permanent residency; or c) left Israel and resided abroad for a period of seven years. The Israeli Interior Ministry then defined as "outside Israel" the West Bank, including Bethlehem and Ramallah, and other Jerusalem suburbs that had not been annexed, and

This status of being "resident but not citizen" allowed Israel to discriminate against [East Jerusalem Palestinians] in a variety of ways and to ensure that their status was even below that of its own second-class Arab citizens within the 1948 borders.

Defining Colonialism in the Israeli Context

...Jews become a people out of a series of experiences: first the experience of slavery, then the experience of Sinai; the experience of being given a code of law, and so there is a moral dimension to being Jewish. It's not only a tribal designation....I think one can argue that the Jewishness of Israel is enhanced by accepting refugees because the notion of our obligation to the stranger is so central to Jewish texts....It's encoded in Israel's declaration of independence; it doesn't just say Jews are going to have a state; it says this will be a state that pursues freedom, justice, and truth as embodied by the Hebrew prophets. It seems to me, we enhance the Jewishness of the state by fulfilling Israel's moral obligations to those in distress.

...The most likely way that Israel will "cease to exist as a Jewish state" is because of its moral collapse....It's simply not tenable in 2017 to be a colonial state. It may be for a while, but ultimately, democracy is what gives you legitimacy, and any non-democratic regime is a regime that's living on borrowed time. If Israel becomes a country that is permanently holding millions of Palestinians as subjects but not citizens, under the control of the Israeli government but no ability to become citizens of the Israeli government, that's the definition of colonialism. That's what colonialism means, to be the subject of a state that you cannot become a citizen of.

Peter Beinart, American liberal Zionist Scholar, in Toronto at the annual symposium of New Israel Fund Canada, September 2017

January 20, 2016. Palestinian children walk on the rubble of their family house in Wadi Qaddum in the East Jerusalem neighborhood of Silwan, demolished after Israeli authorities said it was built without a permit. The building's owner, Samir Nassar, said that Jerusalem municipality bulldozers stormed Silwan's Wadi Qaddum area at 4 a.m. under the escort of Israeli police and tore down the home "without prior notice."

Mahfouz Abu Turk/APA

[Israel] is maintaining a Jewish majority [in Jerusalem] by limiting in every way possible the rights and aspirations of the indigenous non-Jewish population.

proceeded to systematically withdraw Jerusalem identity cards from East Jerusalemites who failed to prove that they continued to reside "inside Israel." Over 14,000 East Jerusalemites lost their status in this manner.

This meant, going forward, East Jerusalemites had to conduct their daily lives, businesses, and family relationships, including marriage and childbirth, with a constant fear of losing their residency and therefore their right to live in Jerusalem. Having lived in Jerusalem for dozens of generations, if they travelled abroad, they had to be in constant fear of losing their residency and being denied re-entry upon returning. Furthermore, this status of being "resident but not citizen" allowed Israel to discriminate against them in a variety of ways and to ensure that their status was even below that of its own second-class Arab citizens within the 1948 borders.

This situation was further solidified as part of the Oslo Peace Process. Israel and the PLO had agreed to postpone dealing with a number of difficult issues, including Jerusalem. As a result, Israel insisted that the newly created Palestinian National Authority would have nothing to do with East Jerusalem, and even passed a law, ostensibly to implement the peace accords, that made it a criminal offense for PA officials to carry out any activity in East Jerusalem. That meant that East Jerusalemites, who did not consider themselves part of Israel, could no longer consider themselves part of the West bank, or its institutions. Israel followed up by pressuring Palestinians and international organizations that served the West Bank to move their headquarters out of East Jerusalem. Even those East Jerusalemites who were elected to represent Jerusalem in the Legislative Council of the PA were prohibited from opening offices in Jerusalem and were chased out to Arram, outside the municipal boundaries. Organizations and Institutions

that continued to be in Jerusalem, including the Chamber of Commerce, the Arab Studies Society, and others were constantly harassed, or simply closed down by administrative orders, originally for six months, but renewed continuously until this day.

The final blow came with the building of the Separation Wall in 2004, which was again meticulously routed in a very political manner to complete the amputation of East Jerusalem from the rest of the West Bank. When this Wall effectively cut off the flow of goods (and people) from the north to the south of the West Bank, the donor nations (including Japan) were pressured to fund a tortuous road throughout the wilderness hills to connect the north of the West Bank to the South by circumventing Jerusalem altogether through Wadi el Nar (the Valley of Fire). Disconnecting Palestinians in the northern West Bank from those in the southern West Bank has been part of an intentional divide and conquer strategy.

East Jerusalem stands today as a case study in the application of Zionist settler colonial policies toward a native population. Its population is truly orphaned with the burdens of Israeli law but few of its benefits. They are cut off from the West Bank, their leadership, economy, and institutions; yet, they have never been included into Israel and its institutions. The 350,000 residents of East Jerusalem are in a terrible no-man's land of neither, nor. Israel has long-ago decreed that it wants to annex all of Jerusalem and keep it united as its capital, but Israel is also concerned about maintaining its "Jewish" character. Israel does not want 350,000 Arabs—Christian or Muslim—added to its ranks in one fell swoop, so it is maintaining a Jewish majority by limiting in every way possible the rights and aspirations of the indigenous non-Jewish population.

The West Bank Now

Kathleen Christison

[Zionism's] objective, from the beginning, has been to take control for the Jewish people, of as much of the land of Palestine with as few of its non-Jewish natives as possible.

The humanitarian context of oPt (the occupied Palestinian territory) is unique amongst today's humanitarian crises and remains directly tied to the impact of the Israeli occupation, now in its 50th year. The occupation denies Palestinians control over basic aspects of daily life....Their ability to move unimpeded within their own country, to exit and return, to develop large parts of their territory, build on their own land, access natural resources or develop their economy is largely determined by the Israeli military.

UN Office for the Coordination of Humanitarian Affairs, Occupied Palestinian Territory (OCHA-oPt), "Fragmented Lives: Occupied Palestinian Territory," *Humanitarian Overview*, May 2017

Aida Refugee Camp in Bethlehem. When the Palestinian refugees of 1948 and 1967 left their homes, they took their house keys with them, thinking return was imminent. Today, the "Key of Return" symbolizes the Palestinian Right of Return enshrined in the Universal Declaration of Human Rights.

Kathleen Christison

In June 2017, as Israel celebrated the fiftieth anniversary of its military victory over armies from Egypt, Syria, and Jordan and its capture and occupation of all Palestinian territory not already under its control, the approximately five million Palestinians in the occupied territories—the West Bank, Gaza, and East Jerusalem—marked another year in the progressive infringement of their aspirations for independence from Israeli domination and, on a more fundamental level, of their ability to control any aspect of their daily lives.

It is impossible to discuss the realities of the West Bank situation and what these mean for Palestinians without reference to Israel's political ideology of Zionism. This is not the place to analyze the political and religious nuances of Zionism,[1] but the key point in considering occupation politics is that, no matter how the meaning of Zionism is fine-tuned, this ideology has no room in practical terms for non-Jews. Its objective, from the beginning, has been to take control for the Jewish people, of as much of the land of Palestine with as few of its non-Jewish natives as possible. It is thus no coincidence that the establishment of Israel in 1948 led to the dispossession of hundreds of thousands of Palestine's Arab inhabitants, constituting two-thirds of the country's population at the time—a massive ethnic cleansing that Palestinians refer to as "the Catastrophe," the *Nakba* in Arabic. Israel would not have become a state with a stable Jewish majority if most of the non-Jewish Palestinian Arabs had not been displaced.

It is also, then, no accident that since its capture of the West Bank, Gaza, and East Jerusalem in 1967, Israel has imposed its full political and military control over these areas but, with the exception of East Jerusalem, has never formally annexed the territories [2]—for the precise reason that annexation would so vastly increase the non-Jewish population that Jews would be very nearly outnumbered. Despite not annexing the West Bank or Gaza, Israel has treated the occupied territories as though they are sovereign Israeli territory, establishing settlements and outposts only for Jews on land expropriated from Palestinians. Settlements in Gaza were dismantled in 2005 when Israel withdrew its military from that territory and claimed to have ended its occupation there despite maintaining a military siege, controlling borders and airspace. But more than two hundred Jewish-only settlements exist in the West Bank and East Jerusalem, housing over 600,000 Jewish Israelis. These are the vanguard of Israel's effort to extend its permanent dominion over all of Palestine.

...the border between Israel and the West Bank has disappeared for all practical purposes, including in all Israeli school textbooks and on most tourist and other maps produced in Israel.

The two-state solution envisioned as part of the peace process begun with the 1993 Oslo peace agreement—which would have seen the establishment of an independent Palestinian state in the West Bank and Gaza existing alongside an Israeli state within its pre-1967 borders—might have obviated Israeli concerns about diluting the Jewish majority inside its sovereign borders. But it now seems clear beyond a reasonable doubt that Israel has never intended to cede control over enough territory to permit establishment of a viable Palestinian state. The clearest evidence of this strategy, although never explicitly enunciated, is that, far from preparing to cede any territory to the Palestinians, Israel has built settlements at breakneck pace and more than doubled the number of Jewish Israeli settlers in the West Bank and East Jerusalem in the quarter century since the Oslo process began. Based on their Jewish identity, Israeli settlers enjoy the legal and political protections of Israeli citizenship; Palestinians living in the same areas do not. Furthermore, the expansion of Israeli settlements has included the construction of a large number of roads—usually limited-access, segregated highways accessible only to Israeli vehicles—that link Israel with the West Bank on an east-west axis as if in a single sovereign territory. In other words, the border between Israel and the West Bank has disappeared for all practical purposes, including in all Israeli school textbooks and on most tourist and other maps produced in Israel. Many settlers are not even aware that they are living in occupied territory taken in the 1967 War. Many commentators note sardonically that Israel is eating the whole pie while negotiating about sharing it with the Palestinians.

Living Under Occupation

Israel's presence in the West Bank, despite constituting only a temporary occupation in international legal terms, is so clearly intended to be permanent that the strategy is evident to the naked eye, without need for maps or signs or boundary markers. Red-tile-roofed settlement houses, very different in style from Palestinian homes, dot hilltops throughout the West Bank, unmistakable from the air and usually easily visible from the ground. The Separation Wall, built primarily inside occupied territory, is an impossible-to-miss eight-meter-high (25ft) concrete structure snaking

in and around Palestinian urban areas near, but not on, Israel's 1967 boundary. In rural areas where concrete is not deemed necessary for separation, the path of the barbed wire barrier is easily identified by the fifty-yard width of open land cleared for military patrol roads paralleling it on either side. The wall functions as a land grab, enclosing the vast majority of Israeli settlers and settlements on the Israeli side. Hundreds of checkpoints manned by Israeli military—ranging from major structures resembling international border crossings to small, impermanent roadblocks—are positioned throughout the West Bank to control and restrict Palestinian movement from one area to the next and in general confine them to small, disconnected segments of territory ringed by Israeli roads and settlements.

For the first two decades of the occupation, until the start of the first Palestinian *intifada*, or uprising, in 1987 and the Oslo peace process that followed, Israel's military presence in the West Bank was relatively unobtrusive; the number of Israeli settlements and settlers was far lower, and restrictions on Palestinian travel around the West Bank, into Jerusalem, and into Israel, were almost non-existent. Until this time, Israel faced no significant pressure to relinquish the territories, either from Palestinian resistance or from diplomatic efforts to reach a peace agreement. Scholars and commentators who study the occupation, including some Israelis, have noted the dramatic shift in the early 1990s. Resistance arose, the peace process began, and Israel was forced to begin negotiating a possible withdrawal from the territories. In response, rather than curtail, Israel markedly expanded settlement construction, establishing a system of separate roads for Israelis and Palestinians, and imposing a regime of permits, closures, and other suppressive measures.

The 1993 Oslo agreement was essentially an agreement to begin negotiations toward a final peace settlement, rather than a peace agreement itself. "Oslo" established as its first order of business, mechanisms for subdividing control of the West Bank. The territory—covering 2,200 square miles, approximately the size of the state of Delaware, and surrounded on three sides by Israel—was divided into three areas of control: in Area A, which includes Palestinian urban centers, Palestinian authorities nominally have full security control; in Area B, covering many rural areas, Palestinians share security control with Israel; and in Area C, which covers fully sixty percent of the West Bank, where most Israeli settlements are located, Israel retains full security control. Area C includes the Jordan Valley, a large fertile area west of the Jordan River that constitutes one-quarter of the entire West Bank.

This division, along with the roads and checkpoints that enforce and define it, has effectively broken up the West Bank into multiple disconnected segments that some Palestinians mockingly call "Swiss cheese." One human rights organization estimated during the

Afflicted with Hope

Peace has two parents: freedom and justice. And occupation is the natural begetter of violence. Here, on this slice of historic Palestine, two generations of Palestinians have been born and raised under occupation. They have never known another—normal—life. Their memories are filled with images of hell. They see their tomorrows slipping out of their reach. And though it seems to them that everything outside this reality is heaven, yet they do not want to go to that heaven. They stay because they are afflicted with hope.

Mahmoud Darwish, *This Is Not a Border: Reportage and Reflection from the Palestine Festival of Literature*. Bloomsbury Publishing, 2006.

Oslo process that the division had created more than two hundred non-contiguous Palestinian areas, many covering no more than two square miles. The territorial fragmentation has caused not only severe impediments to Palestinian movement and the virtually complete disruption of Palestinian commerce and economic development, but the emasculation of any Palestinian political authority. Precisely because the government formed by the Oslo process, the Palestinian Authority (PA), has no administrative or security control except in small, segmented areas, the PA is effectively able to operate only as an agent of Israel. This has set up a "puppet" government that most Palestinians do not trust.

Human Rights Violations

Because it colludes with Israel, the PA has no power to prevent, nor the moral authority even to register a grievance about Israel's violations of Palestinian human rights. Noted Israeli journalist Gideon Levy, who has reported from the West Bank for years for the Israeli paper *Haaretz*, once observed—and makes this clear in all his reporting—that "there is no place in Palestinians' lives that the occupation cannot reach." The occupation has no boundaries; Israel operates in Palestinian daily life with no restrictions.

A campaign of house demolitions hits Palestinians literally where they live. Israel has demolished tens of thousands of Palestinian homes throughout the occupied territories since 1967—including in large swaths of land along Gaza's borders with Israel, where thousands of homes have been bulldozed; in West Bank areas where Israel has chosen to route the Separation Wall through neighborhoods and privately owned agricultural land; and in many neighborhoods in Area C and East Jerusalem, where Israel's intent is clearly to force Palestinians out.

In Gaza and along the Separation Wall, Israel contends that massive demolitions are for security purposes—to clear land adjacent to its borders and prevent infiltration by terrorists. Individual residential demolitions in and near Jerusalem and elsewhere in Area C are fairly capricious: Israel generally refuses to grant residential building permits to Palestinians, and, when a growing family builds or expands a home anyway, Israeli authorities demolish it. Jeff Halper, an American-Israeli anthropologist who co-founded an NGO, the Israeli Committee Against House Demolitions (ICAHD), that tracks demolitions and rebuilds many homes, asserts that the demolition policy is an integral part of Israel's efforts since 1948 to Judaize the entire land and "cleanse" it of its non-Jewish population. Israeli authorities deny all but a minuscule proportion of applications for residential building permits in Area C and Jerusalem and have demolished thousands of unpermitted homes. Note that all areas where Palestinian homes are demolished—whether Area C or Jerusalem or Gaza—constitute Palestinian land in

A mural of Palestinian national poet Mahmoud Darwish lights up a wall in Aida Refugee Camp, Bethlehem.

the occupied territories. Only a very small number of demolitions, fewer than five percent, are carried out for punitive reasons, in retaliation against the families of terrorists.

Israel also denies Palestinians under occupation adequate water, allocating more than five times as much water per person to Israelis as to Palestinians. Studies show that Israel's 600,000 settlers use eighty-five percent of the water available in the West Bank, whereas the two and a half million West Bank Palestinians use only fifteen percent. The gross imbalance is evident in this water-short area: Palestinians often must stand in line for truck delivery of water during typically dry summer months, while many Israeli settlements are connected to running-water systems and enjoy swimming pools and tree- and flower-lined streets, watered mostly by aquifers that are beneath Palestinian land in the West Bank.

Denial of water is not the only serious environmental issue facing Palestinians. Some hilltop settlements, lacking sewage treatment facilities, dump their untreated sewage onto Palestinian villages down the hill. South of Bethlehem, for instance, it has been well documented that the large settlement of Betar Illit—with a population of over 30,000, sitting on a ridge immediately above the agricultural fields of the small Palestinian village of Wadi Fukin, population approximately 1,200—frequently pours its raw sewage onto village lands from a large-diameter pipe clearly visible in the hillside. This occurs elsewhere in the West Bank as well. Other damage to the land and environment is occurring, according to Israeli environmentalists, from significant Israeli trash dumping, uncontrolled industrial waste disposal, uprooting and burning of thousands of mature olive and other trees, water wastage, and the interruption of natural runoff areas by construction of the Separation Wall. The land's hydrology, topsoil, biodiversity, and food production security have been badly harmed, resulting in

[T]he large settlement of Betar Illit—with a population of over 30,000, sitting on a ridge immediately above the agricultural fields of the small Palestinian village of Wadi Fukin, population approximately 1,200—frequently pours its raw sewage onto village lands from a large-diameter pipe clearly visible in the hillside.

adverse health consequences, including reported kidney damage.

With virtually all administrative and security functions under Israel's military control, Palestinians have little or no recourse to the law for redress of grievances. The Israeli High Court has occasionally reversed a military decision—for instance, on one occasion ordering the Separation Wall moved farther away from the Palestinian village of Bil'in—but for

The Poet at the Qalandia Checkpoint

...When he twisted round, briefly, to look at our group, I caught a glimpse of his expression. What I saw was an already pale face bled white by humiliation: that somebody could halt you in your tracks for no apparent reason; that there could be no way you could tell them that you meant no harm or persuade them out of their misbehaviour; that you could end up caught in those unyielding arms hefting a cumbersome suitcase above your head, which you realised as the minutes ticked by and your arms grew tired, was far too big for purpose. When his eyes met mine, he looked away. He was a poet drained of words to describe what he was feeling. He stood, suitcase aloft, no longer trying to get out of there, until at long last a loudspeaker coughed and the turnstile was released, spewing him out so suddenly that he staggered forward. While behind him I thought, what has just happened is not about security. The soldier had frozen the turnstile not because he needed to but because he could. What I had witnessed was the petty exercise of power....

So I try and figure out why this comparatively petty pain I witnessed has stuck so hard. And I realise that what it reminded me of was my childhood in South Africa. At that daily sight of black men and women made to produce their green pass or their blue one, to prove their right to occupy the space in which they were. The expression on the poet's face that I glimpsed was an echo of so many other similar expressions I had noticed as a child. Those downcast eyes and the guilt in them: that they had done something wrong—were pushing a suitcase too big for purpose perhaps—and that is why they ended up being trapped. It is this that stayed with me.

Excerpt from "Qalandia" by South African novelist and playwright Gillian Slovo, from *This Is Not a Border: Reportage and Reflection from the Palestine Festival of Literature,* Bloomsbury Publishing.

Nicholas Adams

Palestinians await passage at the Israeli military checkpoint that controls all traffic in and out of the Wall-encircled West Bank city of Qalandia.

the most part the judicial system is no friend of the Palestinians. Israel uses an old British Mandate system that permits it arbitrarily to detain anyone for renewable periods of six months without bringing charges. Not infrequently, these six-month periods stretch out for years. Israeli military courts have a ninety-nine percent conviction rate in cases that do come to court.

At the same time, Israel itself usually operates outside customary legal strictures without fear of legal action. The Israeli military conducts raids on random Palestinian villages and individual homes on an almost nightly basis, assaulting and arresting so-called suspects, without customary search and seizure warrants or legal charges. Israeli soldiers who have assaulted and injured or killed Palestinian civilians have rarely been indicted or even investigated, and are even more rarely convicted. Israeli settlers who are usually armed, also enjoy relative impunity in their frequent attacks on individual Palestinians, including children. This is especially heightened in Hebron where radical ideological settlers have taken over neighborhoods in the city center and the Israeli military is there in force to protect their illegal land grab. The Israeli military rarely intervenes to stop these settler attacks or to protect Palestinian victims because they are there to protect the settlers.

Israeli Impunity

The Israeli government and individual Israeli citizens operate in the West Bank, and throughout the occupied territories, with virtually total impunity. The noted American scholar, rabbi, and former director of the American Jewish Congress Henry Siegman, who frequently writes critically about the Israeli occupation, noted in a commentary a decade ago (*The Nation* magazine, May 5, 2008) that Israel's continual settlement expansion is part of a deliberate strategy to destroy any possibility of a peace agreement and ultimately to obviate any partition of Palestine. Siegman believed it was obvious that Israel's strategy was to thwart the establishment of any viable, sovereign Palestinian state and that the United States was simply accommodating the strategy by uncritically supporting Israeli policies and refusing to exert any real pressure for compromise.

Siegman's assessment a decade ago remains accurate today, and many other scholars have agreed with his analysis. As Siegman observed then, "the less opposition Israel encounters from its friends in the West for its dispossession of the Palestinians, the more uncompromising its behavior." By essentially winking at Israel's openly and aggressively expansionist policies in the West Bank (and elsewhere in the occupied territories), the United States and the West have for fifty years accorded Israel impunity to do whatever it likes with Palestinian land and lives.

Children Under Attack: The Story of Jubbet adh Dhib School

Laura Siena

During the summer of 2016, I traveled with a Christian Peacemaker Team, a Mennonite-affiliated nonprofit, to East Jerusalem and the West Bank. We met many extraordinary people engaged in various hands-on projects, whose work for justice is intended to directly improve the lives of Palestinians. I was most affected by Hamed Qawasmeh—by the man, his spirit, and his work. His organization, Hebron International Resources Network (H.I.R.N.), raises funds based on the criteria that each project demonstrably enriches Palestinian daily life in a direct and meaningful way. This has included providing firewood for a poor family; outfitting a medical clinic; building a playground; rebuilding a house demolished by the Israeli military; and building a school in an area without one. I was deeply moved by Hamed's can-do attitude, and also amused and inspired by the unusual character of his fundraising efforts. He raises funds primarily through sponsored sporting events such as bungee jumping, swimming with sharks, and running marathons. When I returned from Palestine, I knew I had to tell his story.

Surviving and thriving as a Palestinian in the West Bank is a political act that requires getting up each morning to navigate the stifling layers of restrictions on every movement. Hamed Qawasmeh lives in Hebron, in the heart of the West Bank. His determination to make daily life under Occupation more livable for the Palestinians who are born and live in the West Bank is evidenced in his brainchild, Hebron International Resource Network (H.I.R.N.)[1], a project that raises funds internationally for grassroots projects that directly assist residents of Palestine.

One recent project illustrates the potential and, sadly, the hazard, of trying to help in Palestine. In this case, H.I.R.N. worked in a carefully-constructed partnership with the local Women's Council, the Palestinian Ministry of Education, an international organization funded by the European Union, Citoyen des Rues International (International Street Citizen), an organization supporting local initiatives in favor of street children and vulnerable children, and other groups to plan, build, and equip a school. The school was to be built with modular rooms, on land owned and provided by the community. The idea for the project was issued by and for the community, which was fully involved in its design and implementation. The plans for the facility included six prefabricated structures, with nine classrooms, a room for teachers, and one for the administration. The Palestinian Ministry of Education committed to supporting teacher and administrative salaries.

Jubbet adh Dhib is a small, low-income village in Area C about 6.5 km outside of Bethlehem: Area C is under total Israeli military control subsequent to the Oslo Accords. As residents do not have their own school, children must walk a great distance to schools outside their community. They are frequently unable to get to school on foot (residents do not own cars) because of muddy roads, dogs, and the presence of soldiers. Many children drop out after 7th grade.

The Israeli Civil Administration has refused to connect the village to the electrical grid and village-owned generators operate only two hours a day. Human Rights Watch details life in Jubbet adh Dhib extensively in its 2010 report.[2]

Hamed's fund raising went better than expected. He was able to move the school construction up, with the goal of beginning classes in August 2017. Then reality hit, in this case in the form of the Israeli military. A solar array for the whole village, including the planned school, paid for by the Dutch government and installed in November 2016, was destroyed by the Israeli army in July 2017. Nevertheless, Hamed and his partners persevered with the plans for building the school.

The demolition in Jubbet adh Dhib was one of several recent Israeli attacks on Palestinian schools. According to the Norwegian Refugee Council (NRC), three educational facilities for Palestinian children in the West Bank were demolished or damaged by Israeli authorities in two weeks. In August 2017, occupation forces raided the Palestinian Bedouin community of Jabal al-Baba near the Jerusalem-area village of al-Eizariya and demolished a prefab building that was to serve as a kindergarten for about 25 local children who have no other school. A primary school in Abu Nuwar had its solar panels—the only source of power at the school—dismantled and taken away, the NRC says. According to the Israeli human rights group B'Tselem, about 55 schools in the West Bank are threatened with demolition or so-called "stop work" orders by occupation forces. Many of these schools are donor-funded, including by European Union governments.

> They are frequently unable to get to school on foot... because of muddy roads, dogs, and the presence of soldiers. Many children drop out after 7th grade.

> **Umm Zaid:** "These days, to be illiterate doesn't mean someone who can't read and write, but someone who doesn't know how to use a computer. And our children didn't learn how to work on a computer because they couldn't use a computer for lack of electricity."
>
> **Fadya Wahsh:** "When they went to school (in other villages), the other kids laughed at them and said they were from the Stone Age."
>
> Amira Hass, "Electricity Returns to Palestinian Village," *Haaretz*, October 20, 2017

The Little School That Could

The following passages are excerpted from the emails of Hamed Qawasmeh to supporters of the project he initiated to build a school to serve first through ninth graders in Jubbet adh Dhib, a village near Bethlehem.

August 17, 2017

It was a roller coaster day of devastation that left me with tears and depression; today was the D-Day for Jubbet adh Dhib school construction, a project that we have been planning to carry out for the last ten months at least. Materials were in at dawn and work started as soon as we hit the ground. By midday, the skeleton of four of the eight classrooms was up. It was such a great scene when I received their picture from the contractor who was in the field. My happiness did not last for more than three minutes when the phone rang. It was the contractor. When I saw his number on the screen, I thought to myself "this can't be good"… and it wasn't. The contractor informed me that the Israeli military had arrived at the site, confiscated the building tools (not materials), arrested and maltreated the workers, took away the contractor's two cars and forbade the workers from continuing the work. Silence grew as both of us did not know what to say or do. We left it at that. I called him back four hours afterwards after allowing the news to sink in. The plan is to continue. Tomorrow when the Sabbath starts for Israelis (Friday after sunset), we are going to go back and finish as much as we can throughout the night and into Saturday. Fingers crossed, we can manage to pull this one through. Please, please, please keep us in your prayers as they are much needed as this point.

August 18

I have just received a phone call from the contractor of Jubbet adh Dhib School. He informed me that two additional classrooms were set up without any problem. The hope that all work will be done by 9:00 am Palestine time when (we hope) we can pour the concrete.

August 19, 2017

The settlement guard came at 6:00 pm, accompanied by a military jeep. This has renewed our fears about their intention. As a result, it was decided that school in Jubbet adh Dhib will start tomorrow haphazardly. We will be on location by 8:00 am to move in the tables, school materials, and even the teachers and students. Will make sure to keep you updated on that.

August 20

Ladies and gentlemen—WE DID IT! As of this morning, we have moved into the Jubbet adh Dhib school some of the furniture and desks. The new educational team was at hand, and we are expecting school to start on Wednesday, August 23.

August 22

As of the time of this writing Israeli forces are dismantling the school of Jubbet adh Dhib with a force numbering more than one hundred soldiers. As the people of Jubbet adh Dhib tried to come down to the location of the school, they were met with live fire. None were injured, but currently the community has no access to either adequate electricity or adequate education.

September 9

Well, it seems that Jubbet adh Dhib has become a point of national consensus; yesterday at 9:00 pm a large group of volunteers descended on the site of the school and established FIVE classrooms using bricks and concrete. Now get this....the Minister of Wall and Settlement was present as well as the head of the Bethlehem Directorate of Education in addition to activists from Aida refugee camp.

I believe that we have made a breakthrough. The people who were building the school got into direct confrontation with the Army and managed to push them away. In turn, we got in touch with our lawyer at the Norwegian Refugee Council (NRC)-financed Saint Evyes who managed to get what we believe to be a "Stay Order" that prevents the Army from demolishing the school "without exhausting the legal steps needed for demolitions." This was EXACTLY what we were looking for- to take the issue of school demolition from the hands of the Army into the legal arena. This would mean that years upon years would pass before any action can be taken against the school. So, I think that is safe to say that WE HAVE MADE IT. Tomorrow morning the Minister of Education and Minister of Settlement and the Barrier will be present at the school to officially inaugurate it. Hoping that no bad surprises would come our way. We are keeping our fingers crossed.

Jubbet adh Dhib is located approximately two miles southeast of Bethlehem.

September 26

Ladies and gentlemen: I am THRILLED to announce that the forgotten village of Jubbet adh Dhib was successful in regaining its confiscated solar panels. Not only that the "Civil Administration" was about to be humiliated in court (they settled out of court), the solar panels were re-delivered to the village yesterday. :) :) :). COMET-ME (an Israeli-Palestinian nonprofit organization providing sustainable energy and clean water services to off-grid communities) is awaiting the suitable time to reconnect them once again. My smile is chin-to-chin. Just thought to share this news with you.

October 8

Dear Friends,
We are pleased to announce that, following concerted legal and diplomatic efforts, we have successfully retrieved the equipment from the micro-grid in Jubbet adh Dhib, which was seized by the Civil Administration on June 28, 2017.

As of last week, the system has been reinstalled in its entirety, and power restored to the community of 160 women, children, and men. We would like to take a moment to thank our partners at the Netherlands Foreign Ministry for their untiring diplomatic efforts…and above all the people of Jubbet adh Dhib and in particular the Women's Council, who have weathered this most difficult summer with dignity and persistence.

See also http://bit.ly/PowerRestored

The International Response to the School in Jubbet adh Dhib

By undermining such humanitarian projects, Israel contravenes its international obligations as an occupying power, in particular the Fourth Geneva Convention relative to the Protection of Civilian Persons in Time of War.
Official statement of the Belgian government

It was heartbreaking to see children and their teachers turning up for their first day of school under the blazing sun, with no classrooms or anywhere to seek shelter, while in the immediate vicinity the work to expand illegal settlements goes on uninterrupted.
Itay Epshtain, representative of the Norwegian Refugee Council, after visiting the village

The demolition of a school building the night before the start of the year epitomizes the administrative cruelty and systematic harassment by authorities designed to drive Palestinians from their land.
B'Tselem, Israeli human rights group

Israel denies the majority of Palestinian planning permit requests in Area C, thereby leaving Palestinians with no option but to reconstruct and develop without permits, while Israeli settlements—established in violation of international law—continue to expand.
The Norwegian Refugee Council

Witness to a Silent Emergency in Gaza

Jennifer Bing

The story of Gaza is best told by people who live there, and by the internationals who have devoted time to live among them and deeply listen to their stories first-hand. Accounts of occupation, military invasion, siege, and suffering belie extraordinary complexities in the lived experiences of the people in Gaza, who remain determined against all odds to survive. Previous study guides have focused on events and statistics that document egregious Israeli violations of international law and the human rights of the people in Gaza. Our present intersectional lens demands a different approach. Here we have chosen to highlight the humanity and integrity of a population marginalized as expendable by dominant political forces. Spontaneously, Gazans reached out in solidarity to people attacked by tear gas in Ferguson, Missouri. The global push against capitalism, police brutality, militarization, and the criminalization of resistance knows no boundaries. For all these reasons, we have invited Jennifer Bing, longtime seasoned Israel-Palestine educator and organizer with the American Friends Service Committee, to tell her story of Gaza. —Editors

What I found in Gaza was a passionate determination to live fully despite the perpetual war machine and the way the people have been imprisoned by the siege….

For insights about life in Gaza by young Palestinian writers, see page 91.

had the rare opportunity to visit Gaza with my colleagues from the American Friends Service Committee (AFSC), a Quaker organization with nearly seven decades of work with Palestinians in Gaza. While preparing for my first visit to Gaza in over a decade, I went shopping for small souvenirs in Chicago and began a conversation with a curious shopper who asked where I was headed. When I told him I was going to Gaza, he responded, "Wow. Those people are living in an open air prison. Please tell them that Americans are concerned about their suffering."

While the shopper in Chicago may not represent a majority view, I shared this story with a group of Palestinian college students we met in Gaza in hopes that they would feel like the world was not immune to their hardships living under military occupation and blockade. Our delegation was one of few groups allowed into Gaza and thus the exchange with university students gave us a special opportunity to hear from them how they continued to study and dream of a future beyond the walls sealing off Gaza from the rest of the world. Several Palestinian students told me at the end of our discussion that it was the first time they had ever heard or seen an American show emotion about their lives.

The visit to Gaza in the spring of 2014 was the first for one of my colleagues who reflected that she had not anticipated the deep love and generosity of spirit that we found. In a reflection, she wrote, "I did not expect to find joy and such deep connection. What I found in Gaza was a passionate determination to live fully despite the perpetual war machine and the way the people have been imprisoned by the siege…. I didn't expect to fall in love with Palestinians in Gaza, but when we left, as we walked back through the checkpoint, as we walked through the remote controlled metal doors, as we traversed the maze of security doors that resembled a cattle chute, I wept. As we waited for our luggage in the shadow of an Israeli soldier with a submachine gun, I wept. I didn't know when I would see my friends again; it felt a little like betrayal to leave them behind, imprisoned by the siege, not knowing when the next bombardment might occur, all supported by US tax dollars."[1]

Like my colleague, I promised myself after our brief visit that I would work to increase the knowledge about, and compassion for, life in Gaza, among people living in the United States.

The Flavor to the Ghetto

Rolling into Gaza I had a feeling of homecoming. There is a flavor to the ghetto. To the Bantustan. To the "rez." To the "colored section." In some ways it is surprisingly comforting. Because consciousness is comforting. Everyone you see has an awareness of struggle, of resistance, just as you do. The man driving the donkey cart. The woman selling vegetables. The young person arranging rugs on the sidewalk or flowers in a vase. When I lived in segregated Eatonton, Georgia, I used to breathe normally only in my own neighborhood, only in the black section of town. Everywhere else was too dangerous. A friend was beaten and thrown in prison for helping a white girl, in broad daylight, fix her bicycle chain. But even this sliver of a neighborhood, so rightly named the Gaza Strip, was not safe.

—Alice Walker, 2009

Two months later, Israel began its biggest and most devastating attack on Gaza to date. The 51-day military assault "Operation Protective Edge" killed over 2,200 people (including 539 children), destroyed homes, hospitals, schools, and vital infrastructure in Gaza. Despite distorted mainstream news coverage in the US, many Americans saw the bombings on Gaza without a news filter via their social media outlets. Social media also gave Americans a direct line to people trapped in Gaza pleading for an end to the assault. Some Americans showed their solidarity and outrage by protesting in the streets in July and August of 2014, including linking Gaza with the mass actions following the police killing of Michael Brown in Ferguson, Missouri. Protesters across the country highlighted the connections between the two justice struggles chanting, "From Ferguson to Palestine, Occupation is a Crime." But as in previous Israeli military assaults on Gaza, the American establishment did nothing to hold Israel accountable to international law, nor did the US call for an immediate ceasefire to stop the bloodshed.

Another American colleague visited Gaza two months after the bombing ended and a ceasefire was reached. She reflected on the enormous damage and suffering in northern Gaza that she witnessed as a result of the Israeli military assault:

"The evidence of deadly surgery [surgical strikes] spreads wide to full-scale blocks of destruction, massive piles of rubble, more concrete and rebar skeletons broken and dangling, devastation as far as the eye can see. We stop asking about survivors, but we see them persisting with life amid the wreckage—entire families living in precariously balanced upper floors of smashed and tilted buildings, laundry hung across ruins, kids playing a makeshift game of volleyball on a narrow street between crumbled houses.

"Those houses still standing are riddled with massive bullet and mortar holes. A cemetery wall has been blown apart, gravestones smashed in a grim second death. Clothes, lamps, dolls, and signs of everyday life have been churned into rubble by the man-made tornado that destroyed block after city block. Kids swarm through the street in school uniforms, while many adults simply sit inside their destroyed homes, waiting. Amid the chaos we see a group gathering, then music,… it is a wedding. Here and now, a wedding.

"While we look down from the highest point in Gaza on the site of a destroyed water tank that had served the entire area, the call to prayer echoes across the sprawling city below—we can hear dozens of muezzin each calling out the Adhan at their own pace and cadence in a haunting, discordant chorus. From atop this hill it is clear that the idea of Hamas using the population as 'human shields' is a red herring—there is not a square inch of unpopulated space. Gaza is all humanity."[2]

The belief that "Gaza is all humanity" and thus should be afforded rights guaranteed under international

Gaza, October 2017. Years later, Gaza is still reeling from the 2014 invasion and bombing campaign Israel called "Operation Protective Edge."

law, has yet to permeate American public opinion, even when the World Health Organization reports that the destruction to Gaza's infrastructure will make it "unlivable by 2020." The blockade and inability to travel to Gaza is a huge detriment to building shared experiences and solidarity that has proven so successful in mobilizing support for West Bank and Jerusalem Palestinian communities. The isolation of Gaza has also led to fear and misunderstanding about life in Gaza, which, coupled with growing western anti-Muslim sentiment, makes it difficult for many people to embrace a common humanity with Palestinians in Gaza.

Reports of the worsening humanitarian crisis in the summer of 2017, noting that electricity to Gaza would be further reduced to two to four hours a day—making life unlivable —are rarely picked up in the mainstream news. "We are living a silent emergency," said my colleague in Gaza. The bombing of 2014 may have stopped, but the suffering due to the blockade is rarely in the US news. An exception is a 2017 *LA Times* op-ed by Abier Almasri, a research assistant at Human Rights Watch, who writes about the daily challenges surviving under the blockade with limited electrical power:

"Those four hours structure our days. When we don't have power, life is on hold. We struggle with candles, flashlights, and, if we can afford them, unreliable generators. We wait for the sound of an electric water pump to tell us we're on the clock. I turn on all the light switches before I go to sleep to ensure that I don't miss the electricity. When I hear the water pump and see the lights go on, I jump out of bed. Life becomes a race as we use every last minute to do laundry, finish urgent work tasks, enjoy cold drinking water. Then the lights go out again.

"No electricity means trying to sleep in 95-degree weather without fans or air conditioning, but with the

The human toll of Israel's 2014 attack on Gaza

- Palestinians killed: 2,139
- Palestinian children killed: 490
- Israeli soldiers killed: 64
- Israeli civilians killed: 6
- Israeli children killed: 1
- Palestinians wounded: 11,000
- Palestinian children wounded: 3,000
- Gaza residents displaced: up to 500,000
- Homes destroyed in Gaza: 20,000

Source: United Nations

Evoking Nelson Mandela's struggle for racial equality and recalling the title of his collection of articles, speeches, and letters from underground, a mural on a Gaza University building reads, "There is no easy walk to freedom...."

Jennifer Bing

على هذه الأرض ما يستحق الحياة

وطني ليس حقيبة وأنا لست مسافر

Middle East Children's Alliance

There is no easy walk to freedom · · ·

The government openly admits to having no strategic policy when it comes to Gaza, other than the futile ambition of removing two million Palestinians from the demographic equation, cutting them off from their families in the West Bank, tearing apart Palestinian society, and sentencing the Palestinian economy to a tailspin of de-development.

constant humming of generators. It means showering with only a trickle of water, scrambling to keep phones and laptops charged, and never buying more than a day's worth of meat or milk. It means always taking the stairs to avoid the risk of getting stuck in an elevator. It means planning your outings around blackouts and checking the electricity schedule for a friend's neighborhood before visiting."[3]

Narrative stories like those of Almasri and other Palestinians living in Gaza which appear in online publications like *Electronic Intifada*, the "We are not Numbers" project, or AFSC's "Gaza Unlocked" website (gazaunlocked.org), are critical to building connections between Palestinians in Gaza and the outside world. Almasri describes the impact of electricity cuts on his daily life in terms accessible to many Americans, a key to building empathy across the miles and divide. He also explains that the cause of the power cuts are "man-made" and can be rectified by human action to end the

blockade. This plea is echoed continuously by every writer in Gaza, every relief worker, and every person of conscience who wants to see peace and reconciliation between Palestinians and Israelis.

GISHA (whose name means "access" and "approach") is an Israeli non-profit organization founded in 2005 to protect the freedom of movement of Palestinians. Their work on Gaza is extensive as they advocate for rights guaranteed by international law—including the end to the collective punishment of the blockade. While documenting the impact of Israeli policies, they urge an end to "[Israel] sentencing Gaza residents to a life of ever-growing suffering in a strip of land that will soon be uninhabitable, while at the same time sentencing its own people to repeated cycles of bloodshed."[4]

GISHA explains that Israel is the occupying power, responsible under international law and the Geneva Conventions for life in Gaza and for ending the blockade: "The extensive control [Israel] continues to wield over countless aspects of life in Gaza brings with it the obligations of an occupying power—responsibilities to see to it that the population be able to lead a life of dignity. The arbitrary, punitive, and elusive permit regime is not a policy. The government openly admits to having no strategic policy when it comes to Gaza, other than the futile ambition of removing two million Palestinians from the demographic equation, cutting them off from their families in the West Bank, tearing apart Palestinian society, and sentencing the Palestinian economy to a tailspin of de-development."[5]

Despite the challenges of building compassion for Palestinians in Gaza, I remember the random stranger I met buying souvenirs in Chicago that described Gaza as an "open air prison" and showed empathy for Palestinians. Just as it is difficult for some to build connections with people behind bars in the US, many activists are motivated to work for change when exposed to the humanity of prisoners and the injustice in the system. By touring (when possible) Palestinian speakers and writers from Gaza to diverse US audiences, talking with people at farmer's markets and faith gatherings about the blockade, and sharing stories from Gaza with more US communities, I have seen a growing compassion and desire to speak out about human rights and the Palestinian desire for dignity and freedom. Chicago Rabbi Michael Davis said at a protest against the Gaza blockade in 2016: "We, who have the advantage of seeing the reality of Gaza without this baggage of dehumanizing indoctrination can take a stand for the humanity of the Palestinian people in Gaza."[6]

A painted mural on a Gaza university wall in 2014 stated: "There is no easy walk to freedom." Now is the time to end the cruel and inhumane blockade and work with Palestinians in Gaza on their journey to freedom.

Fatah and Hamas

FATAH and HAMAS are the two largest political parties in Palestine. Both names are acronyms; FATAH stands for the Palestinian National Liberation Movement in Arabic, and HAMAS stands for The Islamic Resistance Movement in Arabic.

Fatah has controlled the Palestinian Authority since its inception and is a secular political party, widely seen as overly supportive of Israeli and US policies in the region.

Hamas is a political party based in political Islam; it promotes its own notions of piety in its attempts to govern the Gaza Strip. Hamas has risen to popularity in Gaza because of its stated refusal to honor past agreements between the Palestinian Authority and Israel and because these agreements give away rights enshrined in international law. Their record of governance is somewhat problematic, and they continue, on and off, to attempt to form a unity government with Fatah.

Gaza: Siege as Warfare

Ron Smith

Luis Astudillo C./Agencia Andes

September 25, 2014. The innocent children of Gaza begin life with steadfast hope, but their life since the blockade and siege has been littered with war, loss, and trauma.

The siege is a system of blockades and sanctions that makes everyday life impossible and unsustainable in Gaza.

In 2005 Israel removed Israeli settlers from the Gaza Strip and relocated them, many to the West Bank. While hailed internationally as an act of good faith, many Palestinians were worried about what the removal of Israeli citizens could portend for Palestinians' future under occupation. What came to pass after this removal is a policy known as the siege.

With the removal of Israeli settlements and the election of Hamas in Palestine in the general election in 2006, Israel began to close off Gaza from the outside world. Much of the infrastructure was already in place, as Israel built a border wall around Gaza in 1995. Israel then began to systematically shut off the spigots of goods and to place harsh, almost impossible limits on travel by Gazans, ostensibly as an effort to encourage the population to overthrow Hamas. The siege, now in its eleventh year, is the most recent form of pressure placed on Gaza, and should be considered part of a larger process of what Harvard researcher Sara Roy calls "De-development."

In Gaza this has long taken the form of import restrictions and the military targeting of industry and infrastructure such as wastewater treatment facilities, electricity distribution systems, and hospitals and clinics.

How Siege Works

The siege is a system of blockades and sanctions that makes everyday life impossible and unsustainable in Gaza. Though the siege has changed numerous times since it was imposed in 2006, the end result is the same: collective punishment for all Palestinians living in Gaza. At its outset, Israel allowed 42 items into the Gaza Strip. Many basic necessities were banned, as well as items like sponges, tahini, and brooms (BBC 2010). After filing a legal demand for documentation of the siege, Israeli NGO GISHA discovered that the Israeli government was, in the words of Dov Weisglas, an adviser to then Prime Minister Ariel Sharon, "Putting Gazans on a diet." The Israeli government did so through a policy they

De-development—the systematic destruction of an independent economy, and the withdrawal of support in that society for even the possibility of the creation of a future independent economy and society.

Sara Roy, *The Gaza Strip: the Political Economy of De-development*

called "breathing space," or the control of food entering the Gaza Strip down to the calories, ensuring that Gaza was maintained just above the humanitarian standards for consumption, approximately 2000 calories per Gazan per day (GISHA 2010).

Some of the most vulnerable populations in Gaza are farmers and fishers who provide desperately needed nutrition to the besieged Strip. One third of Gaza's farm land and all of its maritime territory are within what Israel has deemed "no-go zones" and Gazans are shot and killed, maimed, or arrested for attempting to provide food for the population.

International Complicity

Israel is not alone in maintaining the siege of two million people in the Gaza Strip. This siege is supported by the international community, including Egypt, who shares a border with Gaza, as well as the European Union and the United States who consider Hamas to be a terrorist entity and refuse to allow any funding into Gaza that could eventually end up in the hands of the Government there. In this way, the United States is complicit in the collective punishment of the people of Gaza and is engaged in siege warfare, which has a dubious track record of producing positive political change; consider for example the result of decades of sanctions imposed on Iran, Iraq, and North Korea. The world has turned its back on Gaza, and the UN and other agencies struggle to keep their doors open to provide even a minimum of assistance while Gazans suffer through oppressive heat, often receive no more than two hours of electricity a day, and live in refugee camps in homes where 14 individuals sleep in tiny cinder-block rooms with no ventilation. The siege prevents any attempts at betterment of Gazans'

lives and makes getting quality medical care impossible for the majority living there.

Siege as Warfare

Israel has no need for the two million residents of Gaza and sees them all as hostile captives. As the siege continues, Gazans have no reason to believe that the siege will end, even if they were to overthrow Hamas. Israel targeted Gazans for attack during the previous Fatah administrations, and Israel maintains the siege with international support, keeping Gazans in an open-air prison. Siege is no alternative to war, it is war by other means, targeting a civilian population with shortages, air strikes, and invasions, and preventing their escape through draconian regulations on movement in and out of the strip. Only through pressure from community groups, churches, and local organizations can Israel be expected to loosen the noose of the siege.

Gaza fisherman Rajab Abu Riyala is one of many Gazans trying to keep alive the ancient tradition of making nets by hand. Among the most vulnerable groups in Gaza, fishermen work in more and more danger from the Israeli navy, which fires at Gaza fishermen's boats on a daily basis to force them to fish close to shore—where there are fewer and fewer fish.

If Israel Were Smart

"If the Israelis were smart," one religious Muslim told me, "they would open two or three industrial zones, do a security check, and find the most wanted among us and employ them. Al-Qassem would evaporate very quickly, and everyone would be more secure.... The mosques would be empty." I was told that many young men left al-Qassem after getting a place in one of Gaza's housing projects, not wanting to turn their new home into a possible Israeli target.

"What we need is Israeli factories and Palestinian hands," a local businessman said. "One sack of cement employs 35 people in Gaza; with one worker in Israel you have seven people in Gaza praying for Israel's security. Imagine a 'Made in Gaza' brand. We could market regionally and it would sell like hotcakes. Gaza would benefit and so would Israel. All we want are open borders for export."

Gazans are entrepreneurial and resourceful—and desperate to work and provide for their children once again. Instead they are forced into demeaning dependency on humanitarian aid, which is given by the very same countries that contribute to their incapacity. The policy is not only morally obscene; it is also outrageously stupid....

If the Israelis were thinking clearly, one person said, "everyone could benefit. All they must do is give us a window to live a normal life, and all these extremist groups would disappear. Hamas would disappear. The community must deal with...these groups, not IDF tanks and planes. Our generation wants to make peace, and it is foolish for Israel to refuse. The next generation may not be as willing as we are. Is that what Israel truly wants?"

Sara Roy, "If Israel Were Smart," *London Review of Books*, June 15, 2017

Gaza: Being There

Harry Gunkel

From your very first encounter with Gaza as you pass through the Orwellian Israeli checkpoint at Erez, everything you thought you knew about the world gets upended. Compassion, common decency, the human capacity for cruelty must be redefined.

Now, as you enter and move through the streets of Gaza, the décor of siege and blockade unfolds in front of you: more donkey carts than cars, too many people in too small a space, buildings that are left standing—so many were destroyed by Israeli bombs or missiles—are pockmarked with bullet holes. Modernity is a thing still in the future in this dystopian world that is Gaza. The trappings of civilization and diplomatic niceties on the outside are merely *trompe l'oeil* distractions for a technology-enabled growth spurt of human savagery directed at this ancient, tiny, helpless place.

Children who are supposed to be nurtured and protected are bombed and buried in rubble along with their mommies. The survivors are starved and given water undrinkable by any standards, that further assaults their anemic undernourished bodies with parasites and disease.

The sea has become a cesspool of sewage because the waste treatment facilities were also targets of the occupiers. Fishing, the ancient provider here of food and vocation that always reminds us of Christ—it too is laid waste. Instead of sustaining life, the beautiful Mediterranean breeds illness.

At night, Gaza becomes a shadow world, darkened by destruction of the sole power plant into medieval dependence on the light of stars above and fire on the ground. Fire to cook by and see by that may burn you or fill your lungs with smoke. But don't get injured or sick. The medicines and treatment you need might not be available—prevented from entry by the blockade—and you can't leave to find care elsewhere.

This Gaza is the kind of place you used to know as science fiction, but it isn't. It exists. If you listen closely, you can hear its cry, its keening yearning for someone to look, see, and listen. But the horrors of Gaza, the atrocities in it, don't suit the stories we tell about

ourselves and so we look away and build blockades against the noise. The catastrophe of Gaza is not the result of a natural disaster. It is the result of conscious, intentional, willful decisions. The people of Gaza are suffering because of the people who want them to.

If you are fortunate enough to visit Gaza more than once and to linger there for some time, you will come to know the people of Gaza. And there you will find something other than the poverty, destruction, and disease. You will find steadfast hope. It shares itself in the hospitality offered to visitors and in gratitude for their presence. Despite their nearly incalculable material needs, most people of Gaza ask only one thing of visitors: "Please do not forget about us."

Hope is an intangible thing, as are the endurance, fortitude, courage, and faith that come forth out of every conversation and encounter in Gaza. It is this life force that must seal our bond with the people of Gaza. We must match their insistence on their own humanity. Standing indomitably against the rage of colonialist empire, and in her destitution and homelessness, in her illness and darkness, Gaza offers us her hand. How can we refuse it?

> The trappings of civilization and diplomatic niceties on the outside are merely *trompe l'oeil* distractions for a technology-enabled growth spurt of human savagery directed at this ancient, tiny, helpless place.

wearenotnumbers.org

Chapter 4

A Snapshot of Contemporary Reality Inside Israel's 1948 Borders

4.1

The Palestinian Experience Inside Israel
Jonathan Cook

[T]he Absentee Property Law of 1950...defines all Palestinians displaced during the war as "absentees" and strips them and their descendants of the right to restitution of any property, including buildings, lands, belongings, and bank accounts.

Israel's 1.7 million Palestinian citizens—a fifth of the population—have been called the "forgotten Palestinians" for good reason. Many outside observers are not aware that inside its recognized borders Israel includes a large minority of Palestinians who have citizenship. These Palestinians survived the mass expulsions of 1948—the *Nakba*, or "Catastrophe," as it is known in Arabic—that created a Jewish state.

Four-fifths of Israel's Palestinian population—referred to by Israel as "Israeli Arabs"—are Sunni Muslim, with the rest equally divided between the Druze, a religious sect that broke from Islam in the 11th century, and various Christian denominations. They live in three main areas: the Galilee in the north, a densely populated thin strip of land called the Little Triangle that hugs the north-west edge of the West Bank, and the Negev (Naqab) in Israel's semi-desert south.

The *Nakba*
In 1948 only about 150,000 Palestinians managed to avoid being expelled, from a total population of 900,000 that had been living inside the borders of what became the new state of Israel. The Israeli historian Ilan Pappe has called the expulsions "ethnic cleansing." Those who managed to remain on their land did so for a variety of reasons, in addition to the usual chaotic outcomes of war:
- the failure by a commander, Ben Dunkelman, to carry out the order to expel the inhabitants of the city of Nazareth, leaving it as a sanctuary for its residents and

many refugees who fled there
- the agreement of some Druze to join the Israeli army and fight on its side
- Israel's agreement, under pressure from the Vatican and United Nations, to allow some Christian Palestinians to return to their villages after the fighting
- a renegotiation of the ceasefire lines with Jordan that incorporated the homes of some 30,000 Palestinians inside Israel rather than the West Bank after the war
- and the efforts of many refugee families, living in camps in Lebanon, Syria, and Jordan, to risk their lives and return home clandestinely

Most Palestinian villages —more than 500—were destroyed by Israel either during or after the fighting. Today's Palestinian citizens are still denied access to their former lands, usually by forests planted on the ruins by an international Zionist charity, the Jewish National Fund.

This mass dispossession is permanently enforced through the Absentee Property Law of 1950, which defines all Palestinians displaced during the war as "absentees" and strips them and their descendants of the right to restitution of any property, including buildings, lands, belongings, and bank accounts. Estimates are that about one in five Palestinian citizens are descended from what Israel terms "present absentees," or internally displaced people, who lost all their property under this law.

Citizenship
The Palestinians who remained inside the new Jewish

state may have been unwelcome, but four years later they received citizenship. This change of status was mainly due to pressure from the United Nations and Israel's need to gain acceptance from the international community. Israel's founding father, David Ben Gurion, believed these 150,000 Palestinians would soon become a small fraction of the population after waves of Jewish immigration. He miscalculated. The minority's much higher birth rate meant that it has managed to maintain its demographic weight at 20 per cent of the population.

Israel's complex, bifurcated citizenship legislation from its early years reflected its demographic priorities. Israel passed the Law of Return of 1950 to open its doors to all Jews around the world, allowing mass Jewish immigration. If any Jew landed in Israel, he or she could instantly receive citizenship. But Israel wanted exactly the opposite outcome for Palestinians. So it created a separate law, the Citizenship Law of 1952, for non-Jews. "Separate is inherently unequal," the US Supreme Court ruled in one of its landmark decisions in the civil rights struggle. Israel is no exception to this principle and it enshrined a legal separation of citizenship rights, based on ethnicity, to institutionalize discrimination.

The primary goal of the Citizenship Law of 1952 was to strip the right of return from the 750,000 Palestinians forced into exile by Israel, as well as their descendants. But longer term, it created a legal structure that would guarantee a large Jewish majority in perpetuity by continuing to gerrymander Israel's population.

Today there is only one path by which a non-Jew can gain citizenship in Israel—by marriage to a Jewish Israeli citizen. This exception is allowed only because a few dozen non-Jews qualify each year, posing no threat to Israel's Jewish majority. Under legal challenge, Israel

passed an amendment to the Citizenship Law in 2003 to ensure that Palestinians in the occupied territories did not qualify for Israeli residency or citizenship under the marriage provision.

The Law of Return and the Citizenship Law are two of nearly 70 laws—and the number is growing—hat explicitly discriminate based on whether a citizen is Jewish or Palestinian. An Israeli-Palestinian legal group, Adalah, has compiled a database of such laws [see chapter 2].

Nationality

Palestinian citizens are not only discriminated against in the way many minorities in democratic states are: that is, by the arbitrary, informal, or unregulated decisions of officials and state bodies. In democracies, officials are usually breaking the law when they discriminate against minority groups. In Israel, officials are often breaking the law if they do not discriminate. This institutionalized, state-sanctioned racism is achieved by establishing "nationalities," separate from citizenship. The primary nationalities in Israel are "Jew" and "Arab." The state has refused to recognize an "Israeli nationality," a position supported by the Israeli Supreme Court. In this way, Israel has created a hierarchy of rights.

Individual "citizenship rights" are enjoyed by all citizens by virtue of their citizenship, whether they are Jews or Palestinians. In this regard, Israel looks like a liberal democracy. But Israel also recognises "national rights," and reserves them almost exclusively for the Jewish population. National rights are treated as superior to citizenship rights. So if there is a conflict between a Jew's national right and a Palestinian's individual citizenship right, the Jewish national right will invariably be given priority by officials and the courts.

The primary goal of the Citizenship Law of 1952 was to strip the right of return from the 750,000 Palestinians forced into exile by Israel, as well as their descendants.

A street scene in Nazareth (*an-Nasira* in Arabic). Life in Nazareth appears normal; it's not. Jews and Arabs live segregated lives even within Israel's 1948 borders; by and large, they have separate towns, schools, work, and media.

We need to understand how this hierarchy of rights works in practice. The simplest illustration applies in Israel's citizenship structure. The Law of Return establishes a national right for all Jews to gain instant citizenship—as well as the many other rights that derive from citizenship. The Citizenship Law, on the other hand, creates only an individual citizenship right for non-Jews. Palestinian citizens can pass their citizenship "downwards" to their offspring but cannot extend it "outwards," as a Jew can, to members of their extended family—in this case, Palestinians who were made refugees in 1948.

This hierarchy of rights can also be seen clearly in the treatment of Israel's two most precious material resources: land and water.

Water

In one sense, water is a citizenship right, meaning that Jewish and Palestinian citizens largely enjoy the same access, at the same price and quality. However, this still allows for serious discrimination in water allocation, even as a citizenship right.

More than 100,000 Palestinian citizens live in communities criminalized by Israel under the Planning and Building Law of 1965. These dozens of so-called "unrecognised villages," mainly for Bedouin in the Negev (Naqab), are denied all services by the state, including roads, electricity, and water. All houses in these communities are illegal and under demolition order. This, not some archaic tradition of nomadism, is the reason they are forced to live in tents and tin shacks.

One such village, al-Araqib, has been destroyed more than 100 times by the state in recent years, in an effort to dissuade other Bedouin from trying to continue with their rural lifestyle. Central to Zionist thinking is the idea that only Jews can "redeem" the land through agriculture, or by "making the desert bloom." The Bedouin way of life threatens this settler colonial notion at the heart of Zionism.

According to the authorities, the Bedouin are "trespassers" and "squatters" on state land—even though they often have Turkish or British title deeds to it that predate Israel. Israeli officials insist that the Bedouin's supposed criminality must not be rewarded with access to an essential service like water. There is a problem, however: they are citizens and therefore entitled to water, and its denial could prove life-threatening. With the wisdom of King Solomon, the Israeli courts have settled the matter: the Bedouin must be allowed water, but not where they live. Typically they have to travel several kilometres from their homes to a stand-pipe and collect water in a jerry-can.

Separately, water is also treated as a national resource when used for commercial purposes such as agriculture or industry. For these uses, access is tightly restricted and can usually be accessed solely by Jews. This goal is achieved chiefly by making state-subsidized water available only in specific types of communities, such as the *kibbutz* and *moshav*, rural collectives that control much of the land in Israel.

Here is the catch: these hundreds of rural communities are treated effectively as members-only clubs. To live in one, an applicant must submit to a vetting procedure run by a local admissions committee. The task of the committee is to weed out any Palestinian citizens who try to gain entry. Once this was done openly by denying "Arabs" membership. Today, after legal challenges, the committees reject Palestinian citizens instead as "socially unsuitable."

Land

In the case of land, the situation is even starker. Some 93 per cent has been nationalized—though not for the Israeli populace, as there is no recognition of an Israeli nationality. It is not even nationalized for Israel's Jewish citizens. The courts have rejected efforts to gain status for an Israeli Jewish—or Hebrew—nationality, with judges ruling that the "Jewish nation" is global and cannot be subdivided.

This ruling means that Jewish citizens effectively buy a long-term lease from a government body, the Israel Lands Authority, rather than personally owning land. The state regards them as protecting or guarding the land—typically land taken from Palestinian refugees—on behalf of Jews around the world. This interpretation has led to a situation in which the vast majority of Jewish and Palestinian citizens live in entirely separate communities—a residential segregation that has allowed for huge disparities in the funding and resources allocated by the state to Jewish municipalities compared to Palestinian ones.

In practice, the only place where Jewish and Palestinian citizens live in close proximity is in a handful of so-called "mixed cities," like Haifa, Acre, Jaffa, Lid, and Ramle. But even here, the two populations usually live in segregated areas of the city. With the exception of Haifa, Palestinians typically live in ghetto-like conditions in the mixed cities.

Planning and demolitions

Some 120 Palestinian communities in Israel are recognized under the 1965 Planning and Building Law and are where most Palestinian citizens are supposed to reside. During the state's first two decades, when Palestinian citizens lived under military rule, most of their lands were confiscated. Today, they are largely confined to the 2.5 per cent of Israeli territory that either still belongs privately to them or to their municipal authorities. (The rest is owned either by wealthy Jews who bought land before Israel's creation or by the Churches.)

The same Planning and Building Law has drawn "blue lines" on a planning map designating the expansion area for all communities in Israel. Jewish communities were given room for future growth, whereas Palestinian communities were invariably denied it. Today,

If there is a conflict between a Jew's national right and a Palestinian's individual citizenship right, the Jewish national right will invariably be given priority by officials and the courts.

Palestinian towns and villages are massively overcrowded and facing a land and housing crisis. Desperate families are often compelled to build outside the "blue line."

This "blue-lining" has resulted in some 30,000 homes belonging to Palestinian citizens in Israel being classified as illegal. These families live with the constant threat of demolition of their homes. A few hundred homes, most in the Negev, are demolished each year. The rest must pay annual fines. These households are trapped in a planning Catch-22 that drains them of hope and money.

Jewish "landlords"

The Law of Return, which entitles all Jews to instant citizenship, and Israel's land laws, which reserve ultimate ownership to Jews as a global "nation," effectively mean Israel treats the state as belonging to Jews collectively around the world rather than to Israel's actual citizens. The Jewish state is "owned" by world Jewry, even if individual Jews have failed to actualize their citizenship by coming to live in Israel. Ariel Sharon, a famous general and later prime minister, once termed world Jewry the "landlords" of Israel.

If that sounds improbable, consider this. Israel does not have a constitution but it does have a series of 11 Basic Laws that approximate a constitution. The government has been seeking to pass a 12th Basic Law defining Israel as the nation-state of the Jewish people—that is, as the home of all Jews around the world. This law does not change the existing legal situation, but it does make it explicit.

Palestinian citizens, by contrast, are treated more akin to alien residents, or temporary guest workers, on license so long as they do not threaten the Jewishness of the state. In practice, there are two ways they can do that. The first is by helping more Palestinians to gain citizenship and erode Israel's large Jewish majority. As we have noted, Israel effectively shut the door on that threat in 2003 by passing the Citizenship and Entry into Israel Law that makes it all but impossible for Palestinians in the occupied territories to gain residency or citizenship through marriage. The second is by threatening Israel's image.

Israel's Image

Damaging Israel's international image as a democracy is a political threat posed by unequal Palestinian citizens. This threat became tangible in the late 1990s when a new political party, the National Democratic Assembly or Balad, emerged in the post-Oslo atmosphere to demand that Israel reform from a Jewish state to become a "state of all its citizens." This demand—in different forms—soon became a rallying cry for all Palestinian parties in Israel. It led in 2006 to the publication by the Palestinian leadership in Israel of The Future Vision, a program urging Israel's reform into a "consensual democracy."

The Israeli authorities were deeply troubled by the document—not least, because these demands

strongly suggested that Israel was not the liberal democracy it claimed to be. The prime minister at the time, Ehud Olmert, met with the Shin Bet, Israel's domestic intelligence service, or secret police, to discuss these developments. Exceptionally, the Shin Bet issued a public statement afterwards, decrying these democratization demands as "subversion" and threatening penalties against Israel's Palestinian leadership.

A short time later the leader of the Balad party, Azmi Bishara, who had led the "state of all its citizens" campaign, was out of the country when Israel announced he would be put on trial for treason if he returned. He lives in exile to this day.

Politics

Israel has often claimed that the proof it is a democracy lies in the fact that all citizens, including Palestinian citizens, have an equal vote. This is certainly a necessary condition for a state to call itself a democracy, but it is not sufficient. One should remember that Palestinian citizens had the vote even during the period until 1966, when they lived under martial law and could not leave their communities without a permit from a military official. Despite their having the vote during this period, no one would seriously argue that Israel was a democracy for its Palestinian minority at that time.

Palestinian academics in Israel usually call the minority's right to vote "symbolic" or window dressing. They point out that no Palestinian party has ever been invited to take part in Israel's diverse and often chaotic coalition governments. The dozen or so Palestinian Arab legislators admit that they have no influence on the parliament or the executive. One legislator, Ahmed Tibi, has observed: "Israel is a democracy for Jews, and a Jewish state for Arabs."

With the exception of Haifa, Palestinians typically live in ghetto-like conditions in the mixed cities.

Israeli Arab stopped and ID'd by soldiers in Jerusalem.

Mitzpe Aviv, a community in northern Israel that screens potential residents by ethnicity. In 2014 the High Court upheld the residential screening law, enabling Jewish villages to keep Arabs out, codifying separation/apartheid.

Yaron Kaminsky

Israel has successfully segregated the main resources of land and water to preserve them for the Jewish majority alone.

Nonetheless, increasingly right-wing Israeli governments are exasperated that the parliament continues to serve as a platform for these Palestinian legislators to demand equal rights. In 2014, the government passed a Threshold Law, making it much harder for smaller parties to enter the parliament in Israel's highly proportional voting system. The new threshold was set at a level precisely too high for any of the three main Palestinian parties to pass it.

In a perfect example of unintended consequences, these parties put aside their profound differences and created the "Joint List," which ran in the 2015 general election, becoming the third largest in the parliament. This infuriated many members of the right-wing ruling coalition, and in 2016 they responded with the Expulsion Law, which gives a three-quarters majority of the parliament the right to expel any legislator—not because he or she committed a crime, but because other legislators do not like their political views. It was originally called the Zoabi Law after Palestinian legislator Haneen Zoabi, the most prominent and outspoken member of exiled Azmi Bishara's Balad party.

Its immediate impact has been a chilling effect on the freedom of speech of Palestinian legislators, and the assumption is that this law will be invoked the next time Israel is engaged in an attack on Gaza and Palestinian legislators try to speak out. Given that the three Palestinian parties are in a Joint List, the expulsion of even one of their number will discredit the continuing presence of the rest, making it look as though they are there only on license from the Jewish majority.

Apartheid

There has been a growing debate within Palestinian solidarity activism about whether Israel should be classified as an apartheid state over its treatment of Palestinians in the occupied territories. More controversial at the moment is the claim that this description also applies within the 1948 borders. Let us address this question.

Scholars of apartheid referred to two modes or levels of apartheid in South Africa. The first was what they termed "trivial" or "petty" apartheid. "Visible" apartheid might be a more helpful term. It was the segregation that could be seen by any visitor: separate park benches, buses, restaurants, toilets, and so on. Israel has been very careful to avoid, as far as it can, this visible kind of segregation, even though much of life in Israel is highly segregated for Jewish and Palestinian citizens. Residence is almost always segregated, as is primary and secondary education and much of the economy. But shopping malls, restaurants, and toilets are not separate for Jewish and Palestinian citizens.

Scholars of apartheid, however, also refer to what they call "grand" or "resource" apartheid. They consider this as more fundamental to South Africa's apartheid. This was segregation in relation to the state's key economic resources, such as land, water, and mineral wealth. As we have seen above, Israel has successfully segregated the main resources of land and water to preserve them for the Jewish majority alone. Hundreds of exclusive Jewish communities like the *kibbutz* and *moshav* dominate almost all of the land and restrict the commercial exploitation of land and water for Jews only.

Given this framework, Israel's treatment of its own Palestinian citizens within its internationally recognized borders might justifiably qualify it as a relative or cousin of apartheid South Africa, even if it does not precisely replicate the South African model.

Settler-Colonialism in the Naqab/Negev

Joseph Getzoff

The logic of settler-colonialism is tied to space and identity. Ethnic settler states restrict minority and indigenous populations' land access and land rights. Rights are given and taken based on one's identity. To the casual observer in the Naqab/Negev it may appear that the region is democratic and "multicultural." Often in coffee shops you will hear Arabic and Hebrew (not to mention Russian). Go to a health clinic and your doctor may be Bedouin. At the university, Bedouin young men and women study, hang out in the library, kids enjoying the opportunity to mix and mingle. There are Bedouin towns with Bedouin mayors, Bedouin Members of Knesset. People may say, sure, it is the case that Bedouin are under pressure, but isn't this partly because their society is so illiberal, so traditional? Push deeper and Jewish-Israelis may say, well, why is there so much crime, so little education, such poverty? The rest of us work hard and are rewarded. Often the conflict is assumed to be rooted in cultural difference or ideology and not in land and racial discrimination.

Israeli planners and politicians often say in public that they are working toward a solution to issues in the Bedouin community. Instead of investment in the social infrastructure, or recognizing that land access is often tied to economic privilege, these "solutions" often are focused on "regularizing" Bedouin settlement in the region. For the Israeli planner, "regularization" is the solution for the "dispersion" of Bedouin and implies that they should not be on their land, but stacked in urban housing, no longer farmers, but wage-earners.

Bedouin |ˈbed(ə)wən| (also Beduin) noun
(plural same) a nomadic Arab of the desert.
ORIGIN from Old French *beduin*, based on
Arabic *badawī*, (plural) *badawīn* "dwellers in the
desert," from *badw*, "desert."

Driving along most roads in the Naqab/Negev and you will see Bedouin "unrecognized villages." They appear to be random collections of houses along dirt roads where people cobble together an agrarian livelihood. The unrecognized villages have been the focus of a series of Israeli plans that often try to force people who live in them into the government planned towns, onto smaller plots, off their farms and into an urbanized space. This has not gone unchallenged. In 2013, the infamous Prawer Plan faced widespread community opposition. Bedouin and joint Arab-Jewish civil groups fought back with protests, lawsuits, and international outreach. The plan was shelved, but its logic continues.

Residents of these villages continue to face state pressure, harassment, and demolitions that are designed to get them to "negotiate." The logic of the state is to concentrate as many Bedouin in as little space as possible. There are about 40 unrecognized villages that are home to about 30% of the entire Bedouin population in the south. Bedouin, numbering around 240,000, are about 1/3 of the region's population. The largest such village is Wadi an-Na'am, where 14,000 people are sandwiched between a highway, a power plant, and Neot Hovav, a large chemical industrial waste site.

In the years before 1948, the Bedouin population in the Naqab/Negev reached 90,000-100,000 individuals and was part of a larger, intricate chain of Palestinian life. Beir al-sa'ba (today, Hebraized as Be'er Sheva) was founded in 1901 as an Ottoman administrative center and was part of a larger web of Palestinian life in the south. Bedouin practiced agriculture and sometimes seasonally migrated. They also had specific demarcated territories owned by specific individuals or families. In 1948, most of the Bedouin were expelled by Israeli military forces or fled to the West Bank, Jordan, the Sinai, and Gaza, during the Palestinian *Nakba*.

The new State of Israel instituted a military administration that restricted all Palestinian movement and land-use in the new boundaries. The administration

For the Israeli planner, "regularization" is the solution for the "dispersion" of Bedouin and implies that they should not be on their land, but stacked in urban housing, no longer farmers, but wage-earners.

Bedouin citizens, traditionally agrarian, are pressured to urbanize, while Jewish citizens may (depending on class) choose to live where they like: in the "mixed" cities like Be'er Sheva, towns, agricultural villages, even on single family ranches.

cultivated informants, harassed political figures, devolved economic opportunities, and expanded unemployment. This lasted until 1966, when the administration was "transferred" into the military occupation of the West Bank, East Jerusalem, and Gaza. Bedouin who remained after 1948 were moved by the military into an area known as the Sayig that today is home to most of the Bedouin of the south. Villages that were founded during this time remain unrecognized by the state. They do not appear on official maps, are denied utilities and state services, and are under a near-constant threat of punitive demolitions. In the 1990s and 2000s, the government of Israel began to recognize some, but even today, these "recognized villages" are in similar economic and social straits as their unrecognized neighbors.

There are also seven government planned towns, the largest being Rahat with about 70,000 people. These towns are almost twice as dense as their Jewish counterparts and are lacking the economic and social opportunities that are available to other citizens in Israel. Many Bedouin commute from the towns to work in Be'er Sheva, Tel Aviv, and other places. The government of Israel wants people who live in unrecognized villages

to be transferred into these dense, under-served towns. In doing so, they would also give up their claims to land. People work hard to improve the lives of themselves and others in the government planned towns, but it often feels like an uphill battle.

Settler colonialism in the Naqab/Negev takes this specific form: Bedouin citizens, traditionally agrarian, are pressured to urbanize, while Jewish citizens may (depending on class) choose to live where they like: in the "mixed" cities like Be'er Sheva, towns, agricultural villages, even on single family ranches. Many towns in the Naqab/Negev legally allow for ethnic segregation: of the 126 towns in the region, only 11 (discounting the Bedouin towns) are open to Bedouin residents. This is achieved through "admission committees" that assess the "character" of the applicant to ask if they fit in with the rest of the community. Even towns without admission committees can be cost-prohibitive for Bedouin who, due to the historical and social dynamics outlined above, are more likely than Jews to live in poverty.

Let me now focus on one specific unrecognized village to show you how the logic works on the ground, disrupting peoples' lives and livelihoods. Umm al-Hiran is an unrecognized village, which has already been

Wiping Who Off the Map? Judaization and Memoricide

The Israeli historian Ilan Pappe has coined the term 'memoricide' for Israel's erasure of most traces of the Palestinians' past after it dispossessed them of four-fifths of their homeland in 1948, what Palestinians term their *Nakba*, or Catastrophe.

Israel did more than just raze 500 Palestinian towns and villages. In their place it planted new Jewish communities with Hebraicized names intended to usurp the former Arabic names. Saffuriya

became Tzipori; Hittin was supplanted by Hittim; Muyjadil was transformed into Migdal.

A similar process of what Israel calls "Judaisation" is under way in the occupied territories. The settlers of Beitar Ilit threaten the Palestinians of Battir. Nearby, the Palestinians of Sussiya have been dislodged by a Jewish settlement of exactly the same name.

The stakes are highest in Jerusalem. The vast Western Wall plaza below Al Aqsa mosque was created in 1967 after more than 1,000 Palestinians were evicted and their quarter demolished. Millions of visitors each year amble across the plaza, oblivious to this act of displacement.

Settlers, aided by the Israeli state, continue to encircle Christian and Muslim sites in the hope of taking them over.

Jonathan Cook, *The National,* Oct. 15, 2017. http://bit.ly/memoricide

Tel Aviv's attempt to silence the call to prayer is the latest part of a long history of colonisation in Palestine....According to Israeli scholars, the country's European founders turned the pine tree into a "weapon of war," using it to erase any trace of the Palestinians. The Israeli historian Ilan Pappe calls this policy "memoricide."

Jonathan Cook, http://bit.ly/NoCall2Prayer

Until 1948, Lifta, located in the hills outside Jerusalem, was an affluent Muslim Palestinian village with a population of approximately 2,500. Today, it is a haunting, depopulated village inhabited by the ghosts of those who were not allowed to return.

Ryan Rodrick Beiler/ActiveStills

half-demolished (as of July 2017) by the State of Israel. State planners want to establish a new Jewish town at the location of the village, to be called "Hiran." The Jewish National Fund, and an organization called the Or Movement are heavily involved in the lobbying for and construction of the town. Future residents of Hiran are currently living in trailers in the nearby Yatir Forest.

I've visited the village many times between October 2015 and January 2017. K is a part of the village council that is resisting demolition and transfer. K meets with visitors, diplomats, academics, activists, both international and domestic over and over again. He tells us about a pregnant woman who died in labor because the hospital was too far and they didn't have a clinic (the baby was saved). About the children who died in a storm because the roads washed out and the village flooded. All preventable, if we just had the baseline of what citizens should expect.

On Thanksgiving in 2016, I joined other activists who went to the home of a Bedouin man in Umm al-Hiran, who was under pressure from a demolition order. The man joked with us—internationals and Jewish-Israelis—about how sleepy we looked as they made us coffee and brought out some breakfast. K popped in later and went around with handshakes. The sun was coming up but there was no sign of police yet. In everyone's anxiety and boredom people chatted, joked, and went outside in the cold air for a smoke. On the horizon, above the village, construction equipment buzzed about, flattening land that would become the foundation of Hiran.

Around 9:00 a.m., it was "too late for a demolition" so everyone went home. I wasn't sure how people dealt with the anxiety of never knowing if your home would be gone. Each night people moved things out of their houses to try to save something and moved things back in if the authorities didn't show. A few days later, the man, under pressure from the police, signed away his home and the homes of his sons in return for plots in nearby Hura, a government planned town. It was devastating for everyone and depressingly normal. The man was so overcome, he went to the hospital with a panic attack. A few days later, he and his sons finished demolishing their own homes, in order to try to save their belongings and reduce the trauma on the children.

On January 18, 2017, a large police force and bulldozers arrived at Umm al-Hiran at dawn to carry out demolition orders on another area of the village. A teacher, Yakoub Mousa Abu Al-Qian was driving his truck from his home when police opened fire on him. He lost control of the vehicle and hit a police officer, killing him, as his truck settled at the bottom of a muddy depression. There, Yakoub was left to bleed to death. Almost immediately, much of the Israeli media would report the incident as an ISIS-inspired terrorist attack, knowingly withholding parts of helicopter

Joseph Getzoff

footage that showed the full incident. Even later, when it was revealed that the police had caused the accident, authorities would not release Yakoub Al-Qian's body until the Bedouin community agreed to their demands regarding the funeral: that it should be held at night with only 40 people in attendance. Eventually, the authorities gave up his body and there was a large funeral. At the same incident on January 18th, police also shot Ayman Odeh, leader of Israel's third largest political party, the Joint Arab List, in the head with a rubber bullet.

I visited the village two days later for a large solidarity gathering. Odeh was not there, and recovering, but in the past, I had seen him at all major gatherings, showing Bedouin in the south that they could count on the support of the rest of the Palestinian community in Israel. K showed us around the new wreckage. Roofs, walls, and personal belongings like dolls and books were all packed together in twisted metal. K pointed out where Al-Qian was shot. He seethed at the way the whole village had been painted as "terrorists." He said, all this talk of a country that is democratic, developed, modernized, technological, progressive, and changing, but this only applies to Jews. We don't deserve that.

The category of "citizen" does not do much but normalize how the state pursues settler-colonial policies in the Naqab/Negev. Instead, rights and security in Israel are apportioned depending on one's birth. For Bedouin in the Naqab/Negev, the state has never treated its citizens fairly, instead working to allow for the dominance of land and resources for the Jewish community. Settler-colonialism in the Naqab/Negev, is a long, slow burn that erupts in periodic, normalized violence.

The Bedouins of Umm al Hiran in the Negev have been battling the Israeli authorities for over a decade. Israel wants them to move and refuses to recognize their right to live as generations of Bedouins have. Their village remains unrecognized and ineligible for municipal services, such as connection to the electrical grid and water mains or trash-pickup. Bedouin homes and other structures are routinely demolished by Israeli authorities, as seen with this demolition in January 2017.

For bibliography, see WhyPalestineMatters.org under Further Resources.

The Rightward Shift in Israel

Israel's Arab parliamentary bloc and Knesset members hold signs in protest as security members scuffle with them during the speech of US Vice President Mike Pence in Israel's parliament in Jerusalem on January 22, 2018.

Ariel Schalit/AFP/Getty

Protest for Jerusalem Prompts Expulsion
We protested Mike Pence's speech, and Israel could not tolerate it

Ahmad Tibi, Member, Israeli *Knesset* (Parliament)

The world must finally face the reality that Israel is an apartheid power that rules over millions of Palestinians in the occupied territories without granting them any rights and that systematically discriminates against its non-Jewish citizens.

Earlier this week, I and several other Arab members of the Joint List* were forcibly removed from the Israeli parliament chamber after we attempted to silently protest US Vice President Mike Pence's speech.

As Palestinians indigenous to the land and citizens of Israel, whose families have lived here for countless generations, my colleagues and I felt compelled to act because of the Trump administration's recent recognition of Jerusalem as part of Israel, in contravention of international law and 70 years of US policy, and the complete disregard it has shown for Palestinian rights since taking office.

So, as Pence began his address, we held up signs reading "Jerusalem is the capital of Palestine" before we were swiftly and violently ejected to the cheers of right-wing lawmakers....

Israel has denied Palestinians in the occupied territories the most basic of freedoms, including freedom of movement, freedom of speech, and freedom of religion, for more than half a century....

Palestinian citizens of Israel, who make up about 20 percent of the population (about 1.5 million people) [are] being treated as second-class citizens in the land of their ancestors, subject to dozens of discriminatory laws affecting virtually every facet of life from land ownership and housing rights, to education, health care, employment, and family reunification....

While claiming to be a democracy, our ejection from the Knesset shows that Israel cannot even tolerate a simple democratic protest but rather that they applaud the crushing of dissent. Can one imagine members of the Black Caucus being evicted from Congress in this way for expressing dissent against the Trump administration's policies?...

The world must finally face the reality that Israel is an apartheid power that rules over millions of Palestinians in the occupied territories without granting them any rights and that systematically discriminates against its non-Jewish citizens. We urge all countries and people of conscience to support us as we struggle peacefully for our freedom, justice, and equality.

Newsweek, January 27, 2018, http://bit.ly/2FbLVKb

* The Joint List is the Palestinian coalition party in the Israeli *Knesset* (parliament).

In August 2017 Israel's Supreme Court and its Minister of Justice clashed over what values should be primary in Israeli law. The Israeli judicial system places too much emphasis on individual rights, said Israeli Justice Minister Ayelet Shaked, who criticized the Supreme Court for disregarding the needs of Zionism, which is a political system based on a Jewish majority. Columnist Gideon Levy responded to her moment of transparency in Israel's Ha'aretz.

Israel's Minister of Truth

Gideon Levy, Journalist

Thank you, Ayelet Shaked, for telling the truth. Thank you for speaking honestly. The justice minister has proved once again that Israel's extreme right is better than the deceivers of the center-left: It speaks honestly.... Shaked said, loud and clear: Zionism contradicts human rights, and thus is indeed an ultranationalist, colonialist, and perhaps even racist movement, as proponents of justice worldwide maintain.

Shaked prefers Zionism to human rights, the ultimate universal justice. She believes that we have a different kind of justice, superior to universal justice. Zionism above all. It's been said before, in other languages and other nationalist movements....

What are today's Zionist challenges? To "Judaize" the Negev and Galilee, remove the "infiltrators," cultivate Israel's Jewish character, and preserve its Jewish majority.

The occupation, the settlements, the cult of security, the army—which is primarily an occupation army—that is Zionism circa 2017. All its components are contrary to justice. After we were told that Zionism and justice were identical twins, that no national movement is more just than Zionism, Shaked came to say: just the opposite. Zionism is not just, it contradicts justice, but we shall cleave to it and prefer it to justice, because it's our identity, our history, and our national mission....

Zionism is Israel's fundamentalist religion, and as in any religion, its denial is prohibited. In Israel, "non-Zionist" or "anti-Zionist" aren't insults; they are social expulsion orders. There's nothing like it in any free society. But now that Shaked has exposed Zionism, put her hand to the flame, and admitted the truth, we can finally think about Zionism more freely....

*Ha'aretz,*September 1, 2017, http://bit.ly/MinisterofTruth

> Israel Justice Minister Shaked said the truth loud and clear: Zionism contradicts human rights, and thus is indeed an ultranationalist, colonialist, and perhaps racist movement.

For additional background on Minister Shaked's inflammatory statements on Zionism and human rights, see: http://bit.ly/ShakedZionism

---

In January 2018 in the pages of the New York Times, *Israel's Minister of Education, Naftali Bennett, defended Israel's right to blacklist supporters of nonviolent economic action known as the BDS, calling them enemies of his state. (See pages 86-90 for more on BDS: Boycott, Divestment and Sanctions). Palestinian human rights defender Issa Amro, responded in the pages of* The [Jewish] Forward.

Sorry, [Israel]: "Normal" Democracies Don't Ban Nonviolent Resistance

Issa Amro, Palestinian Human Rights Activist

Issa Amro, an ctivist with Youth Against Settlements in Al-Khalil (Hebron), was hit with 18 charges in an Israeli military court relating to his participation in demonstrations against settlements and Israeli occupation forces in his city.

...Far from normal, Israel is a democracy that is occupying millions of Palestinians. And it is this fact—the denial of civil liberties to millions of people—that BDS uses nonviolent means to oppose.

...Imagine for a moment what it's like being Palestinian and watching the settlements get approved for expansion again and again and again, seeing the new settlements sprout up under the auspices of a country that denies you civil rights.

...Together [with international activists], we protect families being displaced by settlers. We campaign to save villages slated for demolition. We establish infrastructure, like kindergartens and cinemas. We give hope to our community.

For these actions we are attacked, beaten, and arrested. We sit in jail cells under administrative detention with no official charges filed, and we face military court where the conviction rate is over 99%. I am currently facing 18 charges in Israeli military court for such advocacy. And these are punishments for nonviolent actions. What kind of "normal democracy" as Bennett put it jails people for nonviolent advocacy for civil rights?

The Forward, January 29, 2018, http://bit.ly/2BDoNEK

Umm al-Kheir is one of the small scattered communities of Bedouin families here. A handful of people scratch to hang on to their traditional land and way of life, but close enough to overhear conversations is the illegal settlement of Carmel.

June 13, 2014. Bedouin women sit on the ground in Al Arakib, an unrecognized Bedouin village in the Negev desert, one day after the entire village was demolished by the Israeli authorities. According to government figures, 200,000 Bedouin live in the country's southern Negev region, the majority in seven government-planned townships, and several thousand more in eleven Bedouin communities that the government is in the process of "recognizing." Israeli state planning documents and maps exclude 35 "unrecognized" Bedouin communities, where the government estimates that 70,000 to 90,000 people live.

Unwanted: Bedouin in Occupied Territory
Harry Gunkel

Although their geographic locations are separated by only a few miles and a line on a map, and they often belong to the same clans and extended families, the Bedouin residing in the occupied West Bank live under a marginally different system from that of their kinspeople inside Israel. These formerly nomadic goat and camel herders, most now settled in small sedentary villages, were indigenous to Palestine and what is today Israel and followed their own lifestyle and culture for centuries before Zionism and Jewish settlers arrived in Palestine. While Negev Bedouin have Israeli citizenship, at least on a tenuous basis, Bedouin in the West Bank—in the South Hebron Hills and the Jordan Valley— are not Israeli citizens and live at the mercy of Israeli settlers who are building increasingly on land that has always been Bedouin. Harry Gunkel describes the situation in one of these areas.

In the southernmost reaches of the West Bank, beyond Bethlehem and Hebron and verging into an-Naqab (Negev Desert), are the South Hebron Hills. It is an area little known, rarely visited, and hardly spoken of. It is a barren, arid landscape of brown rolling hills and valleys with only the occasional hint of green. A dry wind blows most of the time. It is quite beautiful and full of majesty. In this land of endless vistas, it feels as though there is space for everybody, but there is not.

This is one of the traditional homelands of the Bedouin people. Ancient nomadic people, the Bedouin are among the indigenous of historical Palestine and, like their brethren, are targets of Israeli efforts to displace and dispossess them. Despite the fact that those inside Israel were made citizens in 1954, the Zionist quest to dominate all the land from the river to the sea makes no room for any of these beleaguered people even in this sparsely populated area. They have been pushed, shoved, and moved into ever smaller enclaves of isolation.

Umm al-Kheir is one of the small scattered communities of Bedouin families here. A handful of people scratch to hang on to their traditional land and way of

life, but close enough to overhear conversations is the illegal settlement of Carmel. The settlers in Carmel do not want Umm al-Kheir in the view out their kitchen windows, so the people of this small village suffer. Their few living places are thrown together with the scraps available because nothing permanent will do here. The occupying force will destroy it, and then destroy what is rebuilt. Even the chicken coop here has a demolition order posted on it. In his brilliant book, *The Way to the Spring*, Ben Ehrenreich captures perfectly what goes on here:

> The South Hebron Hills were yet another planet in the solar system of greater Palestine, or perhaps a distant moon, drier and poorer than any other. Even more than in the villages around Nablus, it was the Wild West. The settlers did as they pleased, and almost no one paid attention.[1]

A few miles away, the children of another Bedouin community must walk to the nearest school in at-Tawani. The distance is short but the peril is great because the path passes by a settlement and the children are sometimes attacked by settlers. Now on some days, Israeli soldiers escort the children. The soldiers do not try to stop the settlers or censure them, but even they believe children walking to school are not legitimate targets for violence.

A dedicated few Jewish Israeli dissidents from the organization Tayyush come regularly to these isolated encampments to do what they can to help because their government will not. They fight legal battles in court; they fend off attacking settlers; they help rebuild when a Bedouin encampment is demolished; they walk children to school when army escorts are not around; they provide solar panels; they build cisterns; they spend their spare time away from family and friends because their hearts bring them here to work with their fellow human beings. One Jewish Israeli university professor who spends most weekends with the Bedouin, asked why he does this, noted with a wry grin that he had once been shot by an Israeli settler. "So it's in my gut," he said, rubbing a hand over his abdomen.

Oren Ziv/ActiveStills

Planning Dominance in Israel/Palestine

Joseph Getzoff

Planning is a spatial expression of cultural, social, and economic aims. Planners seek to express their values in the ordering of space, on national, regional, and municipal scales. In Israel, planning is centralized and surprisingly uniform. The overriding logic of the State of Israel's planning regime has been called "Judaization"— that is, the transformation of "Palestinian space'" into "'Jewish space." This ethnocratic logic has treated areas where Palestinians hold a significant demographic presence as frontiers that need to be transformed.

This is achieved through national and local plans that seek to disperse the Jewish population while constricting Palestinian land-use. Israeli plans rarely address Palestinian citizens' concerns, and there has been next to no representation of minorities on planning councils. While Israeli planning has directed the expansion of Jewish towns, the establishment of new ones, as well as industrial zoning, specific urban and rural planning, afforestation, nature reserves and more, Palestinian towns are often ignored, or their planning does not take into account local needs, as in the case of the Bedouin urban towns. In the West Bank, Rawabi, a new suburban development outside of Ramallah, has the distinction of being the only Palestinian town established there since 1948. Even they had trouble securing roads and water pipes to service the town because of the nearby Israeli settlements.

The distribution of the Jewish population throughout all of Palestine/Israel has always been a major obsession of state planners. The coastal plain, where the suburbs of Tel Aviv almost reach north to Haifa, has long been the epicenter of Jewish settlement. In the 1950s, planners worried about the vulnerability of a state wherein a vast majority of the population hugged the coast. Further, they imagined regions where Jewish population was sparse as potentially being lost to the state. In subsequent plans, the state tried to attract Jewish citizens to the "peripheries"—that is, places where the

Hussam 'Abed/B'Tselem

Palestinian citizens of the state make up a significant portion of the population. In the 1970s, planners pushed for the establishment of new cities and settlements throughout the Upper Galilee. Subsequent plans also attempted to develop the Negev/Naqab, focusing on Be'er Sheva as the new capital of the region. In these cases, the state established heavy industry, new centers of commerce, gave out subsidies, sited military bases, and built new towns and housing, in order to attract Jewish residents. Similar processes occur in the West Bank.

In the West Bank, Israeli planning norms function in Area C. Area C was designated under the Oslo Accords as an area of Israeli military and civil administrative control and makes up about 60% of the West Bank. Area C encompasses agricultural fields and open space between Palestinian cities and villages, as well as a number of Palestinian villages and the West Bank Bedouin population. Most Israeli settlements are built in Area C. As a result, the Israeli planning regime

November 2016. Although expulsions of Arab residents are a regular occurrence throughout East Jerusalem, forced dislocation is occurring at the highest rate in Batan al-Hawa, according to B'Tselem, the Israeli Information Center for Human Rights in the Occupied Territories. In 2016 eviction claims were filed against 81 Palestinian families that had been living there for decades. UN research indicates that a third of all Palestinian families in East Jeruslaem live under threat of dispossession on the basis of ethnicity.

restricts Palestinian building here, halting the expansion of already existing towns and/or the building of new ones. Settlers, however, receive expedited planning recognition in order to facilitate "facts on the ground" through the expansion of settlement neighborhoods, transportation lines, utility connections, and military outposts. Palestinians are hardly ever given permits for even mundane expansion. For instance, Palestinians who wish to dig cisterns for water collection even require a permit from Israeli authorities.

As a result of top-down Israeli planning, including in the settlements, Jewish towns tend to appear uniform and suburban, even using similar colors and materials for houses and apartment blocks. Jewish farming villages are usually spread out and planned around large areas of land so there is room for expansion. New suburbs are built according to top-down planning; that is, entire neighborhoods are constructed together, not one house at a time.

In contrast, Palestinian towns in Israel appear denser and unplanned. They do not receive the same services as Jewish towns. Because the state denies building permits to all but a few Palestinians, building is more haphazard and individualized. As they can, people will expand their homes, or build on new plots. And while Palestinians and Jews build structures without permits at roughly a similar ratio, Palestinian structures are categorized as "illegal," and enforcement and demolition is the state's first priority for addressing what is a socio-economic problem and an endemic housing crisis.

Palestinian towns do not have the same kind of centralized, suburban planning of Jewish towns. (Many, in fact, lack any sort of outline plans at all.) This is a result of the Israeli policy of "forced urbanization" of Palestinian citizens. That is, in an attempt to take control of land, the state seeks to concentrate Palestinians into constricting, urban spaces. Palestinian towns do not receive planning license to expand and as their populations grow, people are forced to build upwards (if they receive permits). Furthermore, Israeli regional planning has sited military bases, firing zones, industrial areas, and nature reserves around Palestinian towns, stopping their necessary expansion.

Legal measures are also used to disconnect Palestinians from land and ensure Jewish demographic and spatial dominance. The Planning and Building Law of 1965 is a prime example. The Law allows for the demolition of structures built without permits. Further, it re-zoned much of the rural land in Israel as "agricultural land," purposefully rendering any building on it illegal. This has created the curiously unique Israeli planning designation of an "unrecognized village." Bedouin unrecognized villages are in the south and north of the country and do not appear on maps, do not receive state services, and are under constant threat of demolition, despite the fact that they have long been homes for citizens of the state. State officials refer to these towns as the "diaspora" or "illegal" and seek to push people out of them and into urban localities. While most of the unrecognized villages are in the southern part of the country perhaps the most extreme example of Israeli planning values exists in the north.

Ramiya is an unrecognized village in the middle of the rapidly expanding Jewish city of Karmiel in the Galilee. Karmiel is meant to be a new hub for the development of the region. Surrounded by new apartment buildings, the people of Ramiya have resisted the city's efforts to move them. It is shocking to see the way that planners treat this Bedouin village as a hole in the map: garbage is not picked up, the paved road ends in gravel, utilities are not provided. And yet, people continue to keep gardens, decorate their homes, and persist. These kinds of Kafkaesque situations are all too common because of a planning regime that seeks to transform and control all land for the benefit of the Jewish population.

For bibliography, see WhyPalestineMatters.org under Further Resources.

...Israeli regional planning has sited military bases, firing zones, industrial areas, and nature reserves around Palestinian towns, stopping their necessary expansion.

Area C and the "Temporary" Interim Agreement

...The Interim Agreement in 1995 between Israel and the PLO divided the West Bank into three categories:

Area A, currently comprising about 18% of the land in the West Bank, which includes all the Palestinian cities and most of the Palestinian population of the West Bank; the Palestinian Authority (PA) is endowed with most governmental powers this area.

Area B, comprises approximately 22% of the West Bank and encompasses large rural areas; Israel retained security control of the area and transferred control of civil matters to the PA.

Area C covers 60% of the West Bank (about 330,000 hectares); Israel has retained almost complete control of this area, including security matters and all land-related civil matters, including land allocation, planning and construction, and infrastructure. The PA is responsible for providing education and medical services to the Palestinian population in Area C. However, construction and maintenance of the infrastructure necessary for these services remain in Israel's hands. Civil matters remained under Israeli control in Area C and are the responsibility of the Civil Administration.

The division into areas was to have been temporary and meant to enable an incremental transfer of authority to the Palestinian Authority. It was not designed to address the needs of long-term demographic growth. Yet this "temporary" arrangement has remained in force for nearly twenty years.

Areas A and B were defined by drawing lines around Palestinian population centers at the time the Interim Agreement was signed. Some 2.4 million Palestinian residents live in these areas, which are subdivided into 165 separate units of land that have no territorial contiguity.

B'Tselem - The Israeli Information Center for Human Rights in the Occupied Territories, http://bit.ly/AreasABC

Chapter 5
Rebranding a Country

Whose *Kufiya* Is It, Anyway?
Noushin Framke

Cultural appropriation is familiar to most people when it comes to dominant American culture exploiting Native American rites, traditions, and icons. Using stereotypes, the worlds of fashion, sports, entertainment, and more have capitalized on Native American culture to the point of destroying the original meanings. In other words, the dominant culture has taken over the native identity, which, even if it is distorted, is yet a further continuation of colonization.

One distinct form of colonization is settler colonialism that aims to replace indigenous groups with a new society. Settler colonial countries such as the United States, Canada, Australia, New Zealand, and South Africa were founded by settlers who came to stay and who persisted over decades and even centuries on eliminating local peoples and cultures. Frantz Fanon wrote that

> ...[C]olonialism is not satisfied merely with holding a people in its grip and emptying the native's brain of all form and content. By a kind of perverted logic, it turns to the past of the oppressed people and distorts, disfigures, and destroys it.

Israel as a settler colonial nation intends to be the dominant culture over indigenous people it has colonized. Even as Zionists persisted with the propaganda that they had found "a land without a people for a people without a land," they appropriated the ancient local traditions, foods, embroidery art, and more. In the many appropriations of things Palestinian, Israel has become expert in what is known as "Columbusing," which is what the Urban Dictionary defines as "the art of discovering something that is not new." In this way, the appropriated items take on an Israeli veneer and are stolen out of their native identity. Familiar examples are Arab foods such as hummus and falafel, the Arabic dance, the *Dabka*, and most infuriatingly to the Palestinians, their cotton scarf originally used by farmers as protection from sun and dust, the Palestinian *kufiya*.

The now ubiquitous *kufiya* has become a global symbol of protest and can be found along with Palestinian flags in every corner of the world at protests for human rights and rallies for justice. Palestinians cherish their black and white Palestine-woven scarves, but with the appropriation of the *kufiya* by the fashion industry, cheap copies made in China are now sold all over the world. Palestinians are happy to see authentic kufiya worn by solidarity activists around the world, as long as they are supporting Palestine's struggle for human rights. But it's a cruel insult to see Israeli blue and white versions with the star of David woven into the pattern and adapted into trendy high-fashion dresses. Even the symbol of the Palestinian struggle for justice has not been immune from cultural appropriation.

In a popular hip hop song by the London-born Palestinian Shadia Mansour, who refers to herself as "living in exile in the West," she raps to the beat repeating "*Al kufiya Arabiya*," proclaiming in rhyme, "the *kufiya* is Arab!"[1]

London-based hip hop artist Shadia Mansour, whose hit "The *Kufiya* is Arab" has become a rallying cry against appropriation.

thecultretrip.com

Appropriated Star of David *kufiya*

wearenotnumbers.org

Gaza artist depicts women getting ready for protest with *kufiyas*, highlighting the role of women in the resistance.

For music video, see WhyPalestineMatters.org under Chapter 5 videos, or for full video see: http://bit.ly/kufiya (video is EXPLICIT)

Who's Afraid of Dialogue? Normalizing Oppression

Kathleen Christison

They have treated the wound of my people carelessly, saying "Peace, peace," when there is no peace. —Jeremiah 6:14

Mediating and attempting to reconcile differences often seem to be a natural American inclination. In the Palestinian-Israeli arena, *ad hoc* reconciliatory efforts in the United States proliferate, more or less in inverse relation to the success or lack of success of the long-running, official US "peace process" that has striven off and on since the Oslo peace agreement of 1993 to achieve a final peace settlement. These non-official ad hoc efforts range from small living room dialogue groups that meet regularly to bring Jewish Americans together with Palestinian and other Arab Americans, to summer camps that gather American youth of Jewish and Muslim faith for a few weeks of dialogue, to larger scale, well-funded camps that bring youth from Israel and the Palestinian communities inside Israel and in the Occupied Territories to the US for several weeks of interaction.

The usually well-meaning purpose of these reconciliation efforts is to forge greater understanding between Israelis and Palestinians as people: to facilitate a frank and open exchange of narratives from each side's perspective and discussion of the emotional pain each people feels because of past or present suffering. It is hard to criticize an effort that attempts to bring peoples together when their governments and leaderships are in conflict; in each of these efforts, those who initiate the dialogue groups or the summer camps undoubtedly genuinely hope to take some step to achieve peace between Israelis and Palestinians, and it is true that some level of real understanding is almost always forged on an individual level. But in fact the real-time effect of efforts like these—and specifically in the Israeli-Palestinian instance, when there is virtually no expectation that Israel intends to relinquish territory to the Palestinians

or accord them any measure of justice—is simply to normalize Israel's domination over the Palestinians.

These efforts tend to be feel-good projects that lull supporters and donors into an ineffective complacency, thinking they are helping resolve the political conflict by acting out of a balanced approach toward both sides. But this is actually only myopic self-congratulation. South African Archbishop Desmond Tutu, who oversaw the arduous Truth and Reconciliation Commission hearings in the early 1990s after apartheid had officially ended, has noted that efforts like these that attempt to achieve "balance" or "neutrality" between the two sides are in fact seriously unbalanced. "If you are neutral in situations of injustice," he has said, "you have chosen the side of the oppressor. If an elephant has its foot on the tail of a mouse, and you say that you are neutral, the mouse will not appreciate your neutrality."

Neutrality normalizes the dominant side's actions and policies. Normalization is not balanced; on the contrary, normalization concretizes the status quo, standardizes the dominance of the strong party over the weak party, the occupier over the occupied, the state over any person and group that it oppresses.

From the perspective of the Palestinians, normalization comes across completely differently from the viewpoint of the dominant party and its adherents. Consider, for instance, this analogy with an (imaginary) initiative that would have brought slave youth and the teenage children of slaveholders together for a few weeks of camaraderie at a summer camp. These young people on both sides would probably all enjoy their weeks together and come away with a better attitude, able now to see that they're all young human beings. But then they would return to their own regular lives of being slaves and slaveholders, one over the other, and the institution of slavery would not have been altered. Nothing in the real world would have changed.

One would have to conclude the same thing about any grassroots dialogue or "reconciliation" attempt that does not involve the officials in a position actually to bring about or facilitate a change of government policy.

Palestinian rap poet Remi Kanazi has spoken out specifically about normalization in a dramatic way:

No, I don't want to normalize with you. I don't want to hug, have coffee, talk it out, break bread, sit around the campfire, eat s'mores, and gush about how we're all the same,...talk about how art instead of justice can forge a better path....You're either with oppression or you're against it.[1]

> ...[T]he real-time effect of [dialogue groups and reconciliation efforts] like these...is simply to normalize Israel's domination over the Palestinians.

Palestinian rap poet Remi Kanazi rejects the normalization embedded in reconciliation-through-dialogue initiatives. "Nothing," he says, "is normal about occupation. Nothing is normal about apartheid, ethnic cleansing, siege, blockade, settler-only roads, and bombing water wells, schools, and mosques...."

remikanazi.com

Cultural Appropriation or Theft?

"Israeli" *Hummus* Is Theft, Not Appropriation

Steven Salaita

…[T]he controversy about Israel's appropriation of Palestinian food—most infamously its claim to *hummus*, a lucrative product in Europe and North America—has nothing to do with Jews eating Arabic food. In fact, it has nothing to do with Jews at all. That ludicrous idea is possible only because Zionists aggressively conflate Jewishness with Israel.

Instead, it has everything to do with a deliberate, decades-old programme to disappear Palestinians. Referencing Arab defensiveness about traditional dishes without mentioning colonisation or ethnic cleansing is a whitewash….

When Zionists (or their oblivious collaborators) claim Arabic food as Israeli, it's not a paragon of intercultural harmony but the studious destruction of Palestinian culture. We can mitigate ambiguity by avoiding the word "appropriation," which doesn't adequately capture the dynamics of Israel's voracious appetite for anything that can be marked "indigenous," which it needs to shore up an ever-tenuous sense of legitimacy.

"Theft" is more accurate. It is also rhetorically superior. Discourses of modernity exalt cultural interchange, but no good liberal supports piracy.

We should remember that while chefs, shopkeepers, and propagandists validate the theft, the main culprit is the Israeli government, which brands falafel the "national snack" and advertises a plethora of Levantine dishes as authentically Israeli in tacky Brand Israel campaigns.

State involvement in the pilfer of Palestinian food illustrates that we shouldn't reduce the issue to individual consumption. It's a systematic effort to validate settler colonisation.

It's no shock, then, that Palestinians and their neighbours get salty whenever hearing the phrase "Israeli *hummus.*" Using Arabic food as a symbol of Zionist identity hands over the day-to-day victuals of the native to the coloniser. It's a project of erasure, a portent of nonexistence, a promise of genocide.

No state that destroys olive groves and poisons the environment has a right to claim the objects of sustenance harvested for centuries by other people.

I've never met a Palestinian who is angered by a non-Arab consuming Levantine food. In fact, the vast majority are delighted when outsiders partake of the culture.

Palestinians, like their Lebanese, Jordanian, and Syrian neighbours, are damn proud of their food. (All four groups argue among themselves, along with Greeks and Turks, about the regional provenance of certain dishes—Israel is a non-factor in those arguments, which long predate Theodor Herzl's birthday.)

The problem arises when somebody calls that food "Israeli."

The main argument for "Israeli" food is that Jews prepared and ate staple dishes in Iraq, Morocco, Yemen, and Palestine. This is indisputable. The rootedness of Jews in the Arab World should be acknowledged, studied, and celebrated.

But those Jews weren't eating Israeli food. To say so actually demeans Mizrahi history by suggesting an inability to partake of their own national and cultural milieus, another example of Zionism demanding a narrow sense of identity.

> When Zionists (or their oblivious collaborators) claim Arabic food as Israeli, it's not a paragon of intercultural harmony but the studious destruction of Palestinian culture.

Excerpted from "'Israeli' *Hummus* Is Theft, Not Appropriation," by Steven Salaita, *The New Arab*, September 4, 2017. See http://bit.ly/2h3KlMR

Steven Salaita is an American scholar, author, and public speaker. His latest book is *Inter/Nationalism, Decolonizing Native America and Palestine*, 2016. He successfully sued the University of Illinois over being fired for anti-Israel tweets during the 2014 invasion of Gaza.

US Feminists Wake Up to Palestine

Theo Wargo/AFP

From left: Carmen Perez, Gloria Steinem, and Linda Sarsour onstage during the Women's March on Washington January 21, 2017. Sarsour, the Muslim-American co-founder of the Women's March, is no stranger to right wing anti-Muslim bigotry. Since the summer of 2017 she has been attacked in liberal media outlets for her anti-Zionism.

We Need a Feminism for the 99%. That's Why Women Will Strike This Year

....Racialized gender violence is international, as must be the campaign against it. US imperialism, militarism, and settler colonialism foster misogyny throughout the world. It is no coincidence that Harvey Weinstein, in his long years of trying to silence and terrorize women, used the security firm, Black Cube, which is made up of former agents of Mossad and other Israeli intelligence agencies. We know that the same state that sends money to Israel to brutalize the Palestinian Ahed Tamimi and her family also funds the jails in which African American women like Sandra Bland and others have died....

So, on 8 March we will strike against mass incarceration, police violence, and border controls, against white supremacy and the beating drums of US imperialist wars, against poverty and the hidden structural violence that closes our schools and our hospitals, poisons our water and food, and denies us reproductive justice.

And we will strike for labor rights, equal rights for all immigrants, equal pay, and a living wage, because sexual violence in the workplace is allowed to fester when we lack these means of collective defence.

8 March 2018 will be a day of feminism for the 99%: a day of mobilization of black and brown women, cis and bi, lesbian and trans women workers, of the poor and the low waged, of unpaid caregivers, of sex workers and migrants....

Linda Martín Alcoff, Cinzia Arruzza, Tithi Bhattacharya, Rosa Clemente, Angela Davis, Zillah Eisenstein, Liza Featherstone, Nancy Fraser, Barbara Smith, Keeanga-Yamahtta Taylor, *The Guardian*, January 27, 2018 http://bit.ly/Fem99

"Keep Your Feminism"

The highly publicized rift following the Women's March in January 2017 split feminists according to whether they supported Israel or Palestine. In a Facebook post, excerpted below, Palestinian American March organizer Linda Sarsour eloquently called out feminist "PEPs" for hypocrisy and double-standards when it came to justice for Palestine. PEP has become the term used to describe those who are Progressive Except on Palestine.

If your feminism doesn't include my hijab, my love for and adherence to my Islamic faith,...
If your feminism is about having full unquestionable faith in a system that brutalizes people of color,...
If your feminism doesn't have room for respectful disagreements with substantive debates rooted in facts,...
If your feminism doesn't have room for complex multi-layered identities and experiences of women of color…
[y]ou can "keep your feminism." We promise you, we don't want it.

—Linda Sarsour

Left: Shepard Fairey, creator of the iconic Obama "Hope" poster in 2008, released a series of images of American women before the 2017 Trump inauguration, including this image of an American Muslim woman with patriotic *hijab*.

Palestinian Women: Life Under Israeli Occupation

So long as Western feminists denounce the oppression of Arab women as a result of Islamic fundamentalism, but not as a result of Israeli occupation, I will raise my voice. I will explain that Palestinian women are without any doubt more oppressed by Israel and Zionism than they are by their fellow Palestinian men, that a Palestinian woman's freedom of movement, her right to an education, her right to vote, her right to work, her right to live where she wants, her right to sufficient food, clean water, and medical treatment in her own homeland are denied to her not by her fellow Palestinians but by the illegal occupying power, Israel.

Nada Elia, "The Burden of Representation: When Palestinians Speak Out," in *Arab and Arab-American Feminisms: Gender, Violence, and Belonging*, 2011, p. 158.

Israel's war against the continuance of Palestinian life targets women in every sphere. Certainly it targets women as potential or actual agents of the reproduction of life itself, as mothers and as caretakers, but it also targets women as reproducers of social and cultural life, as if the targeting of women—as so often in colonial regimes—were understood to be the royal road to the destruction of indigenous social and political life.

David Lloyd, Feminists@Law, Vol. 4, No. 1, 2014. journals.kent.ac.uk/index.php/feministsatlaw/article/view/107/282

Pinkwashing and the Politics of Distraction

Noushin Framke

In today's activist lexicon, "pinkwashing" refers to Israel's public relations strategy to "wash" its human rights record by using its supposed LGBTQ-friendly position to rebrand itself. Israel has been using this tactic to change the conversation from the abuses of the occupation to one that brands Israel as progressive and inclusive. This is a campaign that, as CUNY Prof. Sarah Schulman describes, is a well organized and well funded effort for "Winning the Battle of the Narrative," reaffirming the need for re-branding.[1]

The phrase itself goes back to the 1980s when Breast Cancer Action identified corporations who feigned support of breast cancer patients while they were actually profiting from the disease. By 2010, with the rise of solidarity for Palestine, "pinkwashing" took on a new meaning and has been used in the same way as "greenwashing" which refers to cleaning the reputation of non-environment-friendly entities. In this new iteration, Palestine solidarity activists have taken on fighting pinkwashing, along with other PR tactics adopted by Israel to salvage a fast-sliding reputation. In a meeting in 2010, Ali Abunimah, Palestinian-American editor of *Electronic Intifada* is said to have declared, "We won't put up with Israel whitewashing, greenwashing, or pinkwashing."

In a 2016 story about Tel Aviv Gay Pride, Agence France Presse (AFP) reported that the funds spent by Israel to advertise that year's event to European visitors—almost $3 million—was ten times the amount of state funding of LGBTQ associations. The advertising included a rainbow-clad airplane that turned out to be a wakeup call for the community. "'Spending 1.5 million shekels to paint a rainbow on a plane full of tourists, that's ridiculous,' said Imri Kalman, co-chair of Aguda, Israel's largest LGBT NGO. "We finally understood the hypocrisy of this government and this prime minister,

who boasts in English abroad about the freedom enjoyed by homosexuals in Israel but never utters the word in Hebrew when he gets home."[2]

In a 2017 opinion column in *Newsweek*, queer Palestinian Haneen Maikey of alQaws.org calls for a boycott of Tel Aviv Gay Pride. She writes,

> Gay Pride in Tel Aviv is heavily sponsored by the Israeli government and is cynically deployed to divert attention from the occupation of Palestinian lands and the daily violation of Palestinian rights.... [T]he Israeli government has heavily invested in a "Brand Israel" propaganda campaign that uses cultural events and festivities to depict Israel's "prettier face" as a liberal, gay-friendly place. It does so to cover-up and maintain Israel's ongoing system of violence and racial discrimination, enshrined in dozens of laws against indigenous Palestinians, queers and non-queers alike....I know that there is no pink door through Israel's illegal, racist wall that welcomes queer Palestinians while oppressing others. My struggles intersect and cannot be separated. I reject the use of my queerness to erase other sites of oppression around me."[3]

Sa'ed Atshan, Peace and Conflict Studies professor at Swarthmore College who identifies as a queer Palestinian Christian Quaker, has spoken against using the LGBTQ community's hard-won rights to cover-up Israeli crimes. As a member of the community, he also speaks of the intersections of justice of other hard-fought battles. Atshan said in a 2014 lecture at Loyola University in Chicago,

> What I mean by intersectionality is we have to stand up to all systems of oppression. Our fight against colonialism is linked to our fight against racism, classism, abelism, sexism, anti-LGBTQ sentiments, and religious intolerance. When we fight for social justice and human rights, we need to fight for all human beings.[4]

Gay Pride in Tel Aviv is heavily sponsored by the Israeli government and is cynically deployed to divert attention from the occupation of Palestinian lands and the daily violation of Palestinian rights....

"Why we should boycott gay pride in Tel Aviv", Haneen Maikey, *Newsweek*, June 9, 2017

The Israeli Tourism Ministry announced in 2016 that it would invest over $2.9 million in a campaign to attract tourists to the Tel Aviv Gay Pride Parade, including an international competition whose winners would be flown to Israel in a rainbow-painted plane. This simulated picture was posted on Facebook by LGBT activists who were outraged over the huge disparity between the resources allocated to this public relations stunt and the funding support for the Israeli LGBT community. After the blowback, the government backed down.

Rebranding with Sex and Sexuality

Don't Be Fooled by Israel's "Pinkwashing"

Sarah Schulman

... In 2005, with help from American marketing executives, the Israeli government began a marketing campaign, "Brand Israel," aimed at men ages 18 to 34. The campaign, as reported by *The Jewish Daily Forward*, sought to depict Israel as "relevant and modern." The government later expanded the marketing plan by harnessing the gay community to reposition its global image.

Last year, the Israeli news site Ynet reported that the Tel Aviv tourism board had begun a campaign of around $90 million to brand the city as "an international gay vacation destination." The promotion, which received support from the Tourism Ministry and Israel's overseas consulates, includes depictions of young same-sex couples and financing for pro-Israeli movie screenings at lesbian and gay film festivals in the United States....

This message is being articulated at the highest levels. In May Prime Minister Benjamin Netanyahu told Congress that the Middle East was "a region where women are stoned, gays are hanged, Christians are persecuted."

The growing global gay movement against the Israeli occupation has named these tactics "pinkwashing": a deliberate strategy to conceal the continuing violations of Palestinians' human rights behind an image of modernity signified by Israeli gay life. Aeyal Gross, a professor of law at Tel Aviv University, argues that "gay rights have essentially become a public-relations tool," even though "conservative and especially religious politicians remain fiercely homophobic."

Pinkwashing not only manipulates the hard-won gains of Israel's gay community, but it also ignores the existence of Palestinian gay-rights organizations. Homosexuality has been decriminalized in the West Bank since the 1950s, when anti-sodomy laws imposed under British colonial influence were removed from the Jordanian penal code, which Palestinians follow. More important is the emerging Palestinian gay movement with three major organizations: Aswat, Al Qaws and Palestinian Queers for Boycott, Divestment, and Sanctions. These groups are clear that the oppression of Palestinians crosses the boundary of sexuality; as Haneen Maikey, the director of Al Qaws, has said, "When you go through a checkpoint it does not matter what the sexuality of the soldier is."

... Increasing gay rights have caused some people of good will to mistakenly judge how advanced a country is by how it responds to homosexuality.

In Israel, gay soldiers and the relative openness of Tel Aviv are incomplete indicators of human rights—just as in America, the expansion of gay rights in some states does not offset human rights violations like mass incarceration. The long-sought realization of some rights for some gays should not blind us to the struggles against racism in Europe and the United States, or to the Palestinians' insistence on a land to call home.

Sarah Schulman, *New York Times*, Nov. 22, 2011, http://bit.ly/IsraelPink. For fuller history of the Pinkwashing movement by Sarah Schulman, see http://bit.ly/FullStoryPink

Selling "Brand Israel"

Ilan Pappe

In 2007 a poster of an almost naked Miss Israel, Gal Gadot, and a poster of four fit young men, equally barely dressed, were the faces of Israel in a campaign named Brand Israel, commissioned by the government and the Jewish Agency for Israel. The young woman was meant to attract the heterosexual young Americans to a rebranded Jewish State, while the young men became the faces advertising Tel Aviv as the gay capital of Israel. One wonders how Theodore Herzl or even David Ben-Gurion and Menachem Begin would have regarded this presentation of Zionism as a soft-porn wet dream. But policymakers had decided that anything and everything was appropriate in the struggle to fend off Israel's negative image.

Ilan Pappe, excerpt from "Epilogue: Brand Israel, 2013", *The Idea of Israel: A History of Power and Knowledge*, Ilan Pappe, Verso, 2014

Left: Gal Gadot was Miss Israel in 2004, and went on to star in the Hollywood blockbusters *Fast and Furious* in 2009 and *Wonder Woman* in 2017.

It's Brownwashing Time: Self-Orientalizing on the US Campus

Gil Hochberg

A banner displayed by Columbia University group "Students Supporting Israel" during "Hebrew Liberation Week: A Celebration of Semitism." The banner shows semitic people as people of color in an attempt to connect Israel to struggles of other peoples in the picture. Moving beyond pinkwashing in Israel's campaign to rebrand the country, Israel is now pushing a new campaign on US university campuses to promote Israelis as oppressed people.

t is the ninth week for me as a new professor at Columbia University. The move here from UCLA, where I taught for fifteen years, has been full of surprises, and not always of the kind one expects. But nothing prepared me for the sight I encountered recently as I crossed the main plaza of the college on the way to class to teach Edward Said's *Orientalism*

Orientalism reflects a Western, often distorted view of the "East," and not necessarily the views of the inhabitants of what used to be known as the Orient. Orientalism now refers to a racist stereotyping of "Eastern" and North African peoples as inferior to whites, and is used to perpetuate prejudice and discrimination against the colonized.

to a large group of MESAAS (Middle Eastern, South Asian, and African Studies) majors. I was thinking about how best to make them see the political relevance of Orientalism to our present-day reality, and just then, as if by divine intervention, I noticed a flyer: "Hebrew Liberation Week: A Celebration of Semitism." Curiously I approached the plaza. After all, I was about to teach Said's discussion of Semitism as an invented 19th century Orientalist category and this seemed relevant. I soon faced three tall poles mounted with Israeli flags and was surrounded by about a dozen of young men and women wearing *kufiyehs* (a checkered scarf, which has long been a symbol of Palestinian national liberation) that were blue and white (the colors of the Israeli flag). "Things don't look right," I noted to myself. But it was only when I noticed the bombastic billboards covering the borders of the plaza that the effect became truly chilling.

Suggesting, as the posters do, that Jews have been driven out of their land (like indigenous people) and have finally returned to Israel–a trajectory that all indigenous people should unite behind–is a crude and cynical manipulation of (Jewish) history and a vulgar fabrication that not only makes no sense, but is also offensive in its use and abuse of indigenous peoples' histories of oppression.

Another banner, shown on page 65, presented a group of men in indigenous dress with a bearded man in a tallith (a white prayer shawl worn by Jewish men) placed right in the center among them. First I saw a large portrait of a Native American wearing a traditional headdress, with the word "Judah" written across it.

There is, of course, nothing wrong in suggesting an alliance between Jews and Indigenous people, and in the context of Jews living in Europe and elsewhere as "inside outsiders" and as part of internal European colonization (too much has been written about "The Jewish Question" for me to summarize here) it indeed makes sense to compare and point out similarities between the position of Jews as a fragile minority and the position of other oppressed groups, like the indigenous, colonized, enslaved, and more. However, placing such images underneath the Israeli flag makes them, at best, tasteless depictions of a pseudo alliance. Suggesting, as the posters do, that Jews have been driven out of their land (like indigenous people) and have finally returned to Israel–a trajectory that all indigenous people should unite behind–is a crude and cynical manipulation of (Jewish) history and a vulgar fabrication that not only makes no sense, but is also offensive in its use and abuse of indigenous peoples' histories of oppression.

Indigenous people are not the only ones exploited in this campaign, run by SSI (Students Supporting Israel). SSI is the new kid on the block of campus *hasbara* groups (only five years old), but this kid is well funded by the usual suspects. A notable amount of the $319,598 in 2015 contributions SSI reported on tax forms comes, for instance, from the Milstein Family Foundation, which also supports CAMERA, Stand with Us, Hasbara Fellowships, and other right-wing Israel advocates. The mission of SSI, as their webpage indicates, is "to be a clear and confident Pro-Israel voice on college campuses," and for this mission, they even offer scholarships for students "to visit Israel and come back to campus ready for action!" Nothing on the webpage, however, mentions what SSI's current campaign at Columbia University makes clear beyond all doubt: that the organization has decided to shamelessly appropriate histories, narratives, political symbols, and imagery of indigenous people, Native Americans, Africans, and even Palestinians for the purpose of producing a fictitious, if colorful, narrative of Jewish indigeneity and self-Orientalization. By Self-Orientalism I mean, in this context, a certain instrumentalization of Orientalism and its stereotypes for the purpose of producing a figure of a modern Jew/Israeli who is at the same time ancient, biblical, Semitic, Oriental. This figure is in fact an updated and improved version of the early Zionist invention of the Occidentalized "New Jew." If the Occidentalized New Jew was said to bring European civilization and progress to the East, this updated version is no longer associating the Israeli Jew with the West and its promise of modernity and progress. On the contrary, the self-Orientalized Jew/

Israeli embraces his/her position as the son/daughter of the East. He/she is the native indigenous of the east (Palestine, the biblical Holy-land, Israel) whose temporality expands from the biblical time to the present.

In addition to the soldiers, there are images of Arab-Jews (*Mizrahim*) who must not be forgotten, not again. Images of Yemeni families, perhaps making their way to the Promised Land, are shown on other banners. As a bold background to the blue and white *kufiyeh*s being sold on location, there were posters covering the plaza, inundated with images of Brown and Black people and proud Israeli soldiers: Asians (children of mainly Filipino guest workers who became Israeli citizens and "won" the opportunity to serve in the Israeli army), Ethiopian Jews, Bedouins, and overtly joyful Druze. If yesterday's message was that the Israeli army is welcoming of gays, today's message is that the IDF is a place where Brown, Black, African, and Arab people all feel happy. Together.

One must ask: why a "Brown people campaign"? Or: How did all the Israelis (or Jews, the campaign isn't clear) become so Brown all of a sudden? (I ask as a very fair Polish Jew!) Why does an organization like SSI feel the need to "celebrate Semitism" and parade Ethiopians, Yemenites, and Druze in order to make historical claims of belonging and ownership? And why the sudden need to create the pretense of a coalition with the indigenous people in North America?

The answers are to be found in the logic of political tactic and not in the realm of a real existential identity transformation. In other words, Orientalism–which here functions also as self-Orientalism–is meant to do political work, masking settler colonialism with the language and images of nativism. But what is the political work

Student group's "Hebrew Liberation Week" banner showing Yemenite Jewish family.

Orientalism—which here functions also as *self*-Orientalism—is meant to do political work, masking settler colonialism with the language and images of nativism.

of self-Orientalizing? What is gained by associating Zionism with the struggles of Native peoples and people of color? Correctly identifying past and present trends of the liberal and the radical left (the focus of indigenous rights, multiculturalism, and siding with the colonized and the oppressed), SSI disdainfully adopts these characteristics in order to unarm leftist critique. Indeed, if Israelis are indigenous people returning to their colonized lands, their political struggle must be considered valid and progressive.

SSI's Semitic campaign is based on a simple but dangerous manipulation of historical facts. It abuses the historically ambivalent position of the Jew in the West as not-white-not-quite and the Orientalized modern biblical iconography of the Israelites as prototypical Orientals and Semites to create a narrative of a present-day political hallucination, according to which Jews are the colonized natives fighting for their land. If only this fantasy weren't so cynical, offensive, and well-funded, we might have had a good laugh.

This article was previously published in *Mondoweiss* on November 28, 2017. It is republished with permission.

Whose Birthright?

According to *The Tablet*, in 2015, to encourage immigration to Israel by Jews, "billionaire casino magnate Sheldon Adelson donated $40 million to Birthright Israel, a hefty addition to the $120 million the Adelson Family Foundation has given the organization in recent years." As its mission statement says, "The Birthright Israel Foundation, which raises funds in the United States to support Birthright Israel, is a program which currently provides 49,000 young Jewish adults annually the gift of a 10-day trip to Israel, with the goal of strengthening Jewish continuity and providing even more young Jewish adults with a connection to Israel for years to come."

Sources: http://bit.ly/BirthrightAdelson and http://bit.ly/BirthrightMission

Its vision is to enhance Jewish identity, Jewish communities, and solidarity with Israel. The Foundation receives financial support from the Government of Israel, the Jewish Federations of North America, the Jewish Agency for Israel, and a host of family foundations and individuals.

Source: http://bit.ly/aboutbirthright

TAGLIT · תגלית
BIRTHRIGHT ISRAEL

The mission of Taglit-Birthright is to "create solidarity with Israel" through a free 10-day trip. Instead, Birthright made me into a Palestine solidarity activist. I saw a small sample of the violence enacted by Israel in my name as a Jew and I knew I could not stand idly by any longer. I had to extend the pursuit of justice that Judaism taught me to the Palestinian people. Occupation and apartheid are not my Jewish values. When I stand in solidarity with Palestinians, I am doing exactly what Judaism teaches me to do—to seek justice and stand with the oppressed." —Julia Wedgle, Trip participant

Source: http://mondoweiss.net/2015/03/birthright-checkpoint-tollbooth/

Chapter 6
Refugees and the Impact of Geopolitics

6.1

Why the Palestinian Issue Is Still Central to World Stability
Rami Khouri

Many Arabs see Israel as the vanguard and symbol of Western imperial and colonial manipulation in our region. The Israel-Palestine conflict is a constant, painful reminder of our long and difficult history with foreign powers. Indeed, the ongoing Zionist colonization of Palestine, combined with Israel's influence over US policy toward Arab states, reminds most Arabs that the colonial period of the late-nineteenth century never truly ended. Israeli settlements in occupied Arab lands continue a tradition of foreign colonization of our countries that has been unbroken since nineteenth-century Palestine. Foreign powers near and far still seem to dictate events in the region and determine the fate of the lives of hundreds of millions of Arabs—be it the US, Great Britain, France, Russia, Iran, or Turkey, all of which meddle directly and militarily in Arab countries.

The seriously imbalanced support for Israel that defines American policy in the region is a key driver of anti-American government sentiment among Arab publics, which in turn exacerbates tensions between Arab citizens and their (pro-American) governments. Arab weakness and subservience has led repeatedly to humiliating situations in which Arab rights or aspirations were negated by the US in order to satisfy Israel. For ordinary Arab men and women, such humiliations sting; they are left to conclude that the US-Israeli veto strips their governments of the power to safeguard Arab interests. Many Arabs see their own governments as less than sovereign, and they understand that this is due to the indirect impact of the Palestine-Israel struggle....[O]ne reason for the growth across the region of non-violent Islamist movements, above all the Muslim Brotherhood, has been their opposition to Israeli policies in Palestine and other adjacent Arab lands.

Public opinion surveys conducted across the entire Arab world in the past decade, such as those by the Doha-based Arab Center for Research and Policy Studies, repeatedly confirm that the Palestine issue matters deeply to Arabs. Many respondents testify that the best way to achieve positive relations with the US is for Washington to promote a just and lasting resolution of the Palestinian-Israeli conflict. Polls also show that many Arabs assess US conduct on the basis of what the US does in Palestine. So, the Palestine issue is not just one among many that Arabs care about; it is often a litmus test for how they view foreign powers. It touches the lives and hearts of hundreds of millions of ordinary Arab men and women. It will remain a central concern across the region, not just for its historical and symbolic significance, but because it has become implicated in many of the core grievances driving Arab politics. In order to normalize regional politics, as well as for the sake of the long suffering people of Palestine, the conflict needs to be resolved peacefully, equitably, and quickly.

This essay is excerpted with permission from *Moment of Truth: Tackling Israel-Palestine's Toughest Questions*, Jamie Stern-Weiner ed., OR Books, 2018

Children in Dheisheh refugee camp in Bethlehem are always excited upon seeing Western visitors. Originally built in 1949 for 3,000 refugees from nearby Palestinian villages taken over by Israel, Dheisheh has now grown to about 15,000 inhabitants and includes multiple generations. These young children could be the fourth or fifth generation of long-established refugee families.

Kathleen Christison

Palestinian Refugees Today: An Ever-Present Reminder of Western Colonialism

Pauline Coffman

Step by step we shall develop representative institutions leading to full self government, but our children's children will have passed away before that is accomplished.

—Winston Churchill to a Palestinian delegation in Jerusalem in 1921 when they demanded democratic representation, quoted by David Hirst, *The Gun and Olive Branch*, 2003, p. 180.

Between 1947 and 1949 when Israel became a state, approximately 750,000 Palestinians became refugees, expelled from their homes by the Haganah, forerunner of the Israeli regular military, and underground militias including the Irgun and the Lehi (Stern Gang). The majority of these Palestinian refugees, identified as "'48 Refugees" to distinguish them from subsequent waves of refugees, sought refuge in the surrounding Arab states. Others remained within the new Israeli state as permanently displaced persons; approximately 355,000 internally displaced Palestinians reside in present-day Israel. With few exceptions, internally and externally displaced Palestinian refugees were prevented from returning to their homes by the Israeli army; some 530 villages were destroyed to render them uninhabitable.[1]

Spurred by Zionist militia atrocities, the refugees fled to the nearest neighboring countries. Palestinians fleeing the conflict left their homeland by land and sea, assuming their departure was temporary. Approximately 206,000 Palestinian refugees went to Lebanon, 119,500 to Syria, and almost 300,000 to Jordan. These are the official numbers registered by the United Nations Relief and Works Agency, UNRWA; an approximately equal number of refugees were "unregistered." In contravention of International Law, the Declaration of Human Rights, and the Fourth Geneva Convention, they have never been allowed to return.

Oral histories of survivors (both Jewish paramilitaries and Palestinian exiles), as well as declassified official documents, have allowed recent historians to piece together an understanding of what happened in 1948-49 under cover of the fog of war.[2]

Ilan Pappe, an Israeli scholar who has researched the period using archival documents, examined documents declassified fifty years after the state of Israel was established. Zionist leaders, Pappe found, had prepared a series of formal action plans in anticipation of the day when British Mandate troops would exit Palestine, leaving the Zionist colonists with a strong military advantage over the indigenous Palestinians. Within a few months, Zionist forces implemented Plan D or Plan Dalet (the letter D in Hebrew), which was designed to force the "systematic and total expulsion [of Palestinians] from their homeland." Zionist plans to promote large-scale Jewish immigration and creation of a Jewish state depended on the departure of the British Mandate authorities, a condition that explains why pre-state Zionist terrorism was directed at both Arab and British targets.

Nineteen years after the 1948 war that depopulated Palestine of many of its indigenous people, a second wave of external and internally-displaced refugees, known as the "'67 Refugees," was created during the June 1967 Six Day War as the Israeli military advanced into and occupied East Jerusalem, including the Old City, and the West Bank.

The Palestinian Right of Return

Why haven't the refugees living in neighboring countries in the region become citizens of the countries in which they live? After all, there have been four generations of descendants from the original refugees.

To answer this question, it is necessary to know the context. First, several resolutions governing the treatment of refugees have been passed by the United Nations.

Article 13 and Resolution 194

The United Nations was formed three years before Israel became a state in 1948; one of the UN's first acts was to adopt the Universal Declaration of Human Rights (Dec. 10, 1948).[3] Article 13 states that "everyone has the right to leave any country, including his own, and return to his country." Human rights are those that are innate and cannot be taken or given away. The Declaration of Human

Palestinians fleeing the conflict left their homeland by land and sea, assuming their departure was temporary.

continued on page 71

The Legacy of 67 Words

"His Majesty's Government view with favour the establishment in Palestine of a national home for the Jewish people, and will use their best endeavours to facilitate the achievement of this object, it being clearly understood that nothing shall be done which may prejudice the civil and religious rights of existing non-Jewish communities in Palestine, or the rights and political status enjoyed by Jews in any other country." The Balfour Declaration of 1917

Britain's Foreign Secretary, Lord Balfour, on the implications of the declaration: "... [I]n Palestine, we do not propose even to go through the form of consulting the wishes of the present inhabitants of the country....The four great powers are committed to Zionism, and Zionism, be it right or wrong, good or bad, is rooted in age-long tradition, in present needs, in future hopes, of far profounder impact than the desires and prejudices [not the rights] of the 700,000 Arabs who now inhabit this ancient land."

As reported in *Crossroads to Israel, 1917-1948*, Christopher Sykes, p. 5

Refugees and Memory

According to the UN office for humanitarian affairs, attacks by Jewish settlers in the last five years on Palestinians and their property have destroyed around 50,000 fruit trees, mainly olives. Palestinian farmers get a quarter of their incomes from olives, and the trees are the most powerful symbol of Palestinian attachment to the land. bbc.com/news/world-middle-east-30290052

...the loneliness of not-belonging, of being at home nowhere but in an imaginary land, its topography gleaned second hand from sister and brothers, because her mother and father could not speak of it.

Mourid's Story

Like the refugees trying to get back from Jordan, the poet Mourid Barghouti became homeless in 1967. Unlike most of them, he was already out of the country, enrolled as a student in Cairo University and then, suddenly, unable to go home to Ramallah. In 1996 he was allowed to return. He was overwhelmed by the extent of the change and the scars of occupation, at a loss to find points of continuity between the Palestine he remembered and the one before his eyes. Occupation, he wrote, "interferes in every aspect of life and of death; it interferes with longing and anger and desire and walking in the street. It interferes with going anywhere and coming back, with going to market, the emergency hospital, the beach, the bedroom, or a distant capital.... The scene is of rock. Chalk. Military. Desert. Painful as a toothache." That's about how it feels today, if you add the buses backed up at Israeli barriers and the lines of people shuffling slowly through layers of Israeli security.

Jeremy Harding, "Permission To Enter," from *This Is Not a Border: Reportage and Reflection from the Palestine Festival of Literature*, 2009, p. 67.

Maleka's Story

Old Askar refugee camp, northern West Bank.
Maleka's hands chop, slice, and stir, and as she works, she tells me about the house in Jaffa and her grandmother who, as she fed her children with *rijla* (purslane), which grew in the rocky crevices of the long road to exile, dreamed of crabs stuffed with red chilli, stingray soup doused with lemon, squid with golden rice, sea bass, sardines, and everything that swam in the clear waters that bathe Jaffa, the bride of the sea! She dishes up the rice and chicken and says, "I wish that I could offer you such a banquet, but I have never seen the sea. So I offer what I have."... As I take my leave Maleka says, "I am a simple woman, but my daughters will study and grow wise. We'll go back to our land, *inshallah*. And if not us, then our children."

Mercedes Kemp, "The Girl from Jaffa," from *This Is Not a Border: Reportage and Reflection from the Palestine Festival of Literature*, 2009, p. 38.

Nadine's Story

… She has no photographs, neither here nor at home; no known grandfather's house to lament.
Her grandmother Mona, the youngest of four, the afterthought, was transplanted first to Beirut, then to Columbus, Ohio, a child of seven then for whom memories of home were already myth. The details the young woman hears now, over sweating Cokes in the hotel bar—other people's family fables of deeds and rusting keys carefully handed down through generations; of the spreading swallow-tailed willow and the carpet of vermilion pheasant's eye in a summer garden; of long-legged boys splashing along the grassy banks of the al-Zarqa River—loom vivid and dream-like. Her inheritance instead is a grandmother's American immigrant stories: of a childhood in Columbus, trailing through snow behind an older sister and two brothers chattering between themselves in Arabic; of a mother prone to migraines who required quiet and a darkened room, and a laconic father wizened by care, scrabbling to rebuild his family's life in middle age. These, her grandmother's stories, include dinner plates stored for years in their packing crate, carefully returned each night after washing (just in case the family had to move again); a little girl's shame in the mid-century Midwestern playground at the blackness of her glossy braids, the wrongness of her home-made skirt, and her mother's inability to speak English; the loneliness of not-belonging, of being at home nowhere but in an imaginary land, its topography gleaned second hand from sister and brothers, because her mother and father could not speak of it.
This means, the young woman reasons, that her own Palestine is born out of the mists of myriad imaginations. In life her grandmother never returned; nor has her mother made the journey: she blesses but does not understand her daughter's pilgrimage.…

Claire Messud, "The Scattering," from *This Is Not a Border: Reportage and Reflection from the Palestine Festival of Literature*, 2009, p. 281.

Rights was specifically applied to Palestinian refugees through UN Resolution 194, which demands that

the refugees wishing to return to their homes and live at peace with their neighbors should be permitted to do so at the earliest practicable date, and that compensation should be paid for the property of those choosing not to return and for loss or for damage to property....[4]

The United States voted in favor of Resolution 194 every year until 1993 and this Resolution has been reaffirmed every year at the United Nations with near unanimity.

UNRWA Established

After the creation of the state of Israel, knowing the impact that the creation of the state had had upon the indigenous people already living there, the United Nations General Assembly established by Resolution 302 (IV) in December 1949 the United Nations Relief Works Agency (UNRWA) to carry out direct relief and works programs solely for Palestine refugees. Operations began on May 1, 1950. UNRWA is charged with the full support of Palestinian refugees: housing, food, education, and health care. In the absence of a solution to the Palestine refugee problem, the General Assembly has repeatedly renewed UNRWA's mandate, most recently extending it until June 30, 2017. For Palestinian refugees desiring resolution and repatriation, UNRWA's existence has been a blessing and a curse on many levels, allowing the international community to postpone indefinitely a permanent solution for Palestine refugees and, for internal refugees, allowing Israel to renege on the duties incumbent upon an occupying power.[5]

UNHCR established: (Convention on Status of Refugees)

The United Nations High Commission on Refugees (UNHCR) was established in 1951, two years after UNRWA. UNHCR is charged with protecting "the most vulnerable people in the world." In the Middle East, UNHCR serves refugees in Syria, Lebanon, Jordan, and also Greece. The situation for Palestinian refugees is more complicated than that of other refugees; hence UNRWA is designated as the sole aid agency responsible for Palestinians. For this reason, in 2011 and following, when Syrian-Palestinian refugees fled to Lebanon or elsewhere, UNHCR could not serve them as it would for other refugees around the world.

The Right of Return—Palestinians and Jews

Palestinians continue to hold that the right of return must be addressed justly if the conflict is to be resolved. According to UNRWA,

Over decades of international practice, refugee situations have been resolved in three principal ways: local integration, resettlement in third countries, and voluntary repatriation. Of these, the voluntary return of refugees to their country of origin has come to be recognized by refugees, states, and international agencies as the optimal solution to the plight of

refugees. It is equally recognized that for refugees everywhere, a precondition for solutions to refugee situations is the resolution by political actors of the underlying causes of dispute and conflict.[6]

Israel honors the "right of return" for all Jewish people, wherever they live and whoever they are. This is referred to as the "exchange of populations." At the same time, Israel will not allow non-Jewish people the "right of return," even those who have left for only a few years.

Maintaining a Jewish Identity in Israel

When Israel became a state in 1948, it was able to establish its Jewish identity by the successful removal and erasure of the Palestinian population. In the present day, even without allowing Palestinians to return, projections show that it won't be long before Israel's Jewish population will be outnumbered by Palestinians. The desire to maintain a Jewish identity for the state is the reason why Israel fights against allowing a Palestinian Right of Return; this is called "the demographic threat." In a *New York Times* opinion piece entitled "Not All Israeli Citizens Are Equal," Yousef Munayyer wrote "Palestinian babies in Israel are considered 'demographic threats' by a state constantly battling to keep a Jewish majority."[7] The situation eerily parallels White Nationalists in the US calling for limits on non-White immigration in order to maintain the demographics they prefer.

Peace negotiations seldom address the rights of Palestinian refugees, enshrined in the Declaration of Human Rights, and which are regarded as sacrosanct when applied to other peoples [see page 75]. While the United States government has not officially taken a stand against the Right of Return, US officials have pushed Palestinians to give up and/or make the right of return symbolic. This pressure does not comport with the reality that a right is something that one is entitled to and cannot be forced to surrender. Consider the importance of the Bill of Rights to US citizens.

The desire to maintain a Jewish identity for the state is the reason why Israel fights against allowing a Palestinian Right of Return; this is called "the demographic threat."

Girls at an UNRWA-operated school in Lebanon stretch during their daily morning lineup.

6.3

Where Did the Palestinian Refugees Go?

Pauline Coffman

[T]he majority of the refugee children are in the UNRWA schools that are overcrowded, understaffed, and trying to cope with an increasing population and decreasing funds.

By 2014, the numbers had grown from 750,000 displaced to almost 8 million first, second, and third generation registered refugees and IDPs (Internally Displaced Persons). According to BADIL, the Resource Center for Palestinian Residency and Refugee Rights, at the end of 2014, at least eight million (66 percent) of 12 million Palestinians worldwide were forcibly displaced persons.[1]

Among them were six million 1948 refugees and their descendants. This figure includes five million refugees registered with and assisted by the UN Relief and Works Agency for Palestine Refugees (UNRWA) and a further one million unregistered refugees. Also included are more than one million 1967 refugees and 720,000 internally displaced persons on both sides of the Green Line (1949 armistice line). It should be noted that at least 280,000 Palestinian refugees are internally displaced within Syria due to the ongoing conflict in that country. Despite the changes in the pattern of distribution of Palestinian refugees over the last 67 years,

the majority of refugees still live within 100 kilometers of the borders of Israel and the 1967 occupied territories, where their places of origin are located.[2]

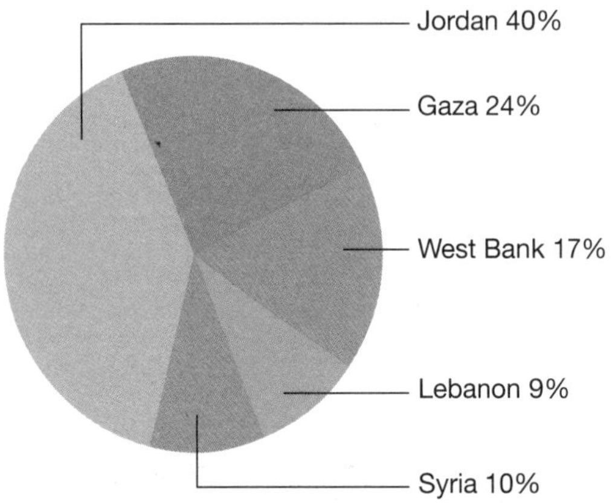

Status of Refugees in Their Host Countries

Lebanon

Lebanon has enacted a series of barriers that deprive Palestinian refugees of the right to work in more than 30 syndicated professions including medicine, law, engineering, and pharmacy. They also do not benefit from social security, which employers have to pay for them in jobs they are allowed to pursue. The UNRWA is responsible for the education of the Palestinian children and has set up 677 schools inside the camps or nearby. These schools provide education from the first grade until the ninth grade when all students in Lebanon whether Lebanese, Palestinian, or other nationalities attending schools in Lebanon sit for a standardized exam known as the "Brevet." This exam marks the end of the intermediate level. Only two schools provided the high school program for the Palestinian refugees until only recently when under much pressure the number was raised to eight schools. Nurseries and kindergartens are provided by NGOs and not UNRWA. The Lebanese public schools are generally not open to Palestinian refugees, but some accept them only after the Lebanese children are registered and places are available. Private schools are open to the refugees if they can afford them, a situation that is very rare. Thus the majority of the refugee children are in the UNRWA schools that are overcrowded, understaffed, and trying to cope with an increasing population and decreasing funds with more and more students dropping out of school. All universities in Lebanon are private except for the government-supported Lebanese University which takes Palestinian refugees only if places allow and in limited fields.

Several factors govern Lebanon's approach to the refugees. First, Lebanon's constitution adopted in 1926,

The pie charts shown on pages 72, 73, and 74 are derived from statistics compiled by BADIL Resource Center for Palestinian Residency and Refugees and published in *Survey of Palestinian Refugees and Internally Displaced Persons*, 2013-2015. Vol. VIII; www.badil.org/en/publicaton/survey-of-refugees.html

Middle East destinations of Palestinian refugees from conflict, 1947-2015. Source: Badil

Jordan 40%

Gaza 24%

West Bank 17%

Lebanon 9%

Syria 10%

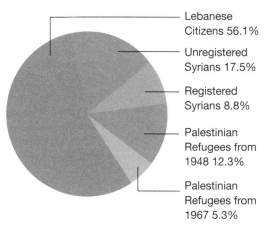

- Lebanese Citizens 56.1%
- Unregistered Syrians 17.5%
- Registered Syrians 8.8%
- Palestinian Refugees from 1948 12.3%
- Palestinian Refugees from 1967 5.3%

Component subpopulations in Lebanon, 2015. Source: Badil

based on 1926 population estimates, mandates that the president must be Christian, the Prime Minister a Sunni Muslim, and the Speaker of the Parliament a Shia Muslim. Although many have emigrated because of long years of civil war and a military invasion by Israeli forces (1982-1990), population statistics have not been published; if an imbalance were documented, these mandates would have to be addressed.

In 1949, the Palestinian refugees in Lebanon represented roughly 10% of the country's total population.[3] As the majority of Palestinian refugees are Sunni Muslims, Christian politicians have long feared that their permanent resettlement would upset Lebanon's uneasy sectarian balance. More than 60 years later, the government of Lebanon still does not provide publicly available statistics for Palestinian refugees in the country. In its January 2010 statistics report, the United Nations Relief and Works Agency for Palestinian Refugees (UNRWA) stated that there were currently 425,640 Palestinian refugees living in Lebanon.[4] Of these, 53% reside in 12 official refugee camps, while the remainder live in Lebanese cities and villages as well as in unofficial refugee camps or "Palestinian gatherings."

Adding to the influx of Palestinians into Lebanon was the Jordanian government's expulsion of Palestinian fighters in the 1970's, which created a new category of refugees known as the Non-ID refugees. These fighters had their identification papers (as Palestinian refugees residing in Jordan) withdrawn by the Jordanian government and were denied any kind of identification papers in Lebanon. The fighters set up makeshift homes near the sea in the south but have suffered greatly and still do, especially since most married into other families with no identification papers. This lack of documentation prevents them from finding jobs or accessing educational services or health care for their children and themselves. In 1982 when Israel invaded Lebanon, the PLO young men were forced to leave Lebanon; the PLO closed its Beirut office and established a new headquarters in Tunis. Shortly thereafter, the

massacre at the Sabra Shatila Palestinian refugee camp occurred.[5] Ariel Sharon's Israeli troops guarded the perimeter of the camp and allowed their Lebanese allies (Maronite Christian Phalangist troops) to enter and slaughter women, children, and elderly men over a three-day period, illuminating their grisly work with flares. Though the casualty numbers vary from 800 to 3,500, all Palestinians know the history of this brutal massacre of Palestinians (mostly Muslims) by Lebanese Christians who were enabled by the Israeli military under the leadership of General Ariel Sharon. (There were Christian families in the camp.)[6]

With the ongoing war in Syria since 2011, Sabra/Shatila, Ein-El-Hilweh, Burj-El Shamali, Beddawi, Dbayeh and other Palestinian refugee camps in Lebanon have become hosts to around 54,000 Syrian refugees of Palestinian origin. These Syrian Palestinian refugees are experiencing the bitterness of being refugees for the second time. Some of them are re-displaced refugees, having been displaced originally out of their homes by Israel into Syria.

Lebanon is a country of about 4 million citizens, with 450,000 Palestinian refugees and with an estimated 1.5 million Syrian refugees having arrived in Lebanon since 2012. An additional number are unregistered and uncounted. Some estimates put the citizen/refugee ratio at an equal level; there are too many informal and formal refugee camps to count. Children beg on the streets of Beirut and social service agencies are overwhelmed.

Syria

Historically, Syria has been more hospitable to Palestinian refugees than Lebanon. After attending UNRWA schools, refugee students achieving tenth grade were required to transfer to public schools and were automatically enrolled in the pro-Assad Baath

Lebanon, with a population of six million [including all refugees], has long given refuge to Palestinians.... [S]ome 450,000 Palestinian refugees are registered in Lebanon, most of them in camps. Even third-generation Palestinians born in Lebanon retain refugee status and live in refugee camps without a pathway to citizenship—almost 70 years after their ancestors arrived. Lebanese law even excludes refugees from most jobs.

"How To Treat Refugees with Dignity: A Lesson from Turkey" by Rula Jebreal, *New York Times*, September 27, 2017, https://www.nytimes.com/2017/09/27/opinion/turkey-syrian-refugees.html

Yarmouk refugee camp on the outskirts of Damascus housed the largest number of Palestinian refugees in Syria before they fled war yet again. In 2015 the UN reported at least six confirmed cases of typhoid in the camp.

AFP

party. These students had ID cards similar to Syrians but with "temporary resident" on top in red. Travel documents looked very much like the Syrian passport but in a lighter shade. They were not confined to camps, although most chose to live near other refugees. Palestinian refugees have been required to fulfill the military service requirement and are usually drafted into the Syrian-aligned Palestine Liberation Army or the Syrian Army.[7]

With the advent of the 2010 Arab Spring movement and demonstrations in Damascus, the Syrian government cordoned off Palestinian refugee neighborhoods in order to contain them. One Palestinian refugee neighborhood in particular, Yarmouk, suffered severe shortages; they did not receive food or medical supplies for months because of government barricades to the north and rebel groups to the south. With the war in Syria approaching its seventh year, it is not only Palestinian refugees who are starving in Syria. It is no surprise then that those Palestinians

Jordanians 46%

Palestinians in Camps 23%

Palestinians— Unregistered and Assimilated 21%

Syrians 10%

Subpopulations in Jordan, 2015. Source: Badil

who are able to do so have left Syria for neighboring countries, becoming refugees once again.

Jordan

Jordan hosts the largest number of Palestine refugees and has been the most hospitable. According to UNRWA, more than 2 million registered Palestinian refugees live in Jordan. Most have full citizenship, including Palestinians who came to Jordan before the 1949 armistice agreement, refugees after 1948, Palestinians who moved from the West Bank to the East Bank (of the River Jordan) in 1967, and finally, Gaza refugees. Daoud Kuttab explains: "The first three groups are Jordanian citizens, the latter, who came from a territory [Gaza] that was not part of the Hashemite Kingdom of Jordan (said to be around half a million), are not Jordanian citizens although they carry a temporary Jordanian passport."[8]

There are ten recognized Palestine refugee camps throughout the country that accommodate nearly 370,000 Palestine refugees, or 18 percent of the country's total population. (In U.S. population terms, that is the equivalent of 58 million refugees in 320 million total). In addition, nearly 10,000 Palestine refugees from Syria have sought assistance from UNRWA in Jordan. Even though UNRWA is working to accommodate their children in its schools and to provide relief and health care to those in need, the majority of these refugees suffer from terrible poverty and live in a precarious legal status.[9]

The War in Syria has further complicated matters for Palestinian refugees. In January 2013 the Jordanian government announced a "non-entry policy" for Palestinian refugees.[10] Human Rights Watch reported in 2014 that Palestinians escaping Syria were being turned away by Jordan.[11] Palestinians who successfully fled to Jordan cannot legally live in the refugee camps established for Syrians escaping the war, but at the same time, the Palestinians cannot legally work to earn money to rent housing outside of the camps either. The one

continued on page 76

In the Sabra Shatila Palestinian refugee camp located south of Beirut, Lebanon, space-starved residents expand their living quarters by building on top of existing structures. On September 16, 1982, Sabra Shatila camp was the scene of a massacre perpetrated through the collusion of the occupying Israeli militia and their Lebanese Phalangist allies. [see page 73].

Pauline Coffman

The Right of Refugees To Go Home

April 2017. Afghan refugees near the UNHCR office in Peshawar, Pakistan, wait for their registration process to cross the Torkham Border Crossing, returning back to Afghanistan after the reopening of the Pakistan-Afghanistan border.

Repatriation and Global Stability

...[E]xperiences from Guatemala and Cambodia to the Balkans and Afghanistan indicate that identifying the state of origin's responsibilities to returnees and ensuring these duties are met is integral to safe and sustainable repatriation and peace-building processes and, in turn, a stable political future.

REPORT: Refugee Repatriation: Justice, Responsibility and Redress, Cambridge University Press, Feb 2013, posted at www.Brookings.edu

The Somali Case

Somali refugees are returning home. Voluntary repatriation remains the main durable solution for refugees applied by the United Nations. As part of the Tripartite Agreement signed between Kenya and Somalia and UNHCR in 2013, Somali refugees—many of whom were born in Dadaab camp and had never set foot in their own country—were being given the chance to return home. In 2016, more than 36,000 of those refugees returned home—alongside small numbers from Yemen. This return contributed to the decrease in Somali refugees in the country from 417,900 in 2015 to 324,000 in 2016. The number of Somali refugees worldwide also declined to one million in 2016.

http://bit.ly/DisplacedQ

Taking a Position on the Palestinian Right of Return

Israel. Israel's position on Palestinian refugees has not changed since 1948. The Israeli government does not recognize Palestinian refugees' right to return and continues to say that Palestinian refugees and their descendants cannot be allowed to return to the homes and communities from which they were displaced because their return would be a threat to the maintenance of a continued Jewish demographic majority in Israel.

United States. The United States government has not officially come out in support of the Israeli position and against the right of return. However, throughout the negotiations process US officials have pushed Palestinians to give up and/or make the right of return symbolic.

Palestinians. Palestinians continue to hold that the right of return must be addressed justly if the conflict is to be resolved.

American Friends Service Committee. AFSC holds that Palestinian refugees' right of return must be recognized and justly addressed if the conflict is to be resolved. Ending the occupation is not enough. If the international community is serious about resolving the conflict it must also recognize the central importance of justly addressing the issue of Palestinians' right of return. Anything less is a denial of justice and will not resolve the conflict.

The American Friends Service Committee (AFSC), http://bit.ly/2wVhsPg

...identifying the state of origin's responsibilities to returnees and ensuring these duties are met is integral to safe and sustainable repatriation and peace-building processes and, in turn, a stable political future.

Thirty percent of the population of the Israeli-occupied West Bank are from other parts of Palestine and live in refugee camps.

exception is Cyber City, which is more of a detention center than a refugee camp, and to which Jordanian authorities have been transferring Palestinians who are in the country clandestinely since April 2012. Unless they decide to return to Syria, they are confined to Cyber City.[12]

Egypt

A relatively small number of Palestinians, 15,500, sought refuge in Egypt. Those who arrived as '48 Refugees during King Farouk's government were not welcomed, but when Gamel Abdel Nasser rose to power as President in the mid-1950's, Palestinians were treated comparably to other citizens of Egypt. According to Oroub el-Abed, [the Palestinian refugees] "enjoy[ed] basic rights, employment in the public sector, and property rights."[13] El-Abed continues, "Under Nasser, children of Palestinians living in Egypt and Gaza were able to enroll in public schools and benefit from discounted university fees." This would later include members of the Palestine Liberation Organization (PLO) and former employees of the Egyptian government. By 1969, Palestinians living in Egypt numbered 33,000, still a small percentage of the total world refugee population compared with Syria and Lebanon, which had smaller total populations to begin with.

As a partner in the struggle, Egypt played an important role in the birth of the movement (in the form of the PLO) for the liberation of Palestine, In 1978 the assassination of Egyptian culture minister Yusif al-Siba'i by the Palestinian Abu Nidal faction aggravated the situation in Egypt for Palestinians. Although Abu Nidal had been expelled from the PLO years before, Egyptians stigmatized the Palestinians in general for the assassination. At al-Siba'i's funeral, Egyptian prime

minister Mustafa Riyad declared, "No more Palestine after today." The fallout was immediate and Palestinians lost a powerful ally.

After the 1978 Camp David Accord and the peace treaty between Israel and Egypt, the standing of Palestinians in Egypt declined further. After signing the treaty with Israel, President Sadat was assassinated by dissatisfied Egyptian Islamists. This assassination changed the perception of Egypt within the Arab world, precipitating the disintegration of a united front. Egypt and Egyptians were less and less interested in mobilizing support for Palestine and the Palestinians. This situation changed again in 2011 with the "Arab Spring" and the ascent of the Palestine-friendly Muslim Brotherhood to the Presidency of Egypt. However, the Brotherhood government did not survive a military coup led by al-Sisi, who became the next president.[14]

West Bank and Gaza

Thirty percent of the population of the Israeli-occupied West Bank are from other parts of Palestine and live in refugee camps. These refugees depend on UNRWA for housing, food, and education through the tenth grade. In the Gaza Strip the refugee population stands at 78 percent. UNRWA's statistics show that Gaza has one of the highest population densities on earth, with almost 3,000 residents per square kilometer. Gaza is now virtually a prison with checkpoints at all entrances. Even the Mediterranean Sea is blockaded, and Gazan fishermen are prevented from plying their income-generating trade beyond six miles from shore.[15]

Gazans are currently suffering from a severe water crisis; salt water from the sea has seeped into its ground water and the 1 to 2-hour per day electricity supply prevents the sewage treatment plants from working. The situation for Gazans is beyond critical.

February, 2011. Egyptian "Arab Spring" anti-government demonstrators protest against President Hosni Mubarak's regime in Cairo's Tahrir Square.

Pedro Ugarte/AFP/Getty

Destabilization and Climate Change

Rain, Drought, Occupation

Israel made the desert bloom. All mantras hide as much as they suggest, and this one is not exceptional. Jewish colonial (and later Israeli) industrial farms have been irrigating parts of the Negev desert for decades, particularly upon completion of the Israeli National Water Carrier in 1964. The implication of the "desert bloom" mantra is that the Palestinian inhabitants of the land either chose not to or could not make it "productive" themselves—thus complementing the "land without a people" myth. In fact, Palestinians had extensively developed agriculture before 1948, and the link with the land was both intimate and life-sustaining. In any case, growing peppers and potatoes in the desert [as the Zionist settlers have done] is unnecessary and poor agricultural practice. It is also illegal when the water used is taken from neighbouring states against their will....

[A look] behind the mantras establish[es] the facts of water development and the water conflict in historic Palestine. The record speaks more of mismanagement, unsustainable pumping rates, and ever-increasing Israeli control of the water resources. The conflict is resolvable, however, according to the water-sharing principles of international water law, or under the management of a single political entity....

The entire system is part of the hydrological cycle and is nourished by rainfall. Next to no rain falls in the Negev desert, only about 50mm per year in Rafah, and about 600mm per year or more around Jerusalem, Jenin, and Nazareth. At the rate at which water is currently extracted for domestic and agricultural use, even a single winter that is dryer than average means the rivers and aquifers are not replenished at a sustainable rate. With each drought, in other words, there is less water available for human use....

Eva Bartlett/IPS

February 2013. Palestinian farmers in the Zeitoun district of Gaza planted olive trees on farmland razed by Israel and renewed their call for the boycott of Israeli agricultural produce. "We grow, they bulldoze, we replant," said Um Abed, 65.

The impact of the restrictions on Palestinian water development was (and remains) felt most by the farmers who must rely on irregular rains, or on villagers with no piped water supply. Water thus became an occupation-related issue, in much the same way that the fate of refugees and the status of Jerusalem became unresolved "issues."...

There is little doubt that the welfare of Palestinians will continue in the future to be linked with water availability. The farming tradition will retain its importance in Palestinian life, while efforts to properly manage the resource take on an increasing urgency due to growing populations and the expected effects of climate change.…

Furthermore, while the agricultural sector in both societies consumes 50 to 70% of all water, this sector is of marginal economic significance in Israel (1.5–2% of GDP) but crucial to the Palestinian economy (20–30% of GDP).

Mark Zeitoun, "A Century of Water Use in Historic Palestine," in Salman H. Abu-Sitta, *The Atlas of Palestine 1917-1966*, 2010, p. 142-146, http://bit.ly/AtlasPal142.

No Is Not Enough

...[M]any of the conflicts driving migration today have already been exacerbated by climate change. For instance, before civil war broke out in Syria, the country faced its deepest drought on record—roughly 1.5 million people were displaced as a result. A great many displaced farmers moved to the border city of Daraa, which happens to be where the Syrian uprising broke out in 2011. Drought was not the only factor in bringing tensions to a head, but many analysts, including former secretary of state John Kerry, are convinced it was a key contributor.

In fact, if we chart the locations of the most intense conflict spots in the world right now—from the bloodiest battlefields in Afghanistan and Pakistan, to Libya, Yemen, Somalia, and Iraq—what becomes clear is that these also happen to be some of the hottest and driest places on earth. The Israeli architect Eyal Weizman has mapped the targets of Western drone strikes and found an 'astounding coincidence.' The strikes are intensely concentrated in regions with an average of just 200 millimeters (7.8 inches) of rainfall per year—so little that even slight climate disruption can push them into drought. In other words, we are bombing the driest places on the planet, which also happen to be the most destabilized.

Naomi Klein, *No Is Not Enough*, Haymarket Books, 2017, p.182-183.

More than 65 million people are displaced from their homes, the largest number since the Second World War, and nearly 25 million of them are refugees and asylum seekers living outside their own country. But that number doesn't include people displaced by climate change.

Under international law, only those who have fled their countries because of war or persecution are entitled to refugee status. People forced to leave home because of climate change, or who leave because climate change has made it harder for them to make a living, don't qualify.

Somini Sengupta, "Climate Change Is Driving People from Home. So Why Don't They Count as Refugees?" *New York Times*, December 21, 2017

Chapter 7

Resistance

Resisting Colonialism and Injustice
Kathleen Christison

The struggle of man against power is the struggle of memory against forgetting.
—Milan Kundera, *The Book of Laughter and Forgetting*

Resistance is a critical act of hope, the essence of that struggle of memory against forgetting.

At this landmark time in Palestinian history, after a century of the struggle of Palestinian memory against the efforts of Power to force forgetting—a century of Power's impositions on the land and the people of Palestine, of Britain's colonial rule and Israel's efforts to erase Palestine and its traces—it is impossible to name a clear victor. The struggle of memory against forgetting of which Czech novelist Kundera speaks is a psychological struggle as much as it is a physical battle using weapons; for that reason, despite Israel's overwhelming strength, neither side has totally prevailed.

But it is clear that the indomitable power of Power has not been able to induce forgetting among Palestinians or halt the persistence of memory. Palestinians have not won the struggle by any means, but their continued existence and their awareness of themselves as a people, after a century-long effort to erase them, is a psychological victory at the most essential level.

Palestine remains, in its people and their memory and, most notably, in their resistance to erasure. Resistance is a critical act of hope, the essence of that struggle of memory against forgetting. Resistance is the very embodiment of the struggle of memory—memory of what was, of what might yet be—against the efforts of Power to erase and forget.

Resistance fueled by memory and hope is in fact the Palestinians' only weapon in the struggle. Any prospect of receiving real support or help from any representative of Power toward achieving justice through a peace agreement appears to have dissipated completely. Israel no longer pays lip service to serious negotiations and continues to expropriate Palestinian land for exclusive Jewish use, in settlements, a limited-access road network, and military bases; the United States exerts no pressure on Israel to limit its control or make concessions and in fact no longer expresses support for Palestinian

statehood at all; neither Israel nor the US any longer treats the occupied territories as occupied illegally, in contravention of international law; Israel makes a concerted effort to hide the realities of Palestinian life under Israeli domination while intensifying control measures against Palestinians and Palestinian allies; and the only official Palestinian leadership, the Palestinian Authority, is corrupt, incompetent, and increasingly authoritarian, basically able to function only as an agent of Israeli Power.

Resistance and Solidarity as Hope
Although Palestinians have no near-term expectation of achieving justice through negotiations—or, certainly, through any Israeli decision to cede control—they have been able to keep their struggle alive and bring it to wider international attention simply by determinedly maintaining their sense of peoplehood: their memory of always having lived in Palestine as a people, their sense of having been wounded as a people, and their hope as a people of maintaining and somehow reviving the uniquely Palestinian character of their ethnicity and their land. Memory is the key: it is the seed of resistance, the inspiration for resistance, and the moral underpinning of the struggle.

Without a credible leadership, Palestinians rely on civil society through which to speak out—through their own popular resistance, as well as the *ad hoc* resistance and solidarity of dissident Jewish Israelis and international individuals and groups allied with the Palestinian struggle. Resistance is their hope and their struggle of memory. Italian Marxist Antonio Gramsci famously spoke of the need to have optimism of the will even if one feels pessimism of the intellect. Palestinians talk about this explicitly: they have no optimism about achieving independence or receiving justice from Israel anytime soon, but they have hope for the longer term. They live on hope; it is what makes getting up every day possible.

Bringing images and stories that portray daily realities of Palestinian life under occupation to international attention is a major aspect of Palestinian resistance, and essential to the task of mobilizing solidarity. The call for Boycott, Divestment, and Sanctions (BDS) against Israel until it complies with international law was issued by Palestinian civil society in 2005. The BDS call is modeled after the boycott that played a critical role in ending apartheid in South Africa. Taking direction from the Boycott National Committee (BNC) in Palestine, the global BDS movement continues to grow, galvanizing support and achieving successes through a range of consumer, academic, and cultural boycotts that target institutions, products, and companies that profit from the occupation. In addition, municipal and divestment campaigns have recorded success on college campuses, in churches, and in cities worldwide.

Unsurprisingly, widespread support for BDS, which demands Israeli accountability for its policies against Palestinians, has aroused concern in Israel and raised alarms among Israel's supporters in the United States and other countries. [See pages 86-90 for more information about the global BDS campaign.] Further, despite bills pending in Congress and in several state legislatures that would criminalize boycott and divestment efforts that target Israel, Palestinian solidarity organizations continue to advocate for BDS as the best way to achieve justice for Palestinians. The US Campaign for Palestinian Rights, a broad national coalition of grassroots advocacy groups, provides organizing and educational resources for BDS activists around the world. In addition, Jewish Voice for Peace is a national organization with local chapters that garner support among predominantly left-of-center Jews who question or outrightly reject Zionism. The American Friends Service Committee, and American Muslims for Palestine increasingly provide leadership and collaborate with other groups on BDS initiatives. There are also Palestine solidarity networks across many church denominations that consistently work on changing church policies on profiting from human rights abuses in Israel/Palestine. All these grassroots groups engage at different levels in legislative lobbying, popular education, protests, demonstrations, social media organizing, and other actions that promote solidarity with Palestinians.

Increasingly in recent years, marginalized populations have come to a greater understanding of the kinds of oppression they face and ways to fight it, as well as a new awareness of similar issues besetting all marginalized groups. Newly conscious of the "intersectionality" of the oppression imposed by allied government-corporate-military agencies, the marginalized are rallying to a new spirit of intersectional cooperation in resistance and a new readiness to position themselves as the active subjects of their struggles rather than the passive objects of oppression. In this way, Palestinians have garnered the support and solidarity of other anti-oppression

Mahmoud Burnat

Since January 2005, the Bil'in Popular Committee against the Wall, led by local activist Iyad Burnat, has organized weekly protests against the construction of the West Bank Barrier and related seizures of Palestinian land, drawing repressive interventions by the Israeli army. The protests have attracted media attention and the participation of international activist organizations. *5 Broken Cameras*, a film by Emad Burnat and Guy Davidi, portrays the protests over many years starting in 2005.

allies and have given back in kind. Palestinians have significant allies among supporters of Black Lives Matter (BLM), the nationwide grassroots political resistance organization formed in 2013 in indignation and protest over the rash of police shootings of young Blacks and the consistent police acquittals. Beginning as nothing more than a social media hashtag, BLM has grown exponentially because it stands for the humanity and dignity of Blacks and gives voice to the need for justice to which all peoples aspire. In this spirit, BLM and the larger Movement for Black Lives have worked together with Palestinians seeking the same justice and human dignity.

The noted Black activist and author Angela Davis has spoken out and written about the linked struggle aimed at collectively envisioning "a more habitable future" through the variously faceted struggle for global justice for all: against the structures of racism, against state violence and police militarization, mass incarceration, economic injustice, colonization and settler colonialism, patriarchy and heteropatriarchy, and ethnic hatreds like antisemitism. Davis consistently proclaims that Palestine is at the forefront of this collective struggle.

Self-Awareness in Resistance

Palestinians may not have intellectualized their resistance in the way Davis does or analyzed the structures of colonialism as their own great intellectual, the late Edward Said, did in numerous books about colonialism's objectification and exploitation of indigenous populations. But since their dispossession during the *Nakba* seventy years ago, Palestinians have experienced a process of consciousness-raising that has always fueled resistance. They have always believed in their struggle as one in which they are the subjects. Yes,

...[T]he marginalized are rallying to a new spirit of intersectional cooperation in resistance and a new readiness to position themselves as the active subjects of their struggles rather than the passive objects of oppression.

Martyr posters in Nablus. A "martyr," or *shahid*, is any Palestinian killed for Palestine; this includes suicide bombers but consists primarily of civilians killed in Israeli actions, ranging from Israel's small-scale night raids on villages to large-scale military assaults.

Could it be that, in spite of everything—in a situation that seems hopeless, when Palestinians are dependent on the political intervention of others—we are left looking to *them*, to the powerless, for hope?

Geoff Dyer, UCLA writer in residence, from *This Is Not a Border: Reportage and Reflection from the Palestine Festival of Literature*, p. 133

they have been objects of colonization and attempted identity theft, but they see themselves as subjects of a decolonizing resistance.

This forward-looking consciousness did not manifest as organized resistance for some years after 1948, when Palestinian society was destroyed and the people scattered in defeat, bereft of homes and livelihood. Even at their lowest period, however, in the immediate aftermath of the *Nakba*, when there was no thought and little possibility of collective organized resistance against Israel, Palestinians in exile consciously preserved their culture and their identity, their dialect, their memories, and their spiritual bond with Palestine. Often, neighborhoods inside refugee camps in Lebanon, Jordan, and Syria were organized according to villages of origin before 1948. Neighborhoods were given the name of a village, and streets were named after village streets or village heroes. Children grew up in refugee camps knowing that they came from such-and-such a village in Palestine and only gradually learned that they were refugees.

A period of violent resistance, including particularly terrorism against Israeli and international targets, followed. The terrorist attacks in the 1960s and '70s by the Palestine Liberation Organization and the suicide bombings by Islamist groups in the '90s and early 2000s have now ceased. These organizations came to realize that Palestinian violence brings massive Israeli violence in response—retaliation that is grossly disproportionate to the terrorism and that ultimately takes a heavy toll on Palestinian lives and resources. Resistance today is primarily nonviolent, except for occasional spontaneous single-person attacks on Israeli soldiers or settlers.

Simply being there is a key form of resistance, for the very reason that Israel is bent on Palestinian removal. *Sumud*, or steadfastness, is their governing philosophy. *Sumud* means remaining on the land, in Palestine, and not fleeing or surrendering to expulsion as occurred

in 1948 and to some extent in 1967; rebuilding when homes are demolished; recreating Palestine through art, poetry, photography; publicly honoring—with elaborate funeral processions, in graffiti on walls, in "martyr posters" plastered on the sides of buildings—any Palestinian, militant or civilian, killed by Israel.

Palestinians exhibited a mass form of *sumud* in the summer of 2017 when Israel blocked access to Jerusalem's al-Aqsa Mosque as a supposed security measure and Muslims throughout the occupied territories and Israel, as well as elsewhere in the Arab world, protested by gathering silently in their thousands to pray in the streets around al-Aqsa and other mosques. Palestinians of all faiths joined together in resistance, refusing to submit to electronic searches to enter their own place of worship. It was a collective refusal to accede to this further attempt to erase one of the most personal aspects of their identity.

Resistance is often its own progenitor. One village protesting the Separation Wall's encroachment on its land inspires other villages similarly affected to speak out. One hero—whether a nonviolent protester killed by Israeli forces, or a noted poet or writer, or a former political leader—inspires activists and heroes elsewhere eager to stand up for Palestine.

Several small villages near the Separation Wall that have lost much of their agricultural land because of the Wall's encroachment stage weekly rallies to protest this land theft. The villages of Bil'in and Nabi Saleh are home to the most prominent and enduring of the protests. Bil'in has held a demonstration faithfully every Friday for over a dozen years, often joined by hundreds of Israeli and international allies. The village gained additional prominence when the film *5 Broken Cameras*, made by village native Emad Burnat, was nominated in 2011 for an Academy Award. The extended Tamimi family has brought Nabi Saleh to prominence through weekly protests against an Israeli settlement's expropriation of a village spring. In December 2017, a Tamimi teenager, Ahed, and her mother were arrested after Ahed slapped an Israeli soldier occupying family property. Mother and daughter face years in prison.

Inspiration

Just as one village inspires another, one hero inspires others. In March 2017 Israeli forces assassinated Basel al-Araj, a non-violent activist who stands out as an exemplar of the courage required to practice and promote *sumud*. A native of the village of al-Walajeh, which lies between Jerusalem and Bethlehem and is being choked by the Separation Wall, al-Araj led widespread protests against the Wall and was imprisoned and tortured by the Palestinian Authority.

Al-Araj knew his work would not bring liberation for his own generation but would lay the groundwork for the next generation. He was described in tributes as a lover of Palestine nurtured by his grandfather's admonition to reclaim Palestinian history, who had studied the history of Palestine's revolutions and the writings of other resisters such as Antonio Gramsci and Frantz Fanon. He was an intellectual visionary who acted, in fact, on Gramsci's teaching that optimism of the will must override pessimism of the intellect. Al-Araj's belief that, to be part of a genuine liberation movement, a leader must love the people, treat them as equals, and think beyond his own individual salvation, made him a model of resistance. One friend pointedly noted that "every Palestinian martyr leaves us with an added sense of responsibility."

Although for decades Palestinians were notably unskilled at making their grievances against Israel for the *Nakba* and the occupation understood outside the Arab world, and they tarred their own credibility with terrorism, the last quarter century has told a different story. Two *intifadas* (uprisings), an intermittent "peace process," and repeated Israeli military assaults in the West Bank and Gaza have brought Palestinians and their situation under occupation to greater international prominence. Although they have not gained anything like strong sympathy, they have garnered a great deal of attention and, with it, enough understanding of their plight, as well as of the ideological Zionist exclusivity that confronts them, to have motivated several noted journalists and authors to publish books sensitively describing what they endure on a daily basis. The number of books published on some aspect of the Palestine struggle in recent decades probably runs in the hundreds—in the scores during the last decade alone.

Social media, along with websites like *Counterpunch. org*, *DissidentVoice.org*, *TomDispatch.com*, *ElectronicIntifada.net* (published by Palestinian American Ali Abunimah), and *Mondoweiss.net* (published by Jewish American Philip Weiss), regularly run news and analysis on Palestine—the last two exclusively so—that rarely appear in the mainstream media.

Probably the most evident sign of resistance—representing continuing struggle and as inspiration for further resistance—is in ubiquitous graffiti throughout the West Bank. Entry to Aida refugee camp in Bethlehem, for instance, is through an archway topped by a large facsimile of an old-fashioned key, symbolizing the keys refugees took with them in 1948, expecting to use them upon their return. Graffiti, some quite artful, adorns almost every wall in the camp, as do various other Palestinian symbols and portraits of Palestinian heroes, from Yasir Arafat, to revered poets, to young children, who have died for Palestine. The young American woman Rachel Corrie, who was run over by a bulldozer driven by an Israeli soldier while she tried to protect a Palestinian home in Gaza from demolition in 2003, is also often honored in posters.

Love of the Arabic language is part of the Palestinian "soul." Virtually all Palestinians fancy themselves poets; they love to write and recite it and they love to listen to it. Poetry has been a tradition, recited at public celebrations for centuries, and its preservation is another sign of Palestinian identity and resistance to efforts to erase it. The Palestinian-American poet Remi Kanazi, who grew up in the US in a family that fled Palestine in 1948 and lived in their exile as a permanent scar, sees his resistance poetry as equally a part of who he is; just as his family lives in the pain of their exile, he lives in his resistance poetry. Kanazi not only writes but performs his poetry, on the stage and in videos, as a powerful way to get across a political message of resistance. "I don't think we can compartmentalize the different aspects of who we are," he told an interviewer. He's a poet and a Palestinian and an organizer but not as separate aspects of himself; he says, "I'm all of these things all at once."

Conclusion

In her most recent book, a 2016 collection of speeches and essays revealingly titled *Freedom Is a Constant Struggle: Ferguson, Palestine, and the Foundations of a Movement*, Angela Davis speaks of resistance as a hopeful imagining of a better future. Calling for an expanding "community of struggle" against oppression everywhere, Davis challenges everyone to recognize the immorality of any nation's claim—the US's or Israel's or Europe's—to exceptionalism, to a special right to kill, oppress, or dominate others. She calls on us all to "make connections" among diverse struggles—Black, Native American, Latina, Palestinian, Muslim—"always foregrounding those connections so that people remember that nothing happens in isolation."

The mere act of resistance, even in the absence of a clear reason for hope, nurtures and builds hope, for without resistance there is only surrender. Without memory, there is only surrender. Palestine's poet laureate, the late Mahmoud Darwish, tells us why there will be no surrender in Palestine:

We did not come to this country from a country
we came from pomegranates, from the glue of memory
from the fragments of an idea.

The mere act of resistance, even in the absence of a clear reason for hope, nurtures and builds hope, for without resistance there is only surrender.

Mimesis

My daughter
Wouldn't hurt a spider
That had nested
Between her bicycle handles
For two weeks
She waited
Until it left of its own accord
If you tear down the web I said
It will simply know
This isn't a place to call home
And you'd get to go biking
She said that's how others
Become refugees isn't it?

—Fady Joudah

Parallels with Puerto Rico

What Puerto Rico's Hurricane Victims Have in Common with Palestinians

It breaks my heart to know that the same crises that make life so difficult every day in Gaza (although here, they are all very much man-made) now are hurting you in Puerto Rico....

The reason why the [US] island territories—not only the Caribbean islands, but also Pacific islands such as Guam and the Northern Mariana Islands—are subjected to separate and unequal treatment, and are not states, is because of the Insular Cases, a series of racist Supreme Court decisions, of which the first were written by the same court that gave us the endorsement of racial segregation in *Plessy v. Ferguson.* These cases established the racist framework governing nonwhite territories of the United States. The island territories, inhabited by so-called alien races, were designed to give the United States control over the seas but second-class citizenship to their inhabitants....

In *Downes v. Bidwell*, the [Supreme] court ruled that Puerto Rico was an unincorporated territory under the control of Congress, but without the full protection of the US Constitution.

"If those possessions are inhabited by alien races, differing from us in religion, customs, laws, methods of taxation, and modes of thought, the administration of government and justice according to Anglo-Saxon principles may for a time be impossible, and the question at once arises whether large concessions ought not to be made for a time, that ultimately our own theories may be carried out and the blessings of a free government under the Constitution extended to them. We decline to hold that there is anything in the Constitution to forbid such action," the court wrote in its opinion....

[Before 1932] US courts regarded the people of the US Virgin Islands not as citizens but as "nationals," which in US colonial policy referred to "inhabitants of colonies to whom the rights of US citizenship were not conferred."...

"The Insular Cases: Why Puerto Rico and the US Virgin Islands Are Colonies and Not States," David Love, *Atlanta Black Star,* October 19, 2017 http://bit.ly/PRColony

Mondoweiss/courtesy Dr. Rabab Abdulhadi

Puerto Rican Women in Solidarity with Palestine

Palestine solidarity is an enduring feature of Puerto Rican intersectional activism. Members of Puerto Rico's Mujeres Con Oscar at the Movimiento Soldario Sindical (the labor solidarity movement), shown here with Palestinian American San Francisco State University professor Dr. Rabab Abdulhadi (center left) raise a banner with the message, "Puerto Rican Women in Solidarity with Palestine."

Letter from Gaza: "We Are All Puerto Ricans"

I know what it's like to struggle with shortages of vital supplies such as electricity, gas, cash, and safe water. I know what it's like to lose everything and have no place to go. I know what it feels like to hope that help will come—and it doesn't. That's why I am writing this letter, to express my solidarity with all of you who are struggling to survive the damage wrought first by years of neglect and now by the furies of Hurricane Maria. It breaks my heart to know that the same crises that make life so difficult every day in Gaza (although here, they are all very much man-made) now are hurting you in Puerto Rico....

Like you, many of us were forced to move into buildings never meant to serve as shelters, like schools. I read about a 31-day-old baby, born just before the hurricane, who is living in a classroom with 64 other people and is suffering from an untreated skin condition. Tragically, we can relate! One of my fellow writers in We Are Not Numbers wrote about one family forced to sleep with nearly 30 other people in the same room after they were forced to flee their home as tanks moved in.

The more I read about the way the hurricane has devastated Puerto Rico, the more parallels I see to Gaza after a war—or actually, even now....

Love, Tarneem from Gaza

Tarneem Hammad, 22, wearenotnumbers.org, October 4, 2017

Liberation Theology as Resistance
Kathleen Christison

Although often thought to enjoy special favor from Israel, Christian Palestinians in Israel and the occupied territories live under the same Israeli oppression as Muslims. They were subjected to ethnic cleansing along with Muslims during the 1948 *Nakba* and face the same limitations today on their liberties. They are as inclined toward resistance to Israeli domination as are Muslims.

And although constituting only a tiny minority among Palestinians because of large-scale emigration during the twentieth century, there remain tens of thousands of Christians in historic Palestine. Palestine and Jerusalem are the very heart of all Christianity. Not only are the regional heads of several Christian denominations seated in Jerusalem, but Palestinian Christians trace their origins to Jesus' time. For those still there, the determination to stay, their *sumud*, arises from the belief that they are descended from the earliest Christians and that their struggle for justice is divinely ordained.

As in Latin America, where liberation theology developed in the 1950s and '60s as a theological balm and empowerment for the poor and oppressed, Palestinian liberation theology focuses on liberating Palestinians from the oppression of Israeli domination through Jesus Christ's example in the gospels. As a modern contextual theology that developed from a range of social and historical contexts, liberation theology is adaptable to any situation in which faith practitioners suffer injustice. Black theology was developed by noted theologian James Cone in several books written over four decades, including the early *Black Theology and Black Power* and his recent *The Cross and the Lynching Tree*. In today's intersectional world, other oppressed populations and groups—for instance, Feminist and Womanist groups, and Latinx[1] populations in the US—have also developed their own liberation theologies.

In its own context, Palestinian liberation theology has been concerned with the central claim of religious Zionists that, in the Old Testament, God made a holy covenant with the Jewish people in which the land Palestinians lived on for centuries was given to the Jews for their exclusive use. Seen through the Palestinian Christian lens, this God is unjust. Their liberation theology concludes that there simply can be no such God because there is one true God who bestows justice on all.

The principal beliefs of Palestinian liberation theology were formulated under the guidance of Palestinian Episcopal priest Naim Ateek and propounded through the organization Sabeel—the Sabeel Ecumenical Liberation Theology Center in Jerusalem. The Arabic word *sabeel*, meaning "the way," was adopted because the first Christians called themselves "people of the Way."

Although his writings are primarily for Christians, Ateek envisions liberation for all Palestinians in everyone's particular context. His own context is Christ-centered, but he feels he has a responsibility to others and works for liberation not only for Palestinian Christians and Muslims, but even for Israelis. He is leading Christians to resist any biblical interpretation, whether by Jewish or by Christian Zionists, that diminishes Palestinian equality by claiming Jewish chosenness and Jewish supremacy in the land.

In his early enunciation of Palestinian liberation theology almost thirty years ago in *Justice and Only Justice,* Ateek voiced questions about God on behalf of Palestinian Christians, noting that the injustice under which they live causes them to question the very character of God. "Is God partial only to the Jews? Is this a God of justice and peace?" he wondered. "The focus of these questions is the very person of God. God's character is at stake. God's integrity has been questioned."

This theology is a resistance that derives from the core of the Christian message as well as the Israeli colonization of Palestine; it therefore speaks to all Palestinians, Muslim as well as Christian. By definition, Palestinian liberation theology challenges Zionist founding principles of exclusive Jewish rights to the land. It is also a resistance to both Christian Zionism and mainstream post-Holocaust Protestant theology, both of which turn a blind eye to Israeli oppression of Palestinians, but for different reasons. Both may be characterized as "orientalist" in their bias against Palestinians and other Arabs.

Church leaders in Palestine have protested the virtually forgotten plight of Christians under Israeli rule, but in 2009 there was an unprecedented gathering of all the heads of churches in Jerusalem and Palestine which resulted in the confessional document they called *Kairos Palestine*. It takes its cue from the 1985 South African Kairos document and is a plea for solidarity and action from Christians around the world for the plight of Palestine. It has been deemed controversial because it calls for nonviolent protest through economic actions such as boycotts, but *Kairos Palestine* stands as a declaration of resistance to Israeli oppression and a challenge to Western Christian churches to cease their acquiescence in that oppression.

Christian Zionism supports Israel uncritically as a part of its doctrine of the "end days" and the second coming of Jesus, while mainstream post-Holocaust Protestant theology overlooks Israeli violations of international law and human rights as a form of repentance for centuries of Christian antisemitism.

Sumud and Palestinian Hospitality as Resistance

Ken Mayers

The taste of the fennel, apples, and oranges from that garden has long outlasted the taste of teargas from Hebron.

A Veterans For Peace delegation to the West Bank in February 2017 had a few dramatic experiences with protests and teargas in Bil'in and Hebron—but to me, the most meaningful experiences were the quiet visits with Palestinians between days of protest.

In Ramallah, we visited a neighborhood in which seven homes and two entire apartment buildings had been demolished. Crews came in the middle of one night with 200 bulldozers to destroy homes. One was still standing, adjacent to a pile of rubble. In a garden next to the house, the owner welcomed us and explained that the rubble had been a four-unit apartment building he had built for his sons and their families. His own residence remained only because it was built before Israel's 1967 conquest of the West Bank.

He sent his younger children inside to get water for us, and we sat down to chat with this kindly, gentle victim of Israeli cruelty. Soon not only water, but coffee, tea, and dishes of fruit, vegetables, and hummus appeared on the table—a miracle of generosity to strangers from a man whose life savings had just been destroyed. The taste of the fennel, apples, and oranges from that garden has long outlasted the taste of teargas from Hebron.

The next day, we visited Al Araqib, one of dozens of Bedouin villages in Israel's Negev region that the government considers "unrecognized" and therefore ineligible for any services, even water. Although the village has existed for centuries, recognized by the Ottomans, the British, even briefly by Israel, Israeli authorities demolished it in 2010, destroying every house and bulldozing 5,400 olive and fruit trees, the cistern, and the electrical generator. The villagers rebuilt with the help of Israeli Jewish activists immediately after this disaster, and in the ensuing years they have rebuilt an incredible 110 more times, more than once a month over this seven-year period, steadfastly refusing to surrender to Israel's demolition campaign.

Each time, the villagers' property deteriorates further, and they become poorer, but they remain as hospitable and generous as ever. The spirit of

thymeandolives.blogspot.ca

Aziz al-Touri, a aresident of Al Araqib, one of dozens of Bedouin villages in Israel's Naqab/Negev region, roasts coffee in the traditional way over an open fire. Serving Arabic coffee is an important aspect of hospitality in Arab societies and considered a ceremonial act of generosity.

Traditionally, coffee is prepared in front of guests. Coffee-making begins with the selection of beans, which are lightly roasted in a shallow pan over a fire, then placed into a copper mortar and pounded with a copper pestle. The coffee grounds are placed into a large copper coffee pot; water is added, and the pot is placed on the fire.

Maqluba, the beloved Palestinian dish typically made of rice, chicken, and vegetables, has become an integral element in protests in Jerusalem and elsewhere, reinforcing Palestinian community and solidarity.

Ammar Awad/Reuters

sumud—steadfastness—is clearly more powerful than the Caterpillar D9 demolition bulldozers. When we arrived, our host, Aziz al-Touri, began preparing coffee from scratch, while describing how important morning coffee is to the community. He started with raw beans, continually flipping them in a skillet as they roasted, all the while telling of his culture and Israel's constant attempts to destroy it and erase their history.

It is this very culture and history that sustain Aziz and his neighbors. First thing every morning when he wakes up, he said, he raises thanks to God for his life, and then gives thanks for the activist Jews who help the community survive. He teaches his son that he must not hate Jews; he may hate the police, the army, the Jewish National Fund—all of which are trying to drive them off the land—but he must not hate the people, or any people.

When the coffee beans were properly roasted and ground with an added handful of cardamom seeds, Aziz poured coffee for us from a beautiful brass pitcher. One colleague declared it the "best coffee ever!" and we all agreed. It had been made with love. After a brief tour of the village fields, we were called back to the welcoming tent, where a feast of Bedouin dishes awaited us.

Once again, people from whom nearly everything has been taken were giving us loving hospitality so deeply rooted in their culture that it survives monstrous abuse. After the feast, we joined them in their weekly Sunday protest at a main highway crossing. Then the long bus ride back to Jerusalem. What amazing human beings these are!

Palestinian National Dish Fuels Al-Aqsa Protests

…Halawani said, "When I was interrogated, Israeli police officers asked me what the goal was behind the Facebook invitation to gather and eat *maqluba* in Al-Aqsa. They were upset, as I do not fight with weapons but with new creative ideas that shook the occupying Israeli forces. They were indeed shocked that a dish could bring so many people together and encourage them to gather at the Damascus Gate."

She went on, "The true *maqluba* is not made with rice, chicken, and vegetables but with steadfastness, persistence, and perseverance and with shouts and cheers when flipped upside down."

Khweis told Al-Monitor, "The goal behind eating *maqluba* in Al-Aqsa is to mobilize and gather Palestinians there, even if just to eat or to have children play. This is our response to Israel's policies on Al-Aqsa and the attempts to remove us from it."

She added, "During our interrogation…they presented pictures of us that were taken while we were flipping the pots and distributing plates to the people who were shouting and chanting."

Eating *maqluba* seems set to remain a prominent feature of the sit-ins in Jerusalem and protests elsewhere, as it not only brings Palestinians together but serves as a symbol of their heritage and culture. The trend has spread to Jordanians as well, and they also flipped pots in front of the US Embassy in Amman during the protests there against Trump's decision.

https://www.al-monitor.com/pulse/originals/2018/01/maqluba-turns-protests-on-trump-upside-down.html

Nonviolent Economic Action as Resistance
Susan Landau

Defining BDS

Boycotts are economic actions on a consumer level. They target Israeli and international companies that profit from violations of Palestinian human rights, or they target sports, cultural, and academic institutions complicit with those violations.

Divestment is economic action by investors. Campaigns urge banks, local councils, churches, endowments, foundations, pension funds, universities, trade unions, and other institutions to withdraw investments from Israeli and international companies involved in violating Palestinian rights.

Sanctions are actions of noncooperation in which governments are pressured to withdraw existing supports and impunity by fulfilling their legal obligation to hold Israel to account, including ending military trade and free-trade agreements and expelling Israel from international forums such as the UN and FIFA, the world governing body of football.

Google "Montgomery Bus Boycott," if you don't know about civil rights history already. We changed our country fundamentally, and the various boycotts of Israeli institutions and products will do the same there. It is our only nonviolent option. —Alice Walker

BDS 101, the Basics

The movement for Boycott, Divestment, and Sanctions (BDS) is a rights-based Palestinian-led movement of nonviolent popular resistance and international solidarity. Palestinians orient their struggle toward Israel, the party responsible for systematically denying their human rights.

After seventy years of Israeli settler colonialism, apartheid, and occupation, Palestinians have appealed to the international community to stop the injustice against them by joining in solidarity with the Palestinian struggle for freedom, justice, and equality.

BDS is a call to action. Inspired by the movement that helped to end apartheid in South Africa, Palestinian civil society issued a call to the international community in 2005 for actions of nonviolent noncooperation against Israeli businesses and institutions until Israel complies with international law and meets three demands:

1. Ending Israel's occupation and colonization of all Arab lands and dismantling the separation Wall.

International law recognizes the West Bank including East Jerusalem, Gaza, and the Syrian Golan Heights as under a belligerent occupation by Israel since 1967. As part of the occupation, Israel confiscates land and forces Palestinians into enclaves, surrounded by checkpoints, settlements, watchtowers, and an illegal separation (Apartheid) Wall. In 2007 Israel imposed a siege on Gaza, where it regularly carries out military incursions and attacks on civilians that constitute war crimes.

2. Recognizing the fundamental rights of the Arab-Palestinian citizens of Israel to full equality.

Twenty percent of Israel's citizens are Palestinians who remained in what became Israel in 1948. They are subjected to a system of racial discrimination codified in more than fifty laws that impact every aspect of their lives. Arab-Palestinian citizens of Israel daily endure the "Judaization of the land," an Israeli policy of decreasing the Palestinian population while increasing the Jewish presence.

3. Respecting, protecting, and promoting the rights of Palestinian refugees to return to their homes and properties as stipulated in UN Resolution 194.

Since its establishment in 1948, Israel has continued the policies of settler colonialism, ethnic cleansing, and systematic forced displacement of the indigenous Palestinian population. Today, more than 7.25 million Palestinian refugees are denied their right to return to

The arrest of Rosa Parks on December 1, 1955, catalyzed the Montgomery bus boycott. The ensuing 13-month mass protest ended with the US Supreme Court ruling that segregation on public buses is unconstitutional. The Montgomery bus boycott sparked other civil rights campaigns in the South and demonstrated the potential for nonviolent mass protest to successfully challenge racial segregation.

their homes or receive compensation for their property.

How Does BDS Work, and What Can I Do?

Dalit Baum, Director of the Economic Activism Program for the American Friends Service Committee, is a consummate researcher in the BDS movement and co-founder of Who Profits, "a research center dedicated to exposing the commercial involvement of Israeli and international companies in the continued Israeli control over Palestinian and Syrian land." According to Baum,

> To urge Israel to comply with international law and uphold Palestinian human rights, people need to learn how BDS works and what they can do to get involved. People ask me all the time for a list of what products to boycott. Of course there are such lists. We publish a list for divestment, too, but the question misses the point. The 2005 Palestinian call is a call for action, and it is addressed to all of us: What is the meaning of the 2005 Palestinian call to me, for us? How do we use our own complicity as leverage? How do we make Palestine relevant to activists all around? How do we move from protest to resistance?

Baum explains BDS as a coordinated strategy of organizing campaigns to educate consumers and investors to pressure institutions and companies to change egregious policies that violate Palestinian human rights, are in contravention of international law, and breach standards of corporate social responsibility:

> Beyond simply being an individual consumer choice, the decision to boycott or divest is contextual, determined by one's community, politics, and values. There is no one-size-fits-all. Based on a range of possible responses to the 2005 call, what needs to be considered is, Of all the possible actions that could be done, we can have an impact here; let's do this.

Baum emphasizes that economic action is an effective tool:

> It works! Big, powerful, noteworthy companies, such as G4S, Hewlett Packard, Sodastream, Orange, Veolia, have moved factories, ended contracts, and changed their policies. It's mind-blowing! Carrying on business as usual by profiting from the occupation and violation of Palestinian human rights was just too controversial. They got out.

The Case for BDS

Ali Abunimah, founder of *Electronic Intifada* writes,

> It is up to Palestinians to debate and decide the best forms of resistance, and in the current situation one of the most powerful means of standing up to Israel is the nonviolent, civil society-led boycott, divestment, and sanctions (BDS) movement....Palestinians may choose not to use armed struggle, just as Nelson Mandela adopted and then suspended armed struggle in South Africa when he and his comrades thought the conditions were appropriate. But they never gave up the right. As the history of South Africa also

shows, the path away from violence is always easier when there are effective alternatives.[1] So those…who apparently find all Palestinian, though not Israeli, violence reprehensible, should be the first in line to promote nonviolent strategies like BDS. But no one… is entitled to strip Palestinians of their fundamental right to resistance and self-defense.[2]

But, Is BDS Antisemitic?

Philosopher and critical theorist Judith Butler explains how using the charge of antisemitism to change the subject and attack the messenger has become a tactic to silence criticism of Israel:

> When the charge of antisemitism is used to censor or quell open debate and the public exchange of critical views on the State of Israel, then it is not exactly communicating a truth, but seeking to rule out certain perspectives from being heard. So whether or not the accusation is true becomes less important than whether or not it is effective. It works in part through stigmatizing and discrediting the speaker but also through a tactical deployment of slander....Those who deploy the charge of antisemitism to discount a point of view and discredit a person clearly fear the viewpoint they oppose and do not want it to be heard at all. It is also a tactic of shaming, seeking to silence those for whom identifying with antisemitism is loathsome.[3]

Making Exceptions for Israel

I often encounter people who express support for boycott movements in the past and present, from the Indian boycott of British goods under colonial rule, to the American boycott of British goods during the struggle for independence, to the Montgomery bus boycott in the Jim Crow South of the US, to the farmworker grape boycott in the US, to the South African boycott under apartheid, to the boycott of states like North Carolina for their transphobic laws and policies, etc.

At the same time, these same individuals attack the Palestinian-led boycott movement of institutions complicit in the Israeli occupation. They fail to see a nonviolent movement based on international law resisting a brutal system of oppression that has gone on for decades now with impunity. The Palestinian boycott movement is in line with the long and rich history of similar nonviolent struggles.

We are accused of singling out Israel, when in fact, it is the US, the world's superpower, that has singled out Israel for large sums of military aid and diplomatic immunity. We call these critics of Palestinian human rights PEP's— progressive except on Palestine. They are committed to human rights except when it comes to Palestinians, and they are the ones who are in fact singling out Israel, and that is for impunity, while also singling out Palestinians as the exceptions to supposedly universal human rights.

Palestinians are not asking for charity or pity or any favors. We're simply asking for moral consistency, for the simple request of boots being taken off of our necks and the discontinuing of investment in institutions that are profiting off of our suffocation. We merely want to breathe.

—A Queer Palestinian (name withheld)

Israel does not have two different economic ecosystems, like, Israel within the green line and Israel over the green line. If you want to divest from the West Bank, Judea, and Samaria, you have to divest from Israel, which means you boycott Israel completely.

Ron Brummer, Chief of Operations, Israeli Ministry of Strategic Affairs and Hasbara, speaking to the Israeli American Council, November 2017

A Report from the BDS Trenches

Susan Landau

Palestine matters. As advocates for Palestinian rights, our work is part of a larger vision rooted in economic, racial, gender, climate, and migrant justice, and toward freedom and equality for all people everywhere.

It was August 14, 2017, and the Philadelphia Coalition for Boycott, Divestment, and Sanctions (Philly BDS) was finalizing plans for an upcoming program, hosting a Sunday morning Coffee & Justice open community event, intended to expand the base of local support for BDS. We had invited allies to meet us, enjoy Arabic pastries and coffee, and learn about our work.

Several of us had launched our group in 2009 with a campaign targeting Sabra hummus and Tribe hummus. This consumer-friendly boycott, with the tagline "No justice, no (chick)peas" immediately took hold on social media, generating enthusiasm and opening conversations about BDS at events and programs on Israel-Palestine, in supermarkets, and on college campuses.

At our meeting, we understood 2017 to be a very different political moment from 2009. The agenda for our Coffee & Justice event included recognition that we are no longer single-issue Palestine solidarity activists. Following the lead of the Boycott National Committee's statement placing the Palestinian cause in the broader context of anti-colonial struggles, March 2017,[1] our mission expanded to become a more inclusive, anti-racist, human rights movement that takes a nonviolent and principled stand against all forms of discrimination, including antisemitism and Islamophobia. This lens linked the Palestinian struggle for justice to other liberation struggles; our organizing had become intersectional.

Our current campaign to boycott Hewlett-Packard (HP) is an example of this shift. We target HP based upon their record of complicity in human rights violations against Palestinians. These same tools of economic action are being utilized across other struggles to hold corporations to account. The demand for compliance with codes of corporate social responsibility is shared by the campaign World Without Walls, as well as movements for prison reform, environmental justice, and rights for indigenous people.

As with the South African struggle against apartheid, BDS is an effective strategy to raise awareness and end Israel's ongoing oppression of Palestinians. Now thirteen years since its launch, BDS is widely supported by unions, academic associations, churches, and justice movements. Across the world, companies, institutions, celebrities, and governments are ending support for Israeli violations of international law.

Sometimes it can be difficult to assess the impact of a movement, but a tell-tale sign may be the efforts to block or silence it. The BDS movement challenges the ways Israel receives unconditional support from much of the international community and calls for Israel to be held to the same standards of international law as any other nation. As a result, BDS is regarded as a "strategic threat," an attempt to de-legitimize Israel; millions of dollars are spent on efforts to suppress BDS action, sabotage BDS initiatives, and advance anti-BDS legislation.

Long-time BDS supporters have witnessed this intensification of backlash. The right to boycott is under attack, with legislative efforts in several states directly

Richard Guffanti

As part of the global campaign to boycott Hewlett Packard, on December 16, 2017, members of Philly BDS, JVP-Philly, and Christian-Jewish Allies Working for Justice in Palestine brave the cold to distribute information about HP complicity in violations of Palestinian human rights at Christmas Village at City Hall in Philadelphia, Pennsylvania.

targeting BDS solidarity. The Israel Anti-Boycott Act (S. 720 and H.R. 1697) in Congress seeks to impose fines and criminal penalties and deny government loans to corporations refusing to do business with corporations in illegal Israeli settlements. The Act infringes on the First Amendment right to effect change through boycotts, divestment, and sanctions, and seeks to legitimize Israel's settlements by imposing penalties on those who oppose them of up to $1 million in fines and 20 years in prison.

The American Civil Liberties Union (ACLU) has entered the fray by opposing this bill, which clearly opposes constitutionally protected political speech.[2] At various points during our meeting, we acknowledged our connections to potential allies who, in the wake of the white supremacy rally in Charlottesville, Virginia, were at that moment organizing, protesting, and holding vigils against racism and hate speech throughout Philadelphia and around the country.

As we were wrapping up, we asked ourselves, "Given our commitment to cross-movement organizing, how do we connect the dots between US racism, white supremacy, and the issue of justice in Palestine?"

Without hesitation, Nathaniel, a founding member, jumped in, "Israel's ethnocentricity is a form of white supremacy. The expulsion of the Palestinian population is racism. The current apartheid situation—the separation barrier, Jewish-only settlements and roads, a two-tiered legal system and education system—all forms of racism. Consider the Israeli treatment of the Mizrahi Jews, Ethiopian Jews, really any Jews of color, and other people of color including migrant workers, African refugees, and of course Palestinians....Isn't that white supremacy?"

Yes, it is. Structures of white supremacy must be challenged, such as colonialism, capitalism, imperialism, neoliberalism, nationalism, racism, Zionism, militarism, gender discrimination, and all others. We must require

Hummus and Human Rights Violations

Sabra hummus and Tribe hummus are each owned by companies complicit in human rights violations against Palestinians. Sabra Dipping Company, owner of Sabra hummus, supports the Golani and Givati Brigades. Founded in 1947-1948, both brigades have long bloody histories of ethnic cleansing, excessive use of force, and human rights violations of Palestinians during wars and military operations.

Tribe hummus is owned by the Osem Group, which partners with the Jewish National Fund (JNF) in "Greenwashing," planting pine forests and national parks to erase destroyed Palestinian homes and villages. Since 1967, the JNF has been the essential partner of the Israeli government and the military in building and sustaining the infrastructure of the Occupation of the West Bank, Gaza, and East Jerusalem, and the displacement of the Bedouin in the Negev.

DON'T BUY INTO ISRAELI HUMAN RIGHTS ABUSES

Sabra
KILLER HUMMUS

SABRA HUMMUS PROFITS FROM WAR & OCCUPATION

Sabra Hummus is co-owned by the Strauss Group, a corporation that supports the Israeli army's elite Golani and Givati Brigades. The Golani and Givati have been cited for numerous human rights violations since 1948, including during Israel's three-week assault on Gaza that killed more than 1,400 mostly unarmed Palestinian civilians.

BOYCOTT SABRA
LET WE SHOP KNOW YOUR MONEY WILL NOT SUPPORT ISRAEL'S VIOLATIONS OF INTERNATIONAL LAW

Students for Justice in Palestine (SJP) / bdsmovement.net

ourselves to show up for other struggles, such as Black Lives Matter, as we work together across movements toward collective liberation, neither exceptionalizing Palestine as unique, nor excluding Palestine from the conversation around ending racism in this country.

Palestine matters. As advocates for Palestinian rights, our work is part of a larger vision rooted in economic, racial, gender, climate, and migrant justice, and toward freedom and equality for all people everywhere.

We must require ourselves to show up for other struggles, such as Black Lives Matter, as we work together across movements toward collective liberation, neither exceptionalizing Palestine as unique, nor excluding Palestine from the conversation around ending racism in this country.

Richard Spenser Might Be the Worst Person in America. But He Also Might Be Right About Israel.

The images of Nazis and white supremacists marching in the streets of Charlottesville with torches chanting "blood and soil" shook me to my core....In the aftermath of these acts of blatant racism and anti-Semitism, one of the march's leaders, Richard Spencer, was invited onto Israeli TV. His words were chilling …

"As an Israeli citizen, someone who understands your identity, who has a sense of nationhood and peoplehood and history and experience of the Jewish people, you should respect someone like me," Spencer said. "I care about my people. I want us to have a secure homeland for us and ourselves,

just like you want a secure homeland in Israel." He told the Israeli [TV] host that he sees himself as "a white Zionist."…

Richard Spencer, whose racist views are rightfully abhorred by the majority of the Jewish community, is holding a mirror up to Zionism and the reflection isn't pretty....There is a disturbing alliance between Zionists and white nationalists in the White House these days, and it doesn't come from nowhere. There is a shared bedrock of anxiety about demographics and racist and Islamophobic fear of "Arabs" that goes hand in hand with both worldviews....

Naomi Dann, *The Forward*, August 17, 2017, [http://bit.ly/WhiteZionist] Dann is the Media Manager at Jewish Voice for Peace.

Meet the BDS Movement

American Friends Service Committee (AFSC)

AFSC offers a fantastic resource for portfolio scanning, information on corporate complicity, and much more related to socially responsible investment or divestment: **afsc.org/investigate**

BDS National Committee

The global guiding body for BDS, it can respond to strategic questions, including whether or not something falls under the boycott, and can keep you up to date with global campaigns and victories: **bdsmovement.net**

Global Exchange

The Economic Activism for Palestine project focuses on corporate accountability for human rights and international law violations by the companies profiting from the occupation in Palestine: **globalexchange.org/programs/economicactivism**

Kairos USA

Kairos USA is dedicated to helping mobilize US churches in response to the Palestinian Christian call for justice and human rights: **www.kairosusa.org**

National Students for Justice in Palestine (SJP)

This network of campus organizations is made up of student activists connected with SJPs nationwide who mentor and support one another: **nationalsjp.org**

Palestine Legal

This organization offers legal support in the face of repression of Palestine solidarity: **PalestineLegal.org**

Palestine Portal

www.palestineportal.org/action-advocacy/direct-action/divestment-campaigns/

Right to Boycott

This US-based coalition produces resources and organizing campaigns to fight anti-BDS legislation: **righttoboycott.org**

US Campaign for Palestinian Rights

This coalition of more than 300 organizations can connect you to other groups and campaigns. The US Campaign also provides resources for campus and church divestment campaigns, organizing advice, targeted online action technology, and other support: uscpr.org. A BDS Toolkit is available at **www.uscpr.org/bdstoolkit**

Who Profits

A list of corporations involved in the occupation: **whoprofits.org**

> **Check these sites regularly to track victories in the global BDS movement**
>
> US BDS victories:
> www.uscpr.org/bdswins
>
> Global BDS impact:
> www.bdsmovement.net/impact
>
> Timeline of church divestment resolution wins:
> www.fosna.org/denominational-divestment-wins

Jesse Rubin/Mondoweiss

FAQ
Learn the arguments for and against BDS!
https://bdsmovement.net/faqs/responding-to-common-arguments-against-bds

BDS Activism Within US Faith Communities

Directory of faith-based initiatives: **https://bdsmovement.net/tags/faith-based**

American Muslims for Palestine
AMPalestine.org

Friends of Sabeel-North America (FOSNA) offers great organizing support, especially for faith-based and municipal campaigns, including HP-Free Churches: fosna.org

The Israel/Palestine Mission Network of the Presbyterian Church (USA) theIPMN.org

Jewish Voice for Peace (JVP)
JVP has a huge base, chapters nationwide, regional staff, and impressive organizing experience. Jewish Voice for Peace provides statements and other visible Jewish support when the label antisemitism is misused to silence criticism of Israel:
jvp.org

Mennonite Central Committee (MCC) US www.mcc.org

The Palestine Israel Network of the Episcopal Peace Fellowship epfnational.org/PIN

Unitarian Universalist Association www.uua.org

United Church of Christ www.ucc.org

United Methodist Church www.umc.org

Other significant contributions of faith-based advocacy and education groups are listed at PalestinePortal.org under Mapping the Movement.

Existence Is Resistance: *Sumud* in Gaza

The following poetry and prose are part of a larger collection available at wearenotnumbers.org, an online publication which lifts up young voices in Gaza.

Siege on Love and Death
Rana Shubair

The first ominous call came in the morning around 10:30. My husband called to tell me his aging and frail aunt had been taken to the hospital. She had fallen two years ago and broken a hip. Her family was told she had other health issues that meant surgery was too risky. Since then, her health had deteriorated and on that Sunday, February 19, her health worsened.

The good thing about my Gaza community is that people stand with and support each other in all types of occasions, whether happy or sad. Maybe that's what I cherish about my Gaza and its people most. For Gazans, family bonds and friendships help sustain and nurture us. So, if you have a problem, you can be sure to find a shoulder to lean on. In this case, the situation was urgent, so I quickly finished some household chores, got dressed and headed to the hospital.

Aunt Fayza lay there numb and helpless, unable to move. I touched her head, prayed for Allah to have mercy on her and left. There was nothing more I or anyone else could do.

The second call came around 5 p.m., with the news of her death. In Islamic tradition, when people pass away, they are prepared for burial by bathing and wrapping them in a white cloth. Family and friends gather to bid them a last farewell. We were weeping non-stop when suddenly two of her daughters who lived in the UAE called to demand that they be able to see their mother via video. They had been unable to come to their mother's side because of the closed borders.

To me, this was the moment that exposed the ugliness and torment of the 10-year-old siege of Gaza. One of the daughters asked that someone put the phone over her deceased mother's ear so she could speak some last words to her. I couldn't hear what the daughter was saying. Incomprehensible words were lost amongst the sobs from anguished hearts. At that moment, the enormity of the blockade loomed large in my mind. Amidst the tears and wailing, I screamed in my head: Damn the siege! God help us! God save us from this madness! I thought about the many others who are denied return to their homeland and who are not allowed to say goodbye to their loved ones.

A Siege Also on Love
The other side of the picture under the living siege of Gaza is not too different, except that it's on happy occasions. Recently I attended my cousin's wedding, or in this case, what we called "a farewell wedding party." My cousin got engaged three months ago, but her fiancé couldn't come into Gaza. He lives in Jordan and his family decided the bride would have to travel to unite with him. Ever since the blockade began, this has been the case with dozens of couples who find themselves trapped, with one of the two unable to come into Gaza or leave. In some cases, the couple have no option but to break up.

The wedding was beautiful and we tried to be happy for the bride's sake. But the absence of the groom was

July 28, 2014. A Palestinian family prays over the grave of a loved one at Sheikh Radwan cemetery in Gaza City.

too tangible to ignore. Nonetheless, we had to pretend it was normal. After an hour and a half, the bride's sisters revealed a surprise. A large TV screen flashed on, and soft, sad music played in the background. A map of the world slowly moved around the screen, with an arrow pointing to different parts of the world, starting with Jordan where the groom lived. Then a short video played in which the groom himself greeted the guests and prayed that he be united with his lovely bride soon. He also said he hoped we would be able to attend the other wedding which was to take place in Jordan. Then, his picture disappeared and the soft music grew more intense. Numerous locations on the map were highlighted, with each one representing one of the bride's aunts or cousins, including one of my sisters, sending warm wishes of happiness and wishes that they could be with us to celebrate this festive occasion.

Tears started rolling down my face and the same was true for the other guests. The scene from the funeral came back to me at that moment. As I watched my aunts and cousins and sister send their wishes, I was devastated. I realized I hadn't seen some of them for over 20 years! And I wondered if I would ever see them again. Was there a superpower that created barriers to separate people from their loved ones in Gaza? Was there an evil spirit who loomed over Gaza at night that forbade two hearts to join in the holy bond of marriage? I've never believed in superstition, and neither have my people.

An illegal siege has been imposed by Israel upon the people of Gaza for no crime at all. It continues to ban most of our people from traveling for any reason, whether medical treatment or studies. The status quo remains: a siege on love, a siege on death.

But why is this life so hard, testing me? Please, Lord, give me release. I am so used to darkness that now the light hurts my eyes.

Basman Derawi, 26

About Rana Shubair

It's true I took my first breath of life in Cairo, Egypt, but I'm a true Palestinian. My passion since childhood has been writing in safely locked diaries. It was only during the summer of 2016 that I shared my writing, when I published my first book, *In Gaza I Dare To Dream*.

I went to school part of my teenage life in the United States, when my father was pursuing his advanced studies. Although it's been a long time since I returned to Palestine, I still hold onto the beautiful memories I shared with my friends in America.

Experiencing Israeli aggression, power cuts, and restrictions on movement can certainly kill one's dreams and extinguish the sparkle of life. But the fact remains that we must stand up to those challenges and refuse to be beaten.

With writing, I also discovered my passion for reading. My nightstand has a pile of books along with my Kindle reader. I'm a stationery hoarder, especially of bookmarks, and I never say no to a good cup of coffee.

Rana's essay was originally posted on March 11, 2017, at https://wearenotnumbers.org/home/Story/Siege_on_love_and_death

Dear Little Boy
Basman Derawi

The world isn't good
like you expected it to be.
You draw your dream on paper,
but time erases it.
Remember when you were a child,
jumping on your bed?
When you were in school,
playing with your friends?
When you ran to the window,
reaching your hand out to feel the rain?
When you and your cousins
threw rotten fruit at each other
in your grandmother's yard?
When you listened to her stories before sleeping?
When you made up scary stories
for your cousins, to frighten them?
When you were in college,
studying hard to achieve your dreams,
Or with friends in a café
talking about the future,
Or celebrating your graduation day
when your dreams reached the sky?

"But why is this life so hard, testing me?
Please, Lord, give me release.
I am so used to darkness
that now the light hurts my eyes.
The pain refuses to leave me,
and I smell my own fear with every breath."

Dear little boy who I still am,
who wants life, wants to travel.
It is not too much to ask:
"Am I wrong for this world,
or is this world wrong for me?"

About Basman Derawi

Basman's essay was originally posted on May 29, 2017, at: https://wearenotnumbers.org/home/Story/Dear_little_boy

Basman, 26, was born in Kuwait and lived there for two years before coming to Gaza. A physiotherapist for the Ministry of Health, he graduated from Al-Azhar University in 2010.

He thinks of writing as a remedy—a tool that can change the world and be used as resistance. Basman began drafting stories a year ago and is inspired by music, movies, and people with special needs. One of his dreams as a Palestinian is to share and show Palestinians' real faces as they struggle and work for their rights. He also loves to read, cook, and play video games and basketball.

Checkmate
Bashar Nabhan

"To live, you need to struggle."

This was what my grandfather told me about when I was a lad of 11. I didn't really understand what he meant, and at the time I didn't actually care. All I wanted was a ball and a space to play football or to watch the skills of Cristiano Ronaldo on YouTube, even though I myself am a goalkeeper.

One year later, my grandfather passed away. But his words didn't.

I always go to the beach—our only sanctuary here in Gaza—to meditate. I go whether I'm feeling content or sad. I sit and whisper my stories to the breeze that touches my face, creating an aura of tranquility that seems to cast me away and to freedom.

I think about what my grandfather told me each time I go there. I repeat them under my breath like a mantra: "To live, you need to struggle." I've lived through three wars at the age of 18; if that isn't struggling what is?

But this year, I faced a struggle that for me, showed me I had not really known what the word really meant. This was my last year in high school, which is when—for Palestinians—we take the Tawjeehi exams. Not only is it the most difficult of all of your studies, but it also determines the rest of your life. I dream of becoming a physician, but without a sufficiently high score on the Tawjeehi, I would not receive a scholarship and even if I was accepted, my family would have to pay about $20,000.

During this year, but mainly during the last two months (April through May), there is no time you can waste; you only have time off to sleep and eat. Otherwise, it's study.

I relinquished almost everything else, including social media. My only occasional escape was to play chess. I played for an hour once. "Checkmate; you lose." This is a sentence I abhor hearing. I never like losing, but I lost that time because of the panic that enveloped me each time I remembered the Tawjeehi. The pressure was not from

my parents; we already had one doctor in the family—my brother. It was from me and my expectations for myself. I felt like I had lost connection with everything else.

However, I finally finished the Tawjeehi and received my result: 96.7 percent! I laugh now when I remember the moment I first saw my result. I seriously went out of my mind. I screamed when announcing the result to my family. Tears poured down everyone's cheeks, and happiness hovered all around.

I won. Checkmate, Tawjeehi; you lose. I have been accepted into the faculty of medicine at Islamic University of Gaza. And, grandfather, checkmate you win. I finally understand the message you wanted to deliver to me.

The future will help me understand it even more because, after all, to live, you need to struggle and learn.

And, grandfather, checkmate you win. I finally understand the message you wanted to deliver to me.

Bashar Nabhan, 18

About Bashar Nabhan

Bashar, 18, is a new high-school graduate who describes himself as "an ambitious Palestinian." He has been accepted into the faculty of medicine at the Islamic University of Gaza, has three brothers and two sisters. "Although young, I have seen planes hovering in the sky and missiles targeting the dreams of 2 million Palestinians living in a prison. I have heard thousands of screams, which follow me in my nightmares. My childhood has been slowly taken from me. But I stood strong as everyone did. What I know as a Palestinian is that nobody can destroy my will. What I know is that I am living to deliver a message; I am a Palestinian, and I am not a number."

Obviously, Bashar loves to write, but he also is avid about swimming, football (soccer), and reading.

Bashar's essay was originally posted on August 12, 2017, at: https://wearenotnumbers.org/home/Story/Checkmate

And Now What? A Realistic Approach to the Current Impasse

Jonathan Kuttab

As hopes for a genuine independent state collapse, and the one-state solution appears even farther away, how do we struggle for our rights and dignity and build for ourselves and our children a better future?

If it is true that the two-state solution is dead, and that the one-state solution is even harder to achieve, then where does that leave us? What is, or should be the agenda for the foreseeable future for those who are concerned with the Israeli-Palestinian impasse? Here are some questions for the two sides:

For Israel, and its ardent supporters: The occupation has gone on for far too long. The excuses for failing to make peace have grown very thin and are no longer believed by its own friends. Yet, for the foreseeable future, Israel holds all the cards and must determine how it wishes to play them. It can no longer "hope for someone on the other side" to come forward. It controls Palestinians completely; their lives, their movement, and even their leadership. It holds levers over all aspects of their lives, and acts as sovereign and owner of the entire land, unrestrained by anything (including international law, or the international community), and has successfully deflected all acts of resistance and all outside pressures. It still needs to determine, for its own purposes, at least, where it should go, and what it should do. The collapse of the moves for Palestinian statehood (celebrated by some) forces the issue of: what now? Do we rule over Palestinians forever, as non-citizens? Can we accept in perpetuity that our Jewish state can only treat Palestinians as unequal in Israel, occupied in parts of the West Bank, totally besieged in Gaza, and in permanent exile for their diaspora? And if so, how do we "manage" this situation as a permanent state of affairs? How can we best deal with another people that we rule but stay in accordance with our own ideals? Palestinians aren't going anywhere, so how we deal with them (*sans* excuses) as part of who we are or have become.

For Palestinians: As hopes for a genuine independent state collapse, and the one-state solution appears even farther away, how do we struggle for our rights and dignity and build for ourselves and our children a better future? Submission to the existing injustice is not an option. Can we find methods that are effective and goals that are achievable? Surely violence has not served us well, and is not likely to succeed against enemies who are immeasurably more powerful, better armed and organized, strategically and tactically dominant in the battlefield, and far better funded. Going by history, we

The Zionist Revolution Is Over

Just as the South African rulers understood, at a certain point, that there was no choice but to dismantle their regime, so the Israeli establishment has to understand that it is not capable of imposing its hegemonic conceptions on 3.5 million Palestinians in the West Bank and Gaza and 1.2 million Palestinians who are citizens of Israel. What we have to do is try to reach a situation of personal and collective equality within the framework of one overall regime throughout the country.

...So I think the time has come to declare that the Zionist revolution is over. Maybe it should even be done officially, along with setting a date for the repeal of the Law of Return. We should start to think differently, talk differently. Not to seize on this ridiculous belief in a Palestinian state or in the fence. Because in the end we are going to be a Jewish minority here. And the problems that your children and my grandchildren are going to have to cope with are the same ones that de Klerk faced in South Africa. The paradigm, therefore, is the binational one. That's the direction. That's the conceptual universe we have to get used to.

...In 1948, Zionism was truly victorious. It succeeded in consolidating itself in 78 percent of historic Palestine. But in 1967, Zionism won one victory too many, and in the 20 years that followed it sealed its fate by implementing the settlements project....It is the victim of its victories, the victim of a terrible history of missed opportunities.

"Cry, the Beloved Two-State Solution," *Ha'aretz*, Meron Benvenisti, Israeli political scientist, June 2003, http://bit.ly/cry2states

A doorway mural by Palestinian artist Ayed Arfeh in Dheisheh Refugee Camp near Bethlehem depicts an iconic thumbprint, the Palestinian flag, and the Key of Return.

cannot expect either the Arab world or the outside world to save us. What else can we do? Can a more assertive and better-planned and organized nonviolent campaign of resistance serve us better?

For third parties, who are concerned about peace and justice, and who perhaps care both for Israelis and Palestinians: Is there a path to actively be supportive of both and work for human rights and dignity in light of the overwhelmingly-depressive political prognosis? Despairing of a peaceful solution, are there interim measures we can support or work for?

There are answers, options, and paths for action for all the above, that may not lay out a complete solution but can be worthwhile effective steps in the right direction. None of them are easy or cost free, or are guaranteed to "solve" the problem, but each can be pursued without either demanding or ruling out a political solution in the future:

Siege of Gaza

Abandonment of the siege of Gaza, and allowing freedom of people and goods into and out of the Strip. The siege, initially undertaken as a political move to punish Gazans for their support of Hamas and to prevent continuity between the West Bank and Gaza as a measure to fragment Palestinians and to prevent Palestinian statehood, cannot be a permanent feature of life. With due consideration for the desire to prevent weapons from entering Gaza (a failed exercise in all cases), draconian controls over the civilian life and economy of two million souls in the Gaza Strip cannot be a permanent state of affairs. It must end. Whatever puny efforts some in Gaza may undertake to militarily resist are strategically insignificant. Given the relative quiet from Gaza's side, the siege must be lifted. This is something all parties must work on now.

Abandonment of armed resistance by Palestinians

Armed struggle is never an end in and of itself. It is only a method for achieving political ends, which seem to be elusive now. However deeply oppressed, and however justly provoked Palestinians are, armed resistance cannot help them in their present situation. No political or national goal can be advanced by acts of desperation, especially if aimed at the civilian "softer targets," and they are definitely bound to be counterproductive. The issue is not legitimacy of armed resistance, but its efficacy. Palestinians will do well (from their own perspective) to suspend any such actions. The emotional rush or satisfaction of "doing something" or "making the other side suffer" is not reason enough to do things that are counterproductive to the cause. (By the same token, continued Israeli reliance on military and deadly force has also proven ineffective, and "deterrence" has not worked. New thinking is required by Israelis as to the efficacy of reliance on military power as well.)

Struggle against collective punishment and administrative measures

Many of the forms of control used by Israel against Palestinians attempt to fashion the behavior of the entire Palestinian community by punishing innocent members of that community and rendering them all subject to the arbitrary acts of Israel. Such actions contravene international law, common morality, and basic human decency. Some say they also contravene the character and morality of Judaism and of the nature of society Jews wish to have for Israel. Such measures may find some justification in times of crisis, but they cannot serve as a permanent feature of any people's existence. If Israel wishes to "manage" this population, it must realize that neither occupation nor segregation and apartheid

However deeply oppressed, and however justly provoked Palestinians are, armed resistance cannot help them in their present situation.

Many of the forms of control used by Israel against Palestinians attempt to fashion the behavior of the entire Palestinian community by punishing innocent members of that community and rendering them all subject to the arbitrary acts of Israel.

Palestinians have not won the struggle by any means, but their continued existence and their awareness of themselves as a people, after a century-long effort to erase them, is a psychological victory at the most essential level. Palestine remains, in its people and their memory and, most notably, in their resistance to erasure.

Accepting Our Human Responsibility

Richard Falk

It requires no great wisdom to observe that the future is a black box. We know that achieving peace and justice for these two peoples will require a lengthy struggle that needs to place its trust in "a politics of impossibility," or as the poet W.H. Auden once put it: "We who are about to die demand a miracle."

And while awaiting such a political miracle, we should accept our human responsibility to aid and abet the Palestinian struggle for rights, self-determination, and a just peace. The attainment of such goals would also inevitably reshape the destiny of Israeli Jews toward a more humanistic and benevolent future.

Conclusion of "The One and Only Path to Palestine/Israel Sustainable Peace," a presentation to the Human Rights Commission of the Italian Parliament, October 11, 2017. http://bit.ly/FalkPath

have permanency. Just as slavery and colonialism eventually had to be abolished, so will this injustice.

If Israel is going to insist, for the foreseeable future, on being in charge of Palestinian lives and affairs, and deny them statehood, it must find a way to acknowledge their humanity and give them a role in deciding their own affairs, both in the West Bank (including areas C) [for information about Area C, see page 58], in Gaza, and in Israel. Israel must lift the measures which subjugate Palestinians to arbitrary actions. A large number of measures do exist which are totally within Israel's control and can be undertaken unilaterally with minimal impact on the ultimate security picture. They do not require negotiation, and they do not determine a particular ultimate political solution. Israel should seriously consider implementing them unilaterally rather than keep them as "potential bargaining chips" in

negotiations over a solution that does not appear on the horizon in the foreseeable future. These include:

1. Ending all administrative detentions, and releasing administrative detainees. Holding people without charging them—sometimes indefinitely—contravenes a just judicial system.

2. Removing all restrictions on normal movement of goods and services between the West Bank and Israel, as well as between Gaza and the West Bank. Specific individuals may still be prevented from movement into Israel by court decree, upon good cause, but the blanket prohibitions must be lifted, especially with respect to access to East Jerusalem. This has actually been tried a number of times with good results. The continued restrictions have a merely political, not a security basis.

3. Removing all barriers, checkpoints, and obstructions within the West Bank, allowing freedom of movement for goods and persons. These restrictions currently hamper economic development and create daily humiliations and harassment, and their contribution to Israel's security is negligible, while their impact on the lives of Palestinians and their contribution to increasing hatred and enmity is enormous.

4. Granting Palestinians permission to build in Area C of the West Bank and turning over zoning and planning authority in those areas to them.

5. Creating new legislative and constitutional guarantees for equality in Israel itself and making the promise of equality in Israel's Declaration of Independence operational and binding.

6. Making all residents of the West Bank, including Jewish settlers, subject to the same laws, administered by civilian and not military courts. This measure does not need Palestinian approval. Those Jewish settlers who wish to continue to live illegally in the West Bank, for whatever reason, must be required as a minimum to "pay the price" of living in equality with Palestinians in that area. This could take the form of extending certain Israeli privileges to West Bank Palestinians or alleviating certain burdens, which would be intolerable to Jewish settlers. Either way, it would promote equality without compromising Israeli security or the eventual political outcome.

Maintaining the Struggle

It may be argued that all these suggestions only beautify and prolong the occupation rather than remove it. My answer is that each and every one of these suggestions can be pursued without abandoning one's own political beliefs or one's own struggle for the ultimate political outcome. Yet, they also address the current intolerable situation that has been bedeviling the local population for half a century while pretending to be temporary. Implementation of these measures will go a long way to alleviate the day-to-day misery in the lives of Palestinians and will also move Israelis toward a more humane and sustainable situation, much more in line with their own Jewish values, and who they want to be.

June 2016. Palestinian women cross through the Israeli military checkpoint of Qalandiya, a main crossing point between Jerusalem and the West Bank city of Ramallah, as they head to Jerusalem's Al-Aqsa mosque for the third Friday prayer of the holy Muslim fasting month of Ramadan. Men over 45 and women in all ages were allowed to enter without permits from the West Bank into Jerusalem to attend the Friday prayer.

Ahmad Al-Bazz/ActiveStills

Discussion Guide: Why Palestine Matters

Katherine Cunningham

Why Palestine Matters: The Struggle To End Colonialism offers a global perspective on the issue of justice for Palestine. In addition to this discussion guide, supplementary educational resources, video clips, and updates designed for home use or a classroom setting are available on a website dedicated to this book. It can be accessed at WhyPalestineMatters.org. Any and all materials can advance self-directed education and be adapted for use in a group setting.

Guidelines for Group Facilitators

Why Palestine Matters is intended to open a space for engaging the cross-currents among some contemporary global justice issues through looking at the history and present-day experiences in Palestine. We suggest some important guidelines for facilitating a study group, including:

- Keep the discussion non-judgmental and open to discovery. The goal is to create a safe space for exploring the intersectional dynamics from the chapters for each session.
- Accept experiences of dislocation from one's comfort zone and accept debate on ideas regarding what is normal or standard.
- Focus on collaborative learning, resisting leadership as "the expert" and allow enough time for processing information and responses.
- Affirm the diversity of perspectives with emphasis on how the material is touching hearts and minds. Try using summary statements to help move discussion to the next questions or topics to be considered.
- Incorporate various facilitation strategies to maximize participation, and be flexible if your approach isn't working. If your group is too large for whole group discussions, transition into working in partners, triads, or small groups before coming together as a whole group.

Why Palestine Matters is intended to open a space for engaging the cross-currents among some contemporary global justice issues through looking at the history and present-day experiences in Palestine.

August 18, 2017. Graffiti artwork, Bethlehem, West Bank.

- Have the following materials available: newsprint, easel, markers, index cards, pens or pencils, tape or gum to attach paper to surfaces or a whiteboard.
- Use video clips or sidebar quotes as discussion prompts.

Suggested Format for Initial Discussion Groups

Tailor the group's format to time available because the quality of learning and interaction on these topics is of greater importance than covering all of the material in the book. This discussion guide is for *an initial run, not a deep dive*, leaving open the possibility of future in-depth topic groups. Most adult groups can commit to 3-4 sessions of 60-90 minutes. Keep the sessions scheduled weekly to maximize energy and commitment to the study. Video clips from WhyPalestineMatters.org can be part of the preparation for the next class along with do-ahead readings.

SESSION 1: Narratives of domination and displacement through a Palestinian lens

ASSIGNMENT FOR FIRST CLASS:

Prior to the first meeting, encourage participants to read the Introduction and Chapter 1.

FACILITATOR INSTRUCTIONS

- As the group first gathers, structure brief participant introductions with time to identify personal expectations.
- State course objectives, what the course will and will not cover. The overarching framework is justice, human rights, and international law. By presenting the history and experience of Palestinians as it intersects current global justice issues, the intention is to provide a counterweight to the dominant narrative and to bring attention to information not readily available through other sources. Disclose that for these reasons the book lifts up the Palestinian narrative.
- Set ground rules for discussions, including keeping confidentiality for what is said within the group. Remind your group about this covenant for each session.
- Be supportive in handling these very difficult and disturbing intersections of histories, including personal experiences of participants.
- Promote an atmosphere that encourages participants to express and honor differences in experience and in response to the book, rather than to make assumptions or judgments.
- Make it clear that doing the homework for each session is critical to getting the most from the course, as is showing up for each session.
- Prior to each class, allocate how much time you want to spend on each item. Use the discussion questions as

a guide. Choose what you want to include, and let go of suggested items that may be too time consuming and impede giving other items adequate time. Do not rush through any discussion in an attempt to cover everything.

FOR DISCUSSION

1. G.J. Tarazi outlines the term "tools of domination" for the parallels he sees as a Palestinian American living with the narratives of his dual homelands.
   - As a group, list some of the inter-connected patterns in the histories he outlines. Evaluate the comparisons he makes.
   - Explore how parallels affected participants, including which contained new ideas, perspectives, or information.
2. Ask each participant to jot down the definition of colonialism, as G.J. Tarazi uses it. Encourage sharing among members of the group.
   - Consider as a group how this shapes the "exceptionalism" of the oppressors and the "dehumanization" of the oppressed.
   - Inquire what is known or imagined about how the oppressor may justify its actions.
3. **Small groups/Personal impact:** Allow ample time for participants to process the personal impact of Chapter 1.
   - Did any of the information in Chapter 1 contradict facts previously understood? How might participants deal with those reactions over the next four weeks? What might the group agree to do as it encounters some of those contradictions?

SESSION 2: Encountering intersectionality: focusing the lens more closely

ASSIGNMENT FOR SESSION 2

Read Chapter 2. Encourage each participant to make note of the quotes or photos that impact him/her/them most strongly, and to come to class prepared to share and discuss these.

FOR DISCUSSION

1. **Personal impact:** What is this lens of intersectionality?
   - Ask a participant to read aloud the beige box quote (page 20) as a prompt for talking about intersectionality, and in preparation for discussing the last paragraph of the text on page 21.
   - Instruct participants to write down on an index card at least one way that intersectionality contributes to their understanding of human rights and justice. In small groups, share and discuss.
2. **Discussion in pairs:** Consider ways that historically, African American women stand at many intersections/struggles.

This 4-5 session discussion guide is expanded on the website, offering options for additional sessions, stand alone sessions, and for designing your own course by selecting what is most appealing to your group.

The towering 26-foot-high Israeli separation barrier has become a canvas for dramatic protest art and political commentary where it severs Bethlehem from the surrounding environs and nearby Jerusalem. This graffiti highlights the insidious significance of the Balfour Declaration on the occasion of its cententennial.

Addie Domske

• What does this tell us about the importance of identities in restorative justice? About coalitions of solidarity in advocacy for change?
• Share with the whole group.

3. **Whole group:** Identifying points of intersection
• Spend 5-7 minutes in silence during which participants individually review all the photos and quotes from page 21-29. Ask each person to explain the personal impact of the photo or quote they identify as most impactful while others in the group listen in silence.

• Record on newsprint the names of the struggles and the intersections that are pictured.
• Share any new perspectives that have emerged in light of the oppression and suffering Palestinians and other communities continue to endure.
• Share additional insights, learning, or reactions.

SESSION 3: Changing the narratives on cultural theft, distortion, and normalization

ASSIGNMENT FOR SESSION 3

Read Chapter 5. Ask each participant to choose the most important issue to him/her/them to discusses in the session, such as kufiya, *appropriation, dialogue, normalization, rebranding, pinkwashing, feminism, and brownwashing. Go to the web site and view Remi Kanazi reciting his poem "Normalize this."*

FOR DISCUSSION

1. **Personal impact/Discussion:** Begin the discussion by asking participants to look again at the banner photos on pages 65-67.
• Imagine yourself seeing these banners on a local university campus. How would you describe to a friend the "narrative" of these banners? Include the concepts of rebranding, indigenous, and intersectionality in your description.
• Ask for two volunteers to briefly argue the pros and cons of whether the banners meet the criteria of cultural theft as Steven Salaita defines it when he refers to "the dynamics of Israel's voracious appetite for anything that can be marked 'Indigenous,' which it needs to shore up an ever-tenuous sense of legitimacy"? (page 61) When they are finished, encourage feedback from others in the class.

2. **Discuss:** "normalization"
• What does the term "normalization" mean in the context of colonization? What new understanding does this reflect?
• Given the discussion from Chapter 1, does the quote from performance poet Remi Kanazi and the discussion in the article on page 60 have any new meaning?
• As a class, list events, groups, books, movies, and other initiatives that you would consider examples of normalization. Based on what you are learning, would you support these in the future? What is the reasoning behind your decision?

3. Small group/whole group: Ask participants to talk about why and how their choice of issues in this chapter impacted the focusing of their own "lenses."

Proposal: (If this is an option) Before proceeding, ask if the class would like to schedule a fifth bonus session. Discuss and decide.

WhyPalestineMatters.org Please visit the website companion to this book for supplementary educational resources, video clips, and updates, all designed for home or classroom use.

SESSION 4: Resistance as a just and moral imperative, now and for the future

ASSIGNMENT FOR SESSION 4

Read Chapter 7. Also read Chapter 4 as background for this discussion. Jonathan Kuttab's article in the Epilogue can be assigned for either Session 4 or Session 5 . As a bonus to enhance study, read the foreword by Richard Falk.

FACILITATOR INSTRUCTIONS

If this is the final class, add #3 from Session 5. Hard choices may be required about which questions to include in this session. In a 4-session course, consider extending time for the last session. It is important to link learning with action.

FOR DISCUSSION

1. **Personal impact:** Find a photo that captures "memory." Share it with another person. Focus on it while the facilitator reads aloud the quote from Kathleen Christison on page 78 under "Resistance and Solidarity as Hope": "Although Palestinians have no near-term expectation of achieving justice,…they have been able to keep their struggle alive and bring it to wider international attention simply by determinedly maintaining their sense of peoplehood….Memory is the key: it is the seed of resistance, the inspiration for resistance, and the moral underpinning of the struggle."

2. **Discussion:** As a class, brainstorm together and record on newsprint examples of how memory grounds resistance for Palestinians.

   - According to Angela Davis, on page 79, Palestinian resistance is connected to the Movement for Black Lives and the struggle for justice and dignity. She claims that Palestine is at the forefront of the collective struggles toward a "more habitable future" for all people. Discuss arguments that support her claim as well as any pitfalls in her statements.
   - Using the examples in Chapter 7, would you agree or disagree that hope and solidarity are linked? What does or does not resonate for you about this assertion?
   - How can the language of intersectionality inform and inspire efforts of creative resistance?

3. **Small groups:** Using one or more of the stories of resistance from Gaza on pages 92-93,
   - Discuss resistance in light of narratives of colonialism and ethnic cleansing.

4. **Discussion:** Review the definitions of BDS on page 86 (beige box) and the three demands of the BDS movement.
   - What strikes you as the intent of the demands? Do the demands seem realistic?
   - What do you know about the history and success of BDS initiatives outside of the Palestinian struggle for justice? Describe any personal experience you

have had with any other boycott or divestment initiatives.
   - On what basis might someone label the BDS movement as antisemitic? What arguments would you make to a friend who described the BDS movement as antisemitic?
   - The SRI movement—socially responsible investing—came out of efforts beginning in the late 1960s to dismantle apartheid. Have you experienced or come across SRI in your workplace or community? If so, how?
   - Imagine discovering that your company, organization, municipality, or faith-based community was invested in contracts that profit from human rights violations today. On what moral, ethical, or investment grounds would you encourage your group to adopt nonviolent economic measures? What if the violations are against Palestinians?

5. **Small groups/whole group:**
In small groups, and then as a whole group, review the options that Jonathan Kuttab proposes on page 96.
   - How do these proposals change the narrative of colonization, oppression, and denial of human rights for Palestinians?
   - Share thoughtful reactions as well as emotions evoked by the content of Kuttab's proposals.

BONUS SESSION 5: Awareness and action

ASSIGNMENT FOR SESSION 5

Read Foreword by Richard Falk.

FOR DISCUSSION

1. **Discussion:** Discuss Richard Falk's Foreword and international law as it impacts on the material in Chapter 1 and throughout the book.
   - List violations of international law these actions and struggles represent.
   - Suggest policies or actions to repair the failures of domination and to restore justice.

2. **Small groups/whole group:**
In small groups, and then as a whole group, review the options that Jonathan Kuttab proposes on page 96.
   - How do these proposals change the narrative of colonization, oppression, and denial of human rights for Palestinians?
   - Share thoughtful reactions as well as emotions evoked by the content of Kuttab's proposals.

3. **Small groups:** Consider and share ways you have shown or will plan to show solidarity through supporting resistance actions by Palestinians or other solidarity groups?
   - Be as specific as possible.
   - Make an action plan of next steps.

4. **Whole group wrap up:** Why concern oneself? What is the value of seeing and knowing? Should we sit on the sidelines or join the struggle?

Affirm the diversity of perspectives in group discussions with emphasis on how the material is touching hearts and minds.

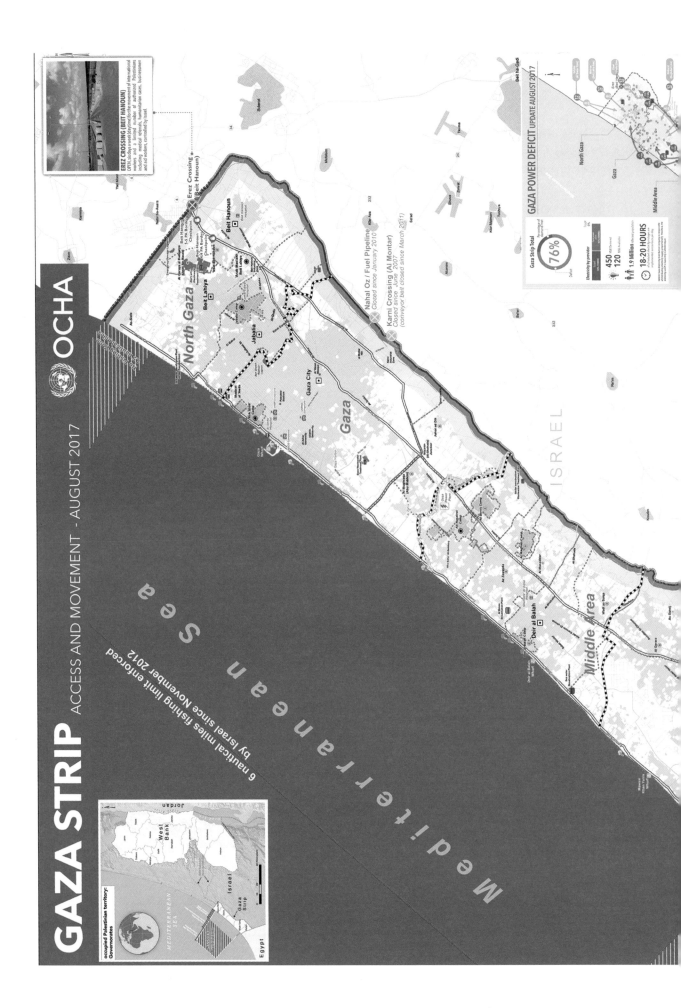

GAZA STRIP ACCESS AND MOVEMENT - AUGUST 2017

6 nautical miles fishing limit enforced
by Israel since November 2012

Mediterranean Sea

occupied Palestinian territory:
Governorates

EREZ CROSSING (BEIT HANOUN)
OPEN, six days a week/daytime) for the movement of international
workers and a limited number of authorized Palestinians
including medical referrals, humanitarian cases, businessmen
and aid workers, controlled by Israel.

Nahal Oz / Fuel Pipeline
Closed since January 2010

Karni Crossing (Al Montar)
Closed since June 2007
(conveyor belt closed since March 2011)

GAZA POWER DEFICIT UPDATE AUGUST 2017

Gaza Strip Total
76%

Electricity by provider

450 MW Demand
120 MW Available

18-20 HOURS

1.9 Million affected population

North Gaza

Gaza

Middle Area

ISRAEL

North Gaza

Gaza

Middle Area

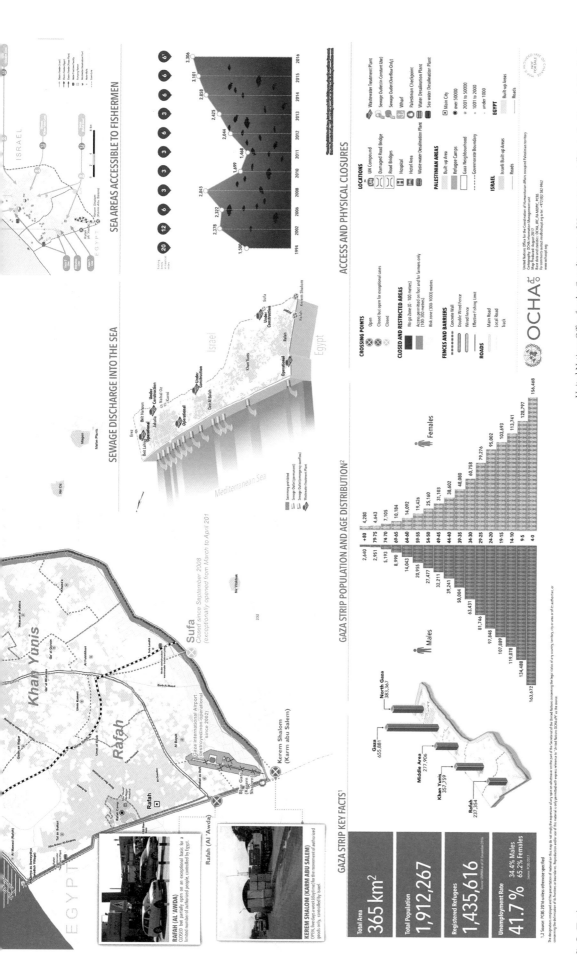

SEA AREAS ACCESSIBLE TO FISHERMEN

SEWAGE DISCHARGE INTO THE SEA

ACCESS AND PHYSICAL CLOSURES

GAZA STRIP POPULATION AND AGE DISTRIBUTION[2]

GAZA STRIP KEY FACTS[1]

Total Area
365 km²

Total Population
1,912,267
Source: UNRWA as of 31 December 2016

Registered Refugees
1,435,616
Source: UNRWA as of 31 December 2016

Unemployment Rate
41.7 %   34.4% Males   65.2% Females
Source: PCBS 2016

1,2 Source: PCBS 2016 unless otherwise specified

RAFAH (AL 'AWDA)
CLOSED but partially open on an exceptional basis for a limited number of authorized people, controlled by Egypt.

KEREM SHALOM (KARM ABU SALEM)
OPEN, five days a week (daytime) for the movement of authorized goods only, controlled by Israel.

United Nations Office for the Coordination of Humanitarian Affairs in the Occupied Territories

United Nations Office for the Coordination of Humanitarian Affairs in the occupied Palestinian territory
Cartography: OCHA. Information Management Unit
Map Produced: August 2017
Base data and statistics: OCHA, JRC, FA NDPMC, PCBS
For comments contact ochaopt@un.org or tel. +972 (0) 582 9962
www.ochaopt.org

To view this map online, visit:
https://www.ochaopt.org/
content/gaza-strip-access-
and-movement-august-2017

West Bank: Settlements and the Separation Barrier

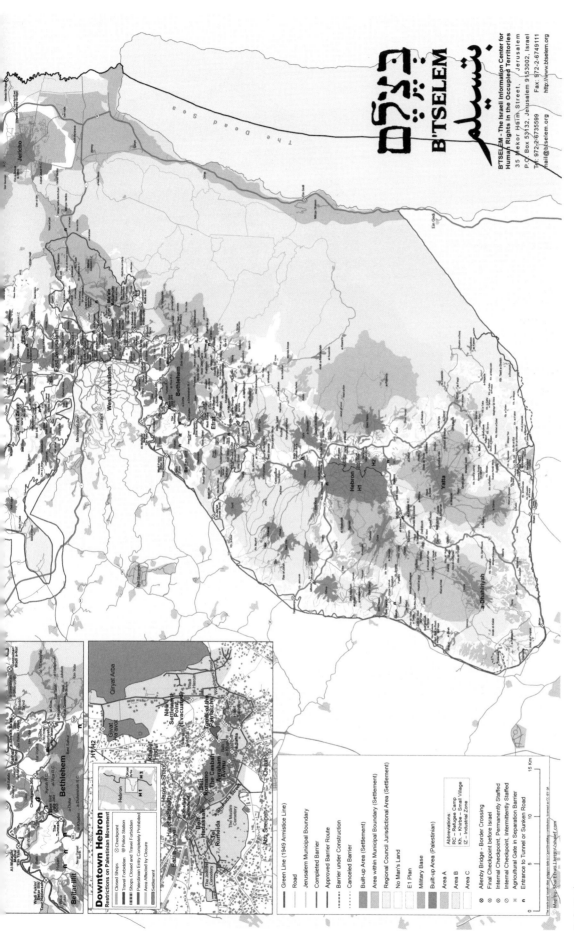

B'TSELEM

B'TSELEM - The Israeli Information Center for Human Rights in the Occupied Territories

35 Mekor Haim Street, Jerusalem
P.O. Box 53132, Jerusalem 9153002, Israel
Tel. 972-2-6735599   Fax: 972-2-6749111
mail@btselem.org   http://www.btselem.org

Downtown Hebron
Restrictions on Palestinian Movement

- Closed Shops
- Travel Forbidden
- Shops Closed and Travel Forbidden
- Palestinian Entry Completely Prohibited
- Area Affected by Closure
- Settlement
- ⊗ Checkpoint
- ⊗ Police Station

- Green Line (1949 Armistice Line)
- Road
- Jerusalem Municipal Boundary
- Completed Barrier
- Approved Barrier Route
- Barrier under Construction
- Canceled Barrier
- Built-up Area (Settlement)
- Area within Municipal Boundary (Settlement)
- Regional Council Jurisdictional Area (Settlement)
- No Man's Land
- E1 Plan
- Built-up Area (Palestinian)
- Area A
- Area B
- Area C

Abbreviations:
RC – Refugee Camp
Kh. – Khirba – Small Village
IZ – Industrial Zone

- ⊗ Allenby Bridge - Border Crossing
- ⊗ Final Checkpoint before Israel
- ⊗ Internal Checkpoint, Permanently Staffed
- ⊗ Internal Checkpoint, Intermittently Staffed
- ⋈ Agricultural Gate in Separation Barrier
- ⌐ Entrance to Tunnel or Sunken Road

0   5   10   15 Km

To view this map online, visit:
https://www.btselem.org/
download/201411_btselem_
map_of_wb_eng.pdf

West Bank Area C

Border

- - -   International Border

- - -   Green Line

   Israeli Unilaterally Declared
         Municipal Area of Jerusalem[1]

1. In 1967, Israel occupied the West Bank and unilaterally annexed
to its territory 70.5 km of the occupied area

Barrier

———   Constructed / Under Construction

- - - - -   Planned

Oslo Agreement[2]

         Area (A), (B) Palestinian Control

         Area C & Nature Reserves
         Full Israeli Control

Oslo Interim Agreement

2. Area A : Full Palestinian civil and security control
Area B: Full Palestinian civil control and joint Israeli-
Palestinian security control
Area C: Full Israeli control over security, planning
and construction

To view this map online, visit:
https://www.ochaopt.org/content/west-
bank-area-c-map-february-2011

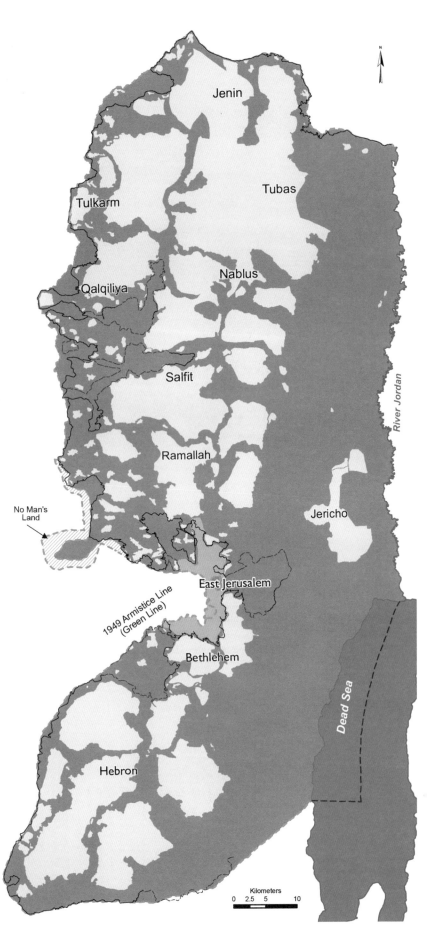

ENDNOTES

FOREWORD

1 Editors: For more on this paradox and anachronism, see Tony Judt in *The New York Review of Books*, "Israel: The Alternative," October 23, 2003, issue. http://bit.ly/JudtOnIsrael "The problem with Israel, in short, is not—as is sometimes suggested—that it is a European 'enclave' in the Arab world, but rather that it arrived too late. It has imported a characteristically late-nineteenth-century separatist project into a world that has moved on, a world of individual rights, open frontiers, and international law. The very idea of a 'Jewish state'—a state in which Jews and the Jewish religion have exclusive privileges from which non-Jewish citizens are forever excluded—is rooted in another time and place. Israel, in short, is an anachronism."

2 "Palestine: Legitimate Armed Resistance vs. Terrorism," John Sigler, *Electronic Intifada*, May 17, 2004. "...However, among these legal forms of violence there is also the right to use force in the struggle for 'liberation from colonial and foreign domination.' To quote United Nations General Assembly Resolution A/RES/33/24 of 29 November 1978: '2. Reaffirms the legitimacy of the struggle of peoples for independence, territorial integrity, national unity, and liberation from colonial and foreign domination and foreign occupation by all available means, particularly armed struggle.' This justification for legitimate armed resistance has been specifically applied to the Palestinian struggle repeatedly. To quote General Assembly Resolution A/RES/3246 (XXIX) of 29 November 1974: 'Reaffirms the legitimacy of the peoples' struggle for liberation from colonial and foreign domination and alien subjugation by all available means, including armed struggle; …7. Strongly condemns all Governments which do not recognize the right to self-determination and independence of peoples under colonial and foreign domination and alien subjugation, notably the peoples of Africa and the Palestinian people.' These two points—that people under colonial and foreign domination have the right to use armed struggle against their oppressors and that this specifically applies to the Palestinian people —has been repeatedly reaffirmed in a myriad of United Nations resolutions. These include UNGA Resolution A/RES/3246 (XXIX; 29 November 1974), UNGA Resolution A/RES/33/24 (29 November 1978), UNGA Resolution A/RES/34/44 (23 November 1979), UNGA Resolution A/RES/35/35 (14 November 1980), UNGA Resolution A/RES/36/9 (28 October 1981), and many others. While these resolutions, coming from the General Assembly do not carry the weight of law *per se*, they do reflect the views of the majority of the world's sovereign states, which is the basis of customary international law. So although General Assembly resolutions are not legally binding in and of themselves, when they address legal issues, they do accurately reflect the customary international legal opinion among the majority of the world's sovereign states."

CHAPTER 1
1.2

1 See *Israeli Practices towards the Palestinian People and the Question of Apartheid*, Richard Falk and Virginia Tilley, a censored UN Report now posted here: http://bit.ly/censoredFalk. See also "The Inside Story on Our UN Report Calling Israel an Apartheid State" *The Nation*, March 2017. http://bit.ly/FalkUNreport

2 Settler violence: Lack of accountability, B'Tselem - The Israeli Information Center for Human Rights in the Occupied Territories. http://www.btselem.org/topic/settler_violence

3 Archive of Discriminatory Laws in Israel, Adalah, The Legal Center for Arab Minority Rights in Israel. https://www.adalah.org/en/law/index

4 *Racial Paranoia: The Unintended Consequences of Political Correctness,* John L. Jackson, Jr., Civitas Books, 2008

5 Addameer, Prisoner Support and Human Rights Association. http://www.addameer.org/statistics

6 "One Rule, Two Legal Systems: Israel's Regime of Laws in the West Bank," November 2014, The Association for Civil Rights in Israel. http://www.acri.org.il/en/2014/11/24/twosysreport

7 Conviction rate for Palestinians in Israel's military courts: 99.74%. http://bit.ly/ConvictionRate

8 Addameer, Prisoner Support and Human Rights Association, Detention Facts. http://bit.ly/10DetenctionFacts

9 "Israel: Hunger Striker's Life at Risk" Human Rights Watch February 2012. http://bit.ly/LifeatRisk

10 "Emmett Till's Casket Goes to the Smithsonian"—Simeon Wright recalls the events surrounding his cousin's murder and the importance of having the casket on public display. http://bit.ly/EmmetCasket

11 "Mandatory Minimum Sentences for Stone-throwing in Israel Will Lead to Injustice - Why should Israeli law include a minimum sentence for stone throwing when there is none for manslaughter, rape, or bribery?" https://www.haaretz.com/opinion/1.677911

12 Statistics on Palestinian minors in the custody of the Israeli security forces - The Israeli Information Center for Human Rights in Occupied Territories. http://www.btselem.org/statistics/minors_in_custody

13 "Israel: Security Forces Abuse Palestinian Children–Chokeholds, Beatings, Coercive Interrogations" Human Rights Watch. http://bit.ly/HRWchildren

14 "Children in West Bank face deadliest year of past decade" Defense of Children International, Palestine. http://bit.ly/32minors

15 DCIP. http://bit.ly/childrenDCIP

16 "The Ferguson/Palestine Connection - As the unrest continues, the St. Louis Police Collaboration with Israel Underscores Connected Struggles" *Ebony*, Aug. 2014. http://bit.ly/FergPal

17 "With Whom Are Many US Police Departments Training? With a Chronic Human Rights Violator– Israel" Amnesty International Human Rights Blog, August 2016. blog.amnestyusa.org

18 See note 14

19 "NYPD Now Has an Israel Branch" *New York Magazine*, September 2012. http://nym.ag/2wV9JAZ

20 Oxfam report on Gaza's water crisis. http://bit.ly/oxfamGaza

CHAPTER 2

1 "The Combahee River Collective: A Black Feminist Statement," in Zillah R. Eisenstein, ed. *Capitalist Patriarchy and the Case for Socialist Feminism* (New York: Monthly Review Press, 1977), pp. 362-372.

2 Crenshaw, Kimberlé, "Demarginalizing the Intersection of Race and Sex: A Black Feminist Critique of Antidiscrimination Doctrine, Feminist Theory, and Antiracist Politics," *University of Chicago Legal Forum*, Vol. 1989, Issue 1, Article 8. http://chicagounbound.uchicago.edu/uclf/vol1989/iss1/8

3 Devon W. Carbado et al., "Intersectionality: Mapping the Movements of a Theory," *Du Bois Review*. Vol. 10, No. 2, Fall 2013, p. 304

4 Devon W. Carbado et al., "Intersectionality: Mapping the Movements of a Theory," *Du Bois Review*. Vol. 10, No. 2, Fall 2013, pp. 303-312

5 *Ibid.*, p. 304

6 *Ibid.*, p. 305

7 *Ibid.*, p. 305

8 *Ibid.*, p. 305

CHAPTER 3
3.1

1 "..the residents either fled or were forcibly evicted, and the homes were razed to the ground by Israeli bulldozers. One resident, a woman, was killed when the house she was in was bulldozed on top of her. Her name was Rasmiya al-Tabaki. The deliberate destruction of civilian infrastructure in occupied territory is prohibited under the Fourth Geneva Convention. For Palestinians, the Western Wall Plaza as we know it today is the site of a war crime." "Reframing the 1967 War," Yousef Munayyer, *The New Yorker,* June 9, 2017. http://bit.ly/reframing67

3.2

1 IPMN enumerated several definitions of Zionism as understood by various early Zionist leaders, as well as by current scholars, in its publication *Zionism Unsettled: A Congregational Study Guide* (IPMN, 2014), p. 11.

2 Although Israel did annex Palestinian East Jerusalem and vastly expand its boundaries immediately after the conclusion of the 1967 war, Israelis have avoided any demographic issue arising from the addition of this Palestinian population to the overall Israeli population by granting Jerusalem Palestinians "residency" but not citizenship. As "residents," Jerusalem Palestinians may vote in Jerusalem municipal elections but not in Israeli national elections.

3.3

1 http://bit.ly/HIRNonFB

2 *Separate and Unequal: Israel's Discriminatory Treatment of Palestinians in the Occupied Palestinian Territories*, pp. 89 and following. http://bit.ly/SepUnequal

3.4.1

1 "Gaza one year on: Does the world wake up?" AFSC.org, Lucy Duncan, Jul.17, 2015. http://bit.ly/leavinggaza

2 "An unnatural disaster: What I saw in Gaza" AFSC.org, Aura Kanegis, Jan. 7, 2015. http://bit.ly/gazadisaster

3 "In Gaza, we get four hours of electricity a day—if we're lucky" *LA Times*, Aug. 20, 2017. http://bit.ly/gazaop-ed

4 "Three years after Protective Edge, Gaza is in free fall," Amir Rotem, Director, GISHA, 972mag.com. http://bit.ly/gazafreefall

5 *Ibid.*

6 "Chicago clergy leaders call for end to blockade of Gaza," Zach Taylor, July 1, 2016, *Mondoweiss.* http://bit.ly/2CkoCze

3.4.2

Sources

BBC, "Guide: Gaza Under Blockade," July 6, 2010. http://bit.ly/BBCgazaguide

Farming the front line, Ron J. Smith and Martin Isleem, *City* Vol. 21, Iss. 3-4, 2017. http://bit.ly/2EGAs7j

Roy, Sara, *The Gaza Strip: The Political Economy of De-Development*, Washington, DC, Institute for Palestine Studies, 1995

CHAPTER 4
4.3

1 *The Way to the Spring: Life and Death in Palestine*, Ben Ehrenreich, Penguin 2016, page 290

CHAPTER 5
5.1

1 For more on appropriation, see "Stealing Palestine: A study of historical and cultural theft," by Roger Sheety, Middle East Eye "The cultural appropriation of books, music, art, cuisine, and dress have been used by Zionists as a weapon against Palestinians." http://bit.ly/culturaltheft

5.2

1 Remi Kanazi, "Normalize This" video at http://bit.ly/Normalizethis, or see WhyPalestineMatters.org under Chapter 5 videos.

5.3

1 Sarah Schulman, "Israel and 'Pinkwashing,'" *New York Times*, Nov. 22, 2011. http://bit.ly/IsraelPink

2 "LGBT campaigners say Israel 'pinkwashing' to distract from Palestinian occupation," *AFP*, June 3, 2016. http://bit.ly/AFPonPink

3 http://bit.ly/HaneenPink

4 http://bit.ly/AtshanPink

CHAPTER 6
6.2

1 See Palestinian Land Society, plands.org

2 A deeper understanding of the history of Palestinian expulsion and dispossession may be found in Sami Hadawi's *Bitter Harvest*, Benny Morris' *The Birth of the Palestinian Refugee Problem*, and Ilan Pappe's *The Ethnic Cleansing of Palestine*, as well as the research and documentation of historian Salman Abu Sitta in *Atlas of Palestine 1917-1966*, posted at plands.org

3 http://bit.ly/unhumanrights

4 UN Resolution 194, article 11. See http://bit.ly/UNRes194

5 http://bit.ly/UNRWAmandate

6 The quotation is from an interview with Chris Gunness, UNRWA's spokesman. The complete interview can be found in: "Exploding the Myths: UNRWA, UNHCR, and the Palestinian Refugees," Ma'an News Agency, June 27, 2011. http://bit.ly/ExplodingMyths

7 "Not All Israeli Citizens Are Equal" Munayyer, *New York Times*, May 23, 2012. http://bit.ly/2wkMkXM

6.3

1 badil.org/en/publication/survey-of-refugees.html

2 *Ibid.*

3 "Unwelcome Guests: Palestinian Refugees in Lebanon" Dalal Yassine, *Al Shabaka*, July 5, 2010. http://bit.ly/UnwelcomeGuests

4 *Ibid.* (Dalal Yassine, a lawyer and advocate for gender and human rights for Palestinian refugees in Lebanon, is a policy advisor for Al Shabaka.)

5 "The United States Was Responsible for the 1982 Massacre of Palestinians in Beirut" Rashid Khalidi, *The Nation*, Sept. 14, 2017. http://bit.ly/USand1982

6 "Why have the killers of Sabra and Shatila escaped justice?" Zeina Azzam, *Electronic Intifada*, Sept. 15, 2015. http://bit.ly/EscapedJustice

7 "Palestinians on the Road to Damascus, Policy Brief," Ahmad Diab, *Al Shabaka*, Sept. 5, 2012. http://bit.ly/2oyKAoD

8 "Jordan and the Palestinian refugees" Daoud Kuttab, *The Jordan Times*, Jan 22, 2014. http://bit.ly/JordanPalRefugees

9 "Insight Into the Socio-Economic Conditions of Palestinian Refugees in Jordan," UNRWA, 20 December 2013

10 "Jordan: Palestinians Escaping Syria Turned Away" Human Rights Watch, Aug. 7, 2014. http://bit.ly/NoMorePals

11 "Not Welcome—Jordan's Treatment of Palestinians Escaping Syria," *Human Rights Watch Report*, 2014. http://bit.ly/NotWelcome2014

12 "Palestinian Refugees from Syria: Stranded on the Margins of Law," Mai Abu Moghli, *Al Shabaka*, October 19, 2015. http://bit.ly/MaiRefugees.

13 "The Invisible Community: Egypt's Palestinians," Oroub el-Abed, *Al Shabaka*, June 8, 2011. http://bit.ly/EgyptPals

14 Aaron David Miller, *Arab States and the Palestine Question: Between Ideology and Self-Interest*, New York: Praeger, 1986, p. 64

15 "Israel reduces fishing zone off Gaza coasts to 6 miles," *Ma'an News*, May 30, 2016. http://bit.ly/Gaza6Miles

CHAPTER 7
7.2

1 Latinx (pronounced lateenex) is a gender-neutral term often used in place of Latino or Latina to designate persons who trace their ancestry to Latin America and/or have social and cultural ties with Latin America.

7.4

1 "Nelson Mandela's legacy: As a leader, he was willing to use violence," Robyn Dixon, *LA Times*, Dec. 6, 2013. http://bit.ly/MandelaTactics

2 Ali Abunimah, *Electronic Intifada*, April 4, 2016. http://bit.ly/caseBDS

3 *On Antisemitism, Solidarity, and the Struggle for Justice*, Jewish Voice for Peace, 2017, pp. x-xii

7.5

1 "Racism and Racial Discrimination are the Antithesis of Freedom, Justice & Equality." http://bit.ly/BDSonRacism

2 ACLU Letter to Senate "Oppose S. 720 – Israel Anti-Boycott Act." http://bit.ly/ACLUletter

For bibliography, recommended books, and related organizations, see this book's website: WhyPalestineMatters.org

CONTRIBUTORS

PRODUCTION TEAM

Co-editors:
Noushin Framke and Susan Landau
Book design: Martina Reese
Proof editor: Don Maclay
Videographer: Jim Tiefenthal
Website: Noushin Framke
Project manager: Noushin Framke

The IPMN Book Project Committee: John Anderson, Pauline Coffman, Walt Davis, Jeffrey DeYoe, Kathleen Christison, Noushin Framke, Katherine Cunningham, Susan Landau, Don Maclay, and Martina Reese

ACKNOWLEDGEMENTS

ActiveStills
Anna Baltzer, *Director, Organizing and Advocacy, US Campaign for Palestinian Rights*
Dalit Baum, *Director, Economic Activism Program for the American Friends Service Committee, and co-founder, Who Profits*
Sylvia Haddad, *Executive Secretary of the Joint Christian Committee in Lebanon*
Elmarie Parker, *Regional Liaison for Syria, Lebanon, and Iraq, Presbyterian Mission Agency of the PC(USA)*
Tova Perlmutter and Adam Horowitz, *Mondoweiss*
Ted Settle, IPMN member and photographer
Don Wagner, *IPMN Education Committee*

CONTRIBUTING AUTHORS

Jennifer Bing

Jennifer Bing is the Palestine-Israel Program director for the American Friends Service Committee (AFSC) in Chicago where she has worked organizing conferences, campaigns, speaking tours, workshops, and internship programs since 1989. Jennifer's first visit to Gaza was in 1982 although Quaker and AFSC engagement began there when Palestinian refugees arrived in 1948. Jennifer currently works on AFSC's project Gaza Unlocked (gazaunlocked.org), which highlights stories from Gaza and the need to end the blockade and Israeli military occupation.

Kathleen Christison

Kathleen Christison has been writing on the Palestinian situation for 45 years, first as a CIA political analyst in the 1970s and since then as a freelance writer. She has traveled to Palestine more than a dozen times, initially in 1963 and with increasing frequency since 2003. She writes often for Counterpunch.org, and is a member of EPF/PIN, the Episcopal Peace Fellowship's Palestine-Israel Network. Her books include *Perceptions of Palestine* (1999 and 2001), *The Wound of Dispossession* (2002), and *Palestine in Pieces* (2009), co-authored with her late husband Bill Christison.

Pauline M. Coffman, Ed.D.

Dr. Coffman is Professor and Director (retired) of the School of Adult Learning at North Park University in Chicago, and an author/editor of *Steadfast Hope: The Palestinian Quest for Just Peace* (2009) and *Zionism Unsettled: A Congregational Study Guide* (2014). Her interest in the Middle East began with a junior year of college at Beirut College for Women (now Lebanese American University) in Beirut, Lebanon. She has led traveling seminars for the Middle East Task Force of Chicago Presbytery to Lebanon, Syria, Jordan, and Israel/Palestine. She is co-chair of the Seraj Library Project, which establishes children's libraries in villages in Palestine (see www.Serajlibraries.org). She was part of the initial group that launched Kairos USA, and has served on the Steering Committee of the Israel Palestine Mission Network of the Presbyterian Church (U.S.A.).

Jonathan Cook

Jonathan Cook, winner of the Martha Gellhorn Special Prize for Journalism, is based in Nazareth, the capital of Israel's Palestinian minority. He is a regular contributor to Al Jazeera and Middle East Eye. His books include *Blood and Religion* and *Disappearing Palestine*. His website is www.jonathan-cook.net.

Katherine Cunningham

Katherine Cunningham is a licensed psychoanalyst and a Presbyterian minister (honorably retired). She is a past moderator of the Israel Palestine Mission Network of the PC(USA) and has been a member of the Core Group of the Palestine Israel Ecumenical Forum of the World Council of Churches. Katherine has also served as the president of the board and executive director of Kairos USA. A committed advocate and educator on Palestinian human rights and justice issues, she has sought to strengthen ecumenical and inter-faith partnerships among faith-based advocacy groups internationally and in the US, especially focusing on the call of Palestinian Christians to the church and the world in the Kairos Palestine document.

Richard Falk

Richard Falk is the Albert G. Milbank Professor of International Law Emeritus, Princeton University, and Former Special Rapporteur for Occupied Palestinian Territories, UN Human Rights Council.

Noushin Framke

Noushin Framke in an Armenian/Iranian writer and editor who is an active Presbyterian advocate for Palestinian rights. She was on the writing and editing teams of *Steadfast Hope,* and *Zionism Unsettled.* Noushin was also involved in the corporate engagement of the Presbyterian Church (U.S.A.) with Caterpillar, Inc., Hewlett Packard, and Motorola Solutions, from all of which the denomination voted to divest its holdings from in 2014, based on their profits from human rights abuses in Palestine. Noushin has been a US citizen since 1986 and splits her time between the US and Canada.

Joseph Getzoff

Joseph Getzoff is a PhD Candidate in the Department of Geography, Environment, and Society at the University of Minnesota. He conducted field work in the Naqab/Negev from 2015-2017 thanks to a Fulbright Fellowship and a University of Minnesota thesis research grant.

Harry Gunkel

Harry Gunkel is a retired pediatrician in San Antonio, Texas, who spent 2007-2012 living in the Palestinian territories as a volunteer with the Episcopal Church, faculty member of Bethlehem University, consultant to a USAID healthcare project, and other volunteer activities. His experiences during those years sealed his bond with Palestine and its people and motivate his ongoing efforts in collaboration with other advocates toward justice in the region. With a colleague, he organizes annual visits to the West Bank and Gaza to offer travelers a different perspective on the "Holy Land."

Gil Hochberg

Gil Hochberg is Ransford Professor of Hebrew and Comparative Literature, and Middle East Studies at Columbia University. Her first book, *In Spite of Partition: Jews, Arabs, and the Limits of Separatist Imagination* (Princeton University Press, 2007), examines the complex relationship between the signifiers "Arab" and "Jew" in contemporary Jewish and Arab literatures. Her most recent book, *Visual Occupations: Vision and Visibility in a Conflict Zone* (Duke University Press, 2015), is a study of the visual politics of the Israeli-Palestinian conflict. She is currently writing a book on art, archives, and the production of historical knowledge.

Rachael Kamel

Rachael Kamel, PhD., is an independent scholar, currently working as an adjunct professor for the Gender, Sexuality, and Women's Studies program at Temple University in Philadelphia, where she teaches a course on gender and globalization. Since the 1980s, Kamel has worked as an editor and writer on a variety of social justice issues. After the beginning of the Second Intifada in 2001, Kamel joined the Jewish anti-occupation movement, which led her to an interest in Jewish Studies. She earned her Ph.D. in Religion in 2016, with research on Zionism, nationalism, and American Jewish history.

Rami Khouri

Rami Khouri is a Senior Public Policy Fellow and adjunct professor of journalism at the American University of Beirut. He is a Syndicated columnist through Agence Global Syndicate, USA, and a Nonresident Senior Fellow at the Harvard Kennedy School.

Jonathan Kuttab

Jonathan Kuttab is a Palestinian attorney, and human rights activist. He grew up in Jerusalem, graduated from University of Virginia Law School, and worked at the Wall Street law firm of Mudge Rose Guthrie & Alexander. He is a member of the Bar Associations in New York, Israel, and Palestine. Mr. Kuttab founded a number of human rights organizations, including Al Haq in Jerusalem and the Mandela Institute for Palestinian Prisoners; he is the Chairman of the Board of Bethlehem Bible College, and of Holy Land Trust. Mr. Kuttab is a recognized authority on international law, human rights, and Palestinian and Israeli affairs; he was the head of the Legal Committee negotiating the Cairo Agreement of 1994 between Israel and the PLO.

Susan Landau

Susan Landau combines her lifelong career as a clinical social worker with her commitment to justice in Israel-Palestine. A founding member and co-convener of Christian-Jewish Allies Working for a Just Peace in Israel-Palestine (Philadelphia, PA), she participates in interfaith teaching teams offering *Steadfast Hope: The Palestinian Quest for a Just Peace* and *Zionism Unsettled* to faith-based communities. Susan helped launch The Philadelphia Coalition for Boycott, Divestment, and Sanctions against Israel (2010; Philly BDS). A former Jewish educator in her congregational school, she left to participate in founding a non-Zionist Tikkun Olam Chavurah, where she serves on the steering committee.

Ken Mayers

Ken Mayers is a graduate of Princeton University in Electrical Engineering and a veteran of the United States Marine Corps who also holds a Ph.D. in Political Science from the University of California, Berkeley. A member of Veterans for Peace since 1986, Ken participated in the Gaza Freedom March in 2010, sailed on "The Audacity of Hope" in the Second Gaza Flotilla in 2011, helped the ICAHD rebuild a home destroyed by the IDF in 2012, and participated in Veterans for Peace delegations to Palestine in 2013 and 2017.

Martina Reese

Martina Reese is a communications professional with a strong interest in the people and politics of the Middle East. She is a past member of the Israel Palestine Mission Network of the Presbyterian Church U.S.A. and has contributed to the development of the IPMN's library of resource materials. Ms. Reese has engaged at the local and national level in educational outreach and activism to promote awareness of the Palestinian narrative and the role of US policy in creating the regional *status quo.*

Laura Siena

Laura M. Siena is a longtime community activist who has had an eclectic professional career in nonprofit management and fundraising. Her particular interests include civil rights, the cooperative economy, and sustainable agriculture.

Ron Smith

Ron J. Smith is a Political Geographer who has conducted research in Palestine for over a decade. His research has focused on the impact of occupation on daily life of Palestinians living in the West Bank and Gaza. His book, forthcoming from University of Georgia Press, details the local geographies of occupation. He is an Assistant Professor of International Relations at Bucknell University.

G.J. Tarazi

Ghassan J. Tarazi is a retired educator, spending 37 years in public education and ending his career as a college professor. He is a founding board member of Palestinian Christian Alliance of Peace and a member of Justice in Palestine & Israel Community of the Alliance of Baptists. He is a member of Ravensworth Baptist Church in Annandale, VA.

Jim Tiefenthal

Jim Tiefenthal is the co-producer of the annual Witness Palestine Film Festival at The Little Theatre in Rochester NY (six years running). He is also a charter member of Christians Witnessing for Palestine, and the Rochester NY, local group of Friends of Sabeel North America.